KNACK
MAKE IT EASY

ROCK CLIMBING

D1313630

KNACK

ROCK CLIMBING

A Beginner's Guide: From the Gym to the Rocks

Stewart M. Green and Ian Spencer-Green

Principal Photography by Mark Doolittle
Additional Photography by Stewart M. Green

KNACK
MAKE IT EASY

Guilford, Connecticut
An imprint of Globe Pequot Press

Copyright © 2010 by Morris Book Publishing, LLC

Editorial Director: Cynthia Hughes
Editor: Katie Benoit
Project Editor: Tracee Williams
Cover Design: Paul Beatrice, Bret Kerr
Interior Design: Paul Beatrice
Layout: Kevin Mak
Front Cover Photos (left to right) by: Mark Doolittle, Stewart M. Green, Mark Doolittle, and Mark Doolittle
Back Cover Photo by: Mark Doolittle
Interior Photos by Mark Doolittle with the exception of those by Stewart Green on pages: xii, 1, 2, 3, 4, 5, 6, 7, 8, 9, 10, 11, 21, 22, 28 (left), 29 (right), 35 (left), 38 (right), 40 (left), 43 (left), 44, 45, 46 (right), 47, 48 (left), 49 (left), 51, 53 (right), 58, 59, 62 (right), 63 (right), 65, 68 (left), 69 (left), 70 (right), 71 (right), 72, 73, 74 (right), 75 (right), 76, 77, 78, 79, 80, 81, 82, 83 (left), 84, 85, 86, 87, 88, 89, 90, 91, 92, 93, 94, 95, 96, 98, 100, 101 (right), 102 (left), 104, 105 (right), 107 (right), 108 (right), 109 (left), 110 (left), 112, 113 (right), 114, 115, 117 (right), 118 (right), 119, 122, 123, 126 (right), 127 (right), 132 (left), 133, 134, 135, 136, 137, 138 (right), 139 (right), 140, 141 (left), 142, 143 (right), 144 (left), 145 (left), 146, 147 (right), 148 (left), 149 (left), 150, 151, 152 (left), 153 (left), 154 (right), 155 (right), 156 (left), 157 (left), 158, 159 (right), 160, 161, 162 (right), 163 (left) 164, 167, 170 (right), 171, 172, 175 (right), 178 (left), 179 (left), 180, 181, 185 (right), 186, 190 (right), 191, 192, 193 (right), 194 (left), 195, 196 (left), 197, 198, 199, 200, 201, 202, 203, 204 (left), 205, 207, 208, 209, 210, 211, 212, 213, 214, 215 (left), 216, 217, 218, 219, 220, 221, 223 (right), and 226 (left); those by Eric Horst on pages: 13 (right), 30 (left), 31, 32, and 33; and those on pages 22 (right): © Tyler Olson | shutterstock; 223 (left): © prism68 | shutterstock; 224 (left): © James "BO" Insogna | shutterstock; 224 (right): © Albert Mendelewski | shutterstock; 225 (left): © Laura Hart | shutterstock.

Library of Congress Cataloging-in-Publication Data

Green, Stewart M.
  Knack rock climbing, a beginner's guide : from the gym to the rocks / Stewart M. Green and Ian Spencer-Green ; principal photography by Mark Doolittle ; additional photography by Stewart Green.
      p. cm.
  Includes index.
  ISBN 978-1-59921-852-6
  1. Rock climbing. I. Spencer-Green, Ian. II. Doolittle, Mark. III. Title. IV. Title: Rock climbing, a beginner's guide.
  GV200.2.G725 2010
  796.522'3—dc22

                                                                    2010002596

Printed in China

10 9 8 7 6 5 4 3 2 1

Dedicated to the memory of Craig Luebben—climber, guide, instructor, and fellow FalconGuides author. Climb in peace on that big rock in the sky.

Acknowledgments

Book writing, by necessity, requires a lot of mental anguish and effort, a lot of field research, and even more putting the seat of the pants to the seat of the chair. This book was no different. We spent four months honing down the essential concepts of climbing and then pounding out words. Many thanks to Maureen Graney, our original project editor, and Katie Benoit, who brought the entire book to fruition. Thanks for your efforts—great editors make great books. Thanks also to our climbing friends who discussed, dissected, parsed, and read parts of the manuscript and gave their dollar's worth, including Brian Shelton with Front Range Climbing Company, Jimmie Dunn, and Dennis Jump. A special thanks also to Susan Joy Paul, who provided superb editing of the book as it progressed.

CONTENTS

INTRODUCTION

Climbing is simply movement across vertical terrain. We spend most of our lives walking upright on sidewalks and trails, but when we climb, we learn about using our arms and legs in new ways. We learn about finding balance in both our movements and our lives, finding equilibrium so we can reach further, so we can climb higher. Climbing is also flow, the concentrated effort to move up a rock face, an effort that requires a unity of mind and body to succeed.

The first time you go rock climbing on a cliff just might change your life forever. Out there on the rocks you discover parts of yourself that you never knew existed—resourceful, strong, brave, and able to do anything you try. Part of the joy of climbing is changing your perceptions of yourself; finding confidence, insight, and hidden strengths; overcoming fears, weakness, and self-doubt; and discovering natural abilities that you've always had but never used.

Climbing includes lots of different disciplines, including mountaineering, traditional climbing, sport climbing, ice climbing, and bouldering. This book concentrates on rock climbing, the sport of ascending cliffs, boulders, and artificial walls. When you climb, you use hands and feet on rock features like cracks, handholds, and footholds to move upward. You also use ropes and other climbing equipment to keep safe on the rock, to hold you in case you fall, and to mitigate the effects of falling and gravity.

To become a climber, you don't need brutish physical strength, the coordination of a monkey, and the courage of a lion. It's far more important to have a desire and enthusiasm for high places tempered by a calm and focused mind and a willingness to stay in the present and not think about work, home, school, and falling. You become a climber by going to the cliffs, by being interested, by always having a beginner's mind, and by a willingness to overcome failure.

When you climb, the risks you take are usually those that you choose to take. Climbing is, of course, dangerous and

risky, but everything you do and all the equipment you use is designed to lessen the risks, to take a lot of the danger out of climbing. Most climbers are not daredevils out on the cliffs trying to cheat death but instead are people who want adventure and challenge.

Climbing is hard work a lot of the time. You get dirty and scared. Your arms get tired and your hands ache. You become a climber by not giving up when the climbing gets difficult or if you become afraid. You can never know what you can climb unless you push through barriers to your outer limits and fall trying to climb harder and higher. If you give up, you'll never know your limits and your possibilities.

Learn to Climb at an Indoor Gym

It's not hard to get started climbing. If you live in a city, find an indoor climbing gym. Many climbing walls are at universities and colleges. The best introduction to climbing is at the gym, where you can learn basic climbing movements and safety skills. Gyms also rent essential climbing equipment, including rock shoes, harnesses, and belay devices with locking carabiners. Later, after you've climbed a few times, you can purchase these items so you can climb on your own.

To progress faster, take a few climbing classes or lessons from an experienced instructor. You can learn how to safely

belay and lower as well as get important tips that will make climbing easier for you. While indoor climbing provides many of the skills needed to climb on real rock, it doesn't prepare you to go outside and have a safe experience. Climbing outside requires a larger set of technical skills and a level of competency that you develop only when you're out there climbing on cliffs.

For this reason, it's important to continue your climbing education beyond the gym. It's easy to think you know more than you do after climbing a few months inside, but don't put yourself or your climbing partners in dangerous situations by overestimating your skills. Your safety skills and knowledge of climbing procedures, including anchor building, placing gear, rigging rappels, and setting up topropes, however, is limited and even dangerous if you've only climbed indoors.

After climbing in the gym a few times, you'll want to venture outside and climb on the real stuff. It's best to go on an outing with a local climbing club, take a trip organized by your climbing gym, or hire a certified climbing guide. You'll do lots of climbing under the guidance of a watchful experienced climber and learn more about being safe on the rocks. Climbing outside is basically like climbing inside except you'll be breathing fresh air, listening to the wind in the pines, and figuring out which hand- and footholds are best to use. You'll climb routes with a top-rope, where the rope is always protecting you from above. Be sure to wear a helmet to protect your head from falling rocks.

As you grow as a climber, you'll learn more about movement, about using different kinds of holds, how to jam a crack, and how to read the rock so you can climb efficiently and with less energy than when you began. More importantly, you'll learn about climbing safety and about all the ways, tools, and techniques you use to stay safe on the rocks and come home at the end of the day.

Always remember that climbing is a serious and dangerous sport. You want to have fun and challenge yourself, but you also never want to compromise either your partner's or your personal safety. Climbing is an unforgiving sport. If you mess up, the consequences can be tragic.

Get Out Climbing to be a Climber

Knack Rock Climbing helps you learn to climb, providing advice, solving problems, and giving a safety framework to allow you to progress and grow as a climber. Through the Knack step-by-step approach, you'll learn about every aspect of climbing, from getting started in the gym to learning how to move across stone to building necessary technical skills. You'll learn about climbing fears and concerns, what equipment you will buy and use, how to improve your technique, and how all your safety systems work. Even experienced climbers will learn new tricks and techniques to improve their climbing experience. As you use this book, you'll come across unfamiliar climbing words. Look them up in the Glossary to understand their meaning.

Remember as you read and study this book that to become a climber, you need to get out climbing. You can't learn to rock climb from a book. You have to put hands and feet to rock to become a climber. Go to the climbing gym and take lessons to learn to move, and practice basic safety skills like belaying, tying into the rope, and lowering. Find experienced climbers or professional guides to take you climbing outside. No instructional book can replace this kind of invaluable experience.

Find a good partner to go climbing with. You can support each other as you learn to climb. Use the buddy system to check and double-check each other's tie-in knot, belay setup, and rappel rigging. Climbing partners will become your best friends. You'll share intense experiences, learn trust, and have loads of fun.

It is important to become a steward of your local climbing area. Respect the cliff environment by following existing trails, by not cutting or damaging vegetation, by keeping your dog leashed, by picking up both your own and other people's trash, and by using restrooms or burying or carrying human waste away. Don't alter the rock by chipping holds, cleaning plants from cracks, placing unnecessary bolts, or marking holds with extra chalk marks.

We need to take care of our cliffs and climbing areas. If we climbers don't do that, we risk having more regulations from management agencies or having our precious areas closed to climbing. Join The Access Fund and get involved in cleanup and trail work days at your local cliff. You can make a difference.

All that said, let's go rock climbing the Knack way!

WHAT IS CLIMBING?

Climbing is moving across rock with your hands and feet—it's lots of fun

Climbing is simply using your hands and feet to ascend natural features like mountains, cliffs, and boulders, and artificial walls. Climbing is a recreational sport, done for fun and enjoyment. It allows you to experience the outdoors differently than other sports. When you climb rocks you develop mental and physical fitness as well as earn lofty views from high places. Climbing also helps you confront and overcome the basic human fears of falling and heights.

Rock climbing is dangerous. Every time you go climbing you have to remember, no matter how much fun you're having, that you could be seriously injured or die. Before you go climbing, especially outside, learn the essential safety

Moving over Stone

- Climbing is using your hands and feet to surmount steep obstacles like cliffs, boulders, mountains, and indoor walls.

- Climbing is done for enjoyment and fun, and allows you to experience the natural world from on high.

- Climbing develops your physical fitness as well as mental health. You learn to overcome two of your natural fears—that of heights and that of falling.

- Climbing equipment is used to protect you from the effects of gravity and falling.

Climbing Is Dangerous

- Remember that every time you go climbing you can be seriously injured or die.

- Learn how to climb from an experienced guide or in a class at your local gym.

- Indoor climbing does not prepare you to climb safely outside on cliffs.

- Learn all the climbing safety systems to protect both your climbing partners and yourself outside.

systems that keep you alive and safe on the rocks. Take climbing classes from your local gym or from an experienced guide. Also remember that climbing inside a rock gym does not prepare you to safely climb outside.

When you climb, you learn to commune with nature in a different way than when hiking or biking. Climbing lets you connect with the natural world in an immediate and intimate way as you learn the nuances of stone and how to utilize rock features to move upward.

GREEN ● LIGHT

American climbers rate routes and climbing moves with the Yosemite Decimal System (YDS), which was created by Sierra Club climbers. Climbs are rated for the hardest moves on a route. Remember that ratings are subjective. They may be harder or easier depending on weather, rock conditions, and your body type. See below for an explanation of the YDS.

Communing with Nature

- Climbing takes you outside to lots of beautiful places.

- Use climbing as an outdoor meditation to connect with nature. Become one with the rock.

- Climbing combines athleticism, agility, balance, and flexibility with mental strength, calmness, and determination to surmount vertical challenges in incredible outdoor venues.

- The adventure of scaling new cliffs, boulders, and mountains is unparalleled.

The Yosemite Decimal System classes:

- 1st Class: Walking on level ground.

- 2nd Class: Hiking on an incline.

- 3rd Class: Scrambling up terrain where hands are used for balance.

- 4th Class: Climbing terrain with hands and feet, where a fall could result in injury or death. Ropes and equipment may be used.

- 5th Class: Technical rock climbing. Climbing gear is always used. Broken down further into a complex scale judging the compared difficulty of climbs from 5.0 (easy) to 5.15 (very hard).

- 6th Class: Aid climbing up faces too difficult to free climb. Equipment is used. Ratings from A0 to A5.

TYPES OF CLIMBING

Different terrain requires specific climbing styles; try them all and find your favorite

Climbing is easily divided into several distinct styles and categories, with each one using its own particular techniques, equipment, and environments.

Rock climbing itself is divided into three separate disciplines—traditional climbing, sport climbing, and bouldering.

Traditional, or *trad*, climbing is the old-style form of climbing where a lead climber places removable gear like cams and nuts, gear that wedges in cracks in the rock, to protect himself and his climbing partners from falling off a cliff. Trad climbing is usually real adventure climbing where you ascend long routes, figuring out where and how to go as you climb.

Sport climbing is a climbing style that emphasizes athletic

Top-rope Climbing

- Top-rope climbing is climbing with the rope anchored above so you're always protected and never at risk when taking a fall.

- Top-roping is the safest way to climb outside for beginners. Go with an expert.

- Top-roping requires only basic climbing equipment, so you don't spend lots of money starting out.

- Top-rope climbing areas are found anywhere there are cliffs. They offer safe climbing in a controlled setting.

Sport Climbing

- Sport climbing is ascending cliffs usually less than 100 feet high that are protected with preplaced bolts that are left in the rock.

- Sport climbing is about pushing your limits, trying hard routes, and making gymnastic moves.

- Most sport routes are safe so you can climb hard without a lot of risk.

- Areas for sport climbing are found everywhere in the United States and Canada.

movements and the pursuit of difficulty in a relatively safe environment. Sport climbing uses permanent bolt anchors that are placed in the rock to protect the climber. Bolts are installed in holes drilled in rock, which permanently alters the rock surface and changes the natural experience.

Bouldering is simply climbing short, difficult boulder routes or problems on boulders and small cliffs up to 20 feet high. Most boulder problems are done ropeless, so the boulderer uses crash pads made from thick foam to cushion bad landings.

Top-rope climbing is ascending cliffs and indoor walls with the safety rope always anchored above the climber, which creates a safe climbing environment with less risk than lead climbing. This is the type of climbing that beginners should do.

Other types of climbing include *aid climbing*, where the climber ascends blank rock faces using climbing equipment to support his weight rather than free climbing with hands and feet; *mountaineering* or *alpinism*, where the climber scales mountain peaks by using rock and ice climbing skills; and *ice climbing*, the winter sport of ascending ice walls, frozen waterfalls, and icy gullies with crampons and ice tools.

Traditional Climbing

- Traditional, or trad, climbing is when a climber places removable gear including cams and nuts for protection as he climbs.

- To climb most multi-pitch routes, a climber needs to have trad skills to climb safely.

- Most trad climbs ascend crack systems that the lead climber wedges gear into for protection.

- Traditional climbing offers real adventure up high cliffs and big walls in places like Yosemite Valley.

Bouldering

- Bouldering is climbing on blocks of rock or small faces without a rope, harness, or gear. It's just you climbing the rock.

- Bouldering is good training, makes you stronger, and enables you to practice climbing moves safely just above the ground.

- Bouldering requires only personal gear—rock shoes, chalk, chalk bag, and a crash pad to cushion landings.

- Boulders and small faces are usually accessible, offering a quick pump and a practice session.

WHY CLIMB?

Climb for mental and physical strength; climb just for fun; or climb to really feel alive!

Why do we climb? It's a natural question. Climbing seems so alien. Aren't humans supposed to walk around with both feet on the ground? The answer is, of course, no. Humans are primates and what do primates do? They climb trees. Climbing is a basic human activity and skill. We once climbed to escape predators and to be safe. We already know how to climb.

We learn to climb as children, scrambling up boulders and monkeying up trees. Later we grow up and unlearn how to climb, preferring instead to walk around on sidewalks and drive cars. But at some point you want to reconnect with that basic childhood instinct to climb. You might visit a national park and see climbers high on a cliff and think, "Wow! How

Climbing Is Fun

- Climbing is a natural activity. Kids scramble on boulders and climb trees. Adults climb rocks.

- Climbing gets you off the couch, out of the house, and onto new and unfamiliar terrain.

- At its best, climbing is like play time for athletes. Get out on the rock and move without thinking. Just have fun.

- You'll find routes of all grades to suit every ability level at your local cliff.

Keeps You Fit

- Climbing offers an all-body workout. After a hard day of climbing, your forearms will be sore but you'll feel fit.

- Climbing gives you flexibility, strength, balance, and endurance.

- Climbing not only tones your arms and shoulders,

but also trims your legs. Hiking to the cliff with a pack filled with climbing equipment and a rope adds to your workout.

- Climbing offers lots of cross-training exercise—hiking to the cliff, climbing, and descending down.

do they do that? I want to go climbing." So you do.

Climbing is a natural sport. It gets you out of the house, off the trail, and out experiencing raw nature. Out there on the cliffs, you grow as a person. You learn what your body and mind can do. You overcome fears and phobias. You tap into the athlete inside you. You become a better and more complete human being.

Climbing offers a whole body workout. When you go climbing, you'll begin to use muscles that you never knew you had. Climbing develops flexibility and strength, and helps you find equilibrium. You can also use climbing as a spiritual exercise like yoga.

When you progress as a climber, you find new confidence as you learn to control anxiety and move upward in ways that you never thought possible. You learn focus and concentration by shutting out negative thoughts and learning to just move without thinking, letting your body loose from your mind. Out there at the cliff, you'll discover that life is only this passing moment as you move across vertical stone.

Builds Confidence

- The only person you compete against when you climb is yourself. Strive to do better every time you climb.

- You get a sense of accomplishment and purpose when you reach the top of a route or after figuring out how to do hard moves.

- The success you find on the cliff can translate to success in life. If you can climb a cliff, you can do anything.

- Climbing teaches you not to give up when the going gets tough. The only way your climbing improves is by hard work.

Teaches Focus

- Climbing, like chess, requires lots of concentration to make the moves. If your focus wanders, you'll get scared or fall.

- When you're climbing, you don't think about work and home but about getting up the rock and reaching the top.

- When you climb, getting up the next 10 feet of rock above is all that matters. The social world ceases to exist.

- The focus, concentration, and mental edge you learn from climbing can translate to other parts of your life.

CLIMBING FEARS

Fear of heights keeps you safe climbing, but don't let it drag you down

Rock climbing seems so improbable. How do climbers cling to walls like spiders, working upward with their hands and feet gripping imaginary holds? Why aren't they afraid of heights? What happens if they fall? Will they get hurt?

Climbing can seem intimidating to the beginner. The new climber has a lot of questions and fears about climbing and not a lot of answers.

If you want to be a climber, you don't have to be super strong or have buckets of courage. All you need is the desire to confront your fears and work at your technique. Climbing is more about using good footwork and body position techniques than about brute strength. Successful climbers use their legs

I'm Not Strong Enough

- "I'm not strong enough to go rock climbing" is a big myth. The best climbers are skinny and lean. Big muscles means more weight to pull up.

- Climbing is all about staying in balance, about finding your center of gravity and using your hands and feet. Move from the core of your torso.

- Good technique and footwork gets you up a lot more routes than brute strength.

- Use your legs to push you up a climb rather than pulling up with your arms. Legs are stronger than arms.

I Weigh Too Much

- You don't have to be stick-figure thin to be a good rock climber.

- Climbing burns a lot of calories, so if you want to lose weight—go rock climbing.

- If you use your legs to propel your body up a cliff, your arms won't have to pull too many extra pounds.

- If you can climb stairs and a ladder, then you will be fine rock climbing.

to push themselves upward rather than pulling up with their arms. It makes sense—your legs are stronger than your arms.

You don't have to be fashion-model skinny and feather light to be a successful climber. It might help if you lose a few pounds, but they won't stop you from getting up moderate climbs. If you get out regularly, you'll probably lose some of those pounds by burning calories while hiking to the cliff and moving across stone.

Climbing is dangerous. That's the truth. But climbing is also incredibly safe. You're more likely to get hurt driving to the cliff than climbing—as long as you use equipment and follow proper climbing safety protocol. Climbing equipment almost never fails. Usually accidents happen because of inattention and inexperience.

The fear of heights and high places is a natural human fear. That fear keeps you alive. Sometimes a fear of heights comes from ignorance of your safety system. If you're afraid, check your knots, your belay anchor (which ties you to the rock), and don't look down. You can build up a tolerance for heights by climbing higher each time you go.

Will I Get Hurt?

- Yes, you can get hurt climbing. But it's safer than driving your car to the mall. Most novice climbers are safe because they don't do stupid things.

- Most climbers are not daredevils trying to thwart death. The risks you take climbing are the risks you choose to take. A safe approach keeps you safe on the rocks.

- Equipment is designed to keep you safe from the effects of gravity and falling.

- Climbers learn and use safety systems that are designed for redundancy and minimizing danger.

Fear of Heights

- The fear of heights is a natural human instinct. We're wired to be afraid of heights for self-preservation.

- If you're afraid of heights, take baby steps when climbing. Build a tolerance for heights by climbing as high as you're comfortable.

- Fear of heights is often based on not understanding and trusting the safety systems, rope, knots, and belayer.

- If you're afraid of heights— don't look down!

MORE CLIMBING FEARS
It's okay to be afraid; climbing is scary, but you'll grow when you confront fear

Being afraid is a natural response to the world. There are lots of scary things, and when you're climbing, you're going to meet some of them. It's okay to be afraid when climbing. If you're not afraid, then maybe climbing is the wrong sport for you, because a healthy fear keeps you alive.

First, admit that you're afraid when you climb. By admitting it, you take some of its power away. Don't fight your fear of heights or falling. Accept it. Say, "Okay, I'm scared. What can I do about that feeling? How can I feel safer?"

Next, accept that climbing is scary. Trust your equipment, rope, and your belayer. Build a strong relationship with your partner and you'll trust him implicitly. Concentrate on the

What Happens If I Fall?

- The fear of falling is a basic and natural human instinct. We don't want to fall because we can be injured or die.

- Your first fears about falling are usually because you don't understand the safety systems or trust your partner.

- If you're afraid of falling, take a few falls on a top-rope. Just let go and let the rope catch you. No big deal!

- Injuries from climbing falls are caused by hitting ledges or protruding rocks, or falling upside down. Always wear a helmet and don't take unnecessary risks.

I'm Too Old

- If you're in good cardiovascular condition and reasonable shape, you're never too old to go climbing.

- Lots of good climbers began in their fifties and sixties.

- Climbing is all about technique rather than strength. Don't worry about muscling up hard routes. Set achievable goals and have fun.

- Climb for life. Climbing allows you to find new parts of yourself as you move through the vertical world.

moves ahead of you. Make goals like, "I'll just climb to that next ledge." Take it slow and don't be afraid to come down. And practice falling.

The fear of falling is climbing's biggest fear. Every climber experiences this no matter how good they are. Climbers don't like to fall. Most falls you take will be on a top-rope, which is secured to anchors above you. If you're afraid of falling, then have your belayer hold you tight while you fall off. See, it's not so bad. The rope stretches and then catches you.

You might also be afraid that you're too old to start climbing, but you're never too old. Remember that climbing is more about technique than strength. If you've been an athlete most of your life, you won't have any problem learning to climb.

If you don't know any climbers, get a membership at your local rock gym. You'll meet lots of folks there of all abilities. A good place to find partners is on the gym bulletin board, local outdoor shop, or on an Internet climbing site. Also consider taking a class. You'll find others of your skill level that want to climb, too.

I Don't Know Any Climbers

- The best way to meet climbers is to start climbing.

- Meet other climbers of similar ability at your local climbing gym. Check the partner board or tell a gym employee that you're looking for a partner.

- Take a group lesson. You'll meet other students and can practice climbing and belaying together.

- After learning basic climbing skills, other climbers will be receptive to climbing with you since you know the ropes.

There's No Gym Nearby

- Believe it or not, people once learned to climb outside. Climbing gyms have only been around since about 1990.

- Every state except Louisiana, which is a delta with no exposed bedrock, has outdoor climbing on cliffs and boulders.

- Look more closely where you live. Lots of YMCAs, universities, and schools have climbing walls.

- You want to climb? Build your own climbing wall in your garage, basement, or backyard.

CLIMBING FOR LIFE

The climbing lifestyle brings many benefits, including lifelong friends and a lifetime of adventures

Climbing has become one of the fastest growing outdoor sports in the world, going from a fringe activity with a few thousand devotees in the 1960s to over a million climbers in the United States today. The artificial wall is the main reason that climbing has become popular. Now indoor gyms, with a safe environment, let beginning climbers understand and practice essential skills, including belaying, using equipment properly, and technique, before making the jump to outside cliffs.

As you learn to climb, you meet a lot of fellow climbers who share your view of the world as a place of adventure and renewal. Some of your best and most long-lived friendships

Fast-growing Sport

- Climbing is one of the fastest growing outdoor sports. There are now over a million climbers in the United States.

- Climbing gyms are found in almost every major city. Look at colleges, schools, and outdoor centers for one near you.

- Many people use indoor gyms for an all-around physical workout and for the excitement of moving across vertical terrain.

- Climbing classes, courses, and guided climbing trips are available all around the world. Take a trip and go climbing.

Social Community

- Climbing introduces you to new friends who share a love of the outdoors and a thirst for adventure.

- The intense nature of climbing and the partnership of the rope often lead to long friendships.

- Climbers everywhere love to get together, socialize, and talk about climbing and routes.

- Your local climbing gym is where you meet your first climbing partners and friends. Go climbing. Have fun. Be good to each other.

will grow from climbing partnerships, where you share intense experiences on vertical walls and forge bonds of trust and understanding. You'll also get together with climbing buddies and recount past deeds and make future plans.

When you're a climber, the whole world becomes a climbing area. You can travel to historic American climbing sites like Yosemite Valley, Joshua Tree National Park, Eldorado Canyon, and the Shawangunks to sample classic climbs. Or you can jet off to limestone cliffs in southern France and Thailand, sandstone walls in Jordan and Australia, or the mountains of

Nepal and Peru to sample more adventurous climbs.

As a climber, you learn to move through the world without leaving a trace of your passage. Follow a zero-impact ethic. Hike to the cliffs on existing trails and durable rock surfaces. Pick up trash you find along the way. Keep a low profile so you don't bother other users like hikers and fishermen. Respect private property and wildlife and don't damage trees and vegetation. Lead by example, and join The Access Fund to support efforts that keep climbing areas open.

Lifetime of Routes

- Climbing allows you to travel to other parts of the United States as well as the world for more vertical adventures.

- Developed climbing areas are found in many wonderful places, including France, England, Australia, Thailand, and Japan.

- You can climb your favorite routes again and again on your home cliff. Each time, you can find a new way to move across the same rock.

- You improve your climbing skills by climbing on different rock types like pockets in limestone, cracks in sandstone, and granite slabs.

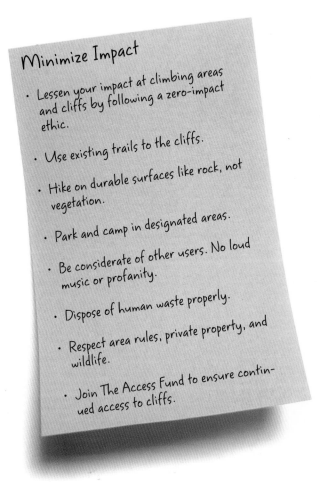

Minimize Impact

- Lessen your impact at climbing areas and cliffs by following a zero-impact ethic.

- Use existing trails to the cliffs.

- Hike on durable surfaces like rock, not vegetation.

- Park and camp in designated areas.

- Be considerate of other users. No loud music or profanity.

- Dispose of human waste properly.

- Respect area rules, private property, and wildlife.

- Join The Access Fund to ensure continued access to cliffs.

INDOOR CLIMBING

Indoor climbing provides a social atmosphere, a fun learning environment, and limited risk

You've decided to try rock climbing. These days it's easy to get your climbing career off the ground at any indoor climbing gym. Before gyms, climbers trained for climbing by ascending stone walls, buildings, trees, and anything else they could put hands and feet on. Now indoor gyms are in every major city, offering a safe environment to learn how to climb.

Indoor climbing walls are built from either textured plywood sheets or prefabricated fake-rock panels. Climbing handholds and footholds of various shapes and sizes are bolted onto the wall, forming routes or a combination of climbing moves of different difficulties up the wall. The walls offer lots of climbing terrain from smooth slabs to arching overhangs. Gyms have

Place to Start

- Indoor climbing gyms are the best places for beginners to learn how to climb.

- Climbing gyms are convenient, accessible, and not intimidating.

- You can rent all the climbing equipment you need from the gym when you're starting out.

- Climbing gyms are great places to meet other beginner climbers and to hook up with more experienced partners.

Safe Environment

- Climbing gyms offer a safe, controlled place to learn to climb. Experienced personnel usually monitor you to make sure you keep things safe.

- Most indoor routes are top-rope climbs. The climber is always protected by a rope from above.

- Climbing gyms have soft spongy floors and few extremely high walls to scare you.

- It's easy to communicate with your climbing partner—as long as the music isn't too loud!

walls from 20 to 50 feet high that are outfitted with top-rope and lead climbs. Additionally, many gyms have low walls for bouldering. Climbing gyms may also offer weight equipment, stretching areas, coffee bars, and pro shops.

Indoor gyms are the best places to learn to climb. They're safe, convenient, fun, and weather is never a problem. They also offer lots of learning opportunities with classes, private lessons, clinics, as well as a chance to observe experienced climbers. Gyms are also great places to meet other climbers, find partners, and to socialize with your local climbing community.

YELLOW LIGHT

Although gyms are safe, accidents still occur. Be responsible for your own safety. Start by mastering all the basic climbing skills, including belaying, lowering, knot-tying, and proper communication.

Learning the Basics

- Climbing gyms are great places to learn the basics of climbing movement as well as how to belay and lower.

- Most climbing gyms offer lessons, clinics, and customized classes to suit your ability.

- Instruction in gyms is cheaper than taking an outside class or hiring a guide.

- In a gym you quickly master the basics by regularly climbing and getting instruction.

Practice Makes Perfect

- Climbing in the gym makes you stronger on the rock when you go climbing outside.

- Climbing gyms are great places to practice specialized moves like back steps, side pulls, and dynamic moves.

- You can climb year-round in gyms with no worries about bad weather or darkness.

- As you progress you can learn lead climbing without the hazards of real rock.

CLIMBING GYMS

With indoor climbing gyms in almost every city, you can start climbing and having fun

As climbing has grown exponentially since 1990, indoor gyms have become commonplace in most cities. Now there are gyms of almost every shape and size. The gym walls are made of fiberglass or wood panels with artificial climbing holds bolted on. The holds are easily switched to different locations and spun to different angles, creating new routes and sequences for practice.

Some gyms boast walls as high as 75 feet, while others have short bouldering walls for solo climbing without a rope. Some gyms are part of a regular health club with weights, machines, and a coffee shop. Others are tucked in the corner of a shopping mall or on the deck of a cruise ship. No matter

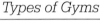

Types of Gyms

- Climbing gyms come in lots of sizes and shapes. Some are a single wall in a health club while others are huge facilities made for climbing.

- Walls, between 20 and 75 feet high, are either made from plywood or prefab panels with holds bolted onto them.

- Most gym routes are top-rope climbs with the rope anchored above the wall and the climber.

- Some gyms are for bouldering only, with overhanging walls to increase your pump.

Before Starting

- If you already know how to belay and lower, ask to take a belay test. If not, take a belay class and learn.

- Most gyms rent rock shoes and harnesses for a reasonable fee.

- Take an introductory climbing lesson and learn how

to tie into the rope, belay, lower, and climb.

- Warm up by stretching for five minutes. Concentrate on your upper legs, hips, arms, and torso. Climb for ten minutes to warm up. Start with easy climbs or use all the holds rather than just the ones marking the route.

what the type of gym, most are made to please the modern climber.

To climb at a gym, you'll have to sign a waiver before you start. The friendly staff will make sure you have proper instruction in basic skills before you jump on your first climb. It's recommended that you take an introductory class before getting off the deck.

Gym Safety

- Gyms are generally safe, but accidents do occur.

- Pay attention to others around you, especially if the gym is crowded. A climber can fall and swing into you.

- Always anchor yourself to the ground, if possible, when belaying and have your belayer anchored when you're climbing. Not all gyms have ground anchors.

- If you're lead climbing, don't skip bolts. Clip into all of them to avoid hitting the ground if you fall. Most gyms require you to clip all bolts.

Avoiding Injury

- Most gym injuries are to muscles and tendons in the hands, arms, and shoulders from overuse.

- Don't overdo it. Gym climbing stresses your joints. Don't overtrain, and take rest days.

- Let go of a hold if you feel finger or elbow pain or numbness. Injuries occur when making extreme moves.

- Small finger holds can strain, damage, and pull tendons and muscles. Use big holds whenever possible.

YOUR FIRST TIME

It's easier to start climbing than you think, especially if you live near an indoor gym

You'll find climbing gyms in most major cities and at universities and colleges, making it easy to start rock climbing. Just go in and check it out. Ask at the front desk about climbing, what equipment you can rent, and if they offer basic lessons. Come back with a friend and start climbing. It's lots more fun to share the experience, plus you need a partner to swap belays with and for encouragement.

You'll learn all the basic safety skills your first time at the gym. You'll learn how to put on the equipment, how to tie into the rope, how to belay and lower, and basic climbing movements.

Most gyms rent all the basic gear—shoes, harness, and

Your First Climb

- Getting started is easier than you think, especially if your city has a climbing gym. Call or check their Web site to find out how to climb.

- Climbing indoors is like outdoor climbing, but without the risks and objective dangers found outside.

- Climb with a friend—it's more fun and you'll get up lots of routes.

- Remember to warm up. Do easy climbs to find a rhythm. Keep your weight on your feet as you climb. If your arms tire, hang on the rope to recover and then climb to the top. Way to go!

Gearing Up

- A climbing gym can outfit you with all the rental gear you need to climb.

- Make sure the rock shoes snugly fit your foot but are not uncomfortable.

- Most gyms rent one-size-fits-all climbing harnesses

so that you can easily adjust them to fit your waist and legs. Make sure it doesn't slide down over your hips.

- Get a belay device attached to a locking carabiner so you can learn to belay and lower.

belay device. Take a class and learn how to belay, one of climbing's most important safety skills. Gyms don't supply belayers. Bring a friend and learn together. Then learn how to lower your partner with the rope from the top of the wall until she's safely on the ground. It's another important skill to know. Lastly, climb the easiest routes to start. Learn different moves and how to use your hands and feet. That will give you a good foundation to build upon.

······· RED●LIGHT ·······

After putting on your harness, pass the waist strap back through the buckle. If you do this, the harness won't come undone. If you don't double it back, the waist strap can come apart. Make sure the strap extends a couple inches past the buckle.

Belaying Basics

- Belaying is one of the most important climbing skills you will learn in the gym. The belay skills you learn in a gym are easily transferred outside.

- Belaying is holding the rope through a belay device, which holds the climber if they fall or hang on the rope.

- If you don't know how to belay, take a class at the gym to learn the essentials. The controlled environment at a gym makes it an excellent place to learn to belay.

- Most gyms require a belay test to prove that you're a competent and attentive belayer.

Climbing and Lowering

- Start on vertical walls, not overhanging. Ask what the best routes are for beginners.

- Use your hands and feet to climb. Keep your weight over your feet. Try using handholds in different ways.

- Celebrate at the top, then have your belayer take the rope tight. Lean back and let him slowly lower you.

- To lower, sit down in your harness and keep your legs straight and shoulder-width apart.

BASIC SKILLS

Learn climbing skills like knots, belaying, and lowering at a local gym

An indoor gym is the perfect place to learn the basic climbing skills—tying into the rope, belaying, lowering, and safety techniques—that you need to know to safely climb outside. In a gym you learn and practice them in a controlled setting, often under the eye of a gym employee.

The first skill you need to know is how to tie into the rope.

The figure-8 follow-through knot is the knot most climbers use to attach the rope to their harness. This is the strongest climbing knot, won't come untied if properly tied, and is easy to check. Learn the knot and practice it until you can tie it without thinking. Remember to tie the knot into your harness at the leg loops and tie-in point on the waist belt. Never

Tying into Rope

- One of the first things to learn is how to tie the rope onto your harness.

- The best knot to use is a figure-8 follow-through knot (see Chapter 7). It's easy to check, easy to tie, and won't come untied.

- Learn to tie the knot so you don't rely on other climbers for your safety.

- Practice tying into the rope until you know the knot— your safety depends on that knot!

Belaying

- You want to go climbing? You need to learn how to belay. Belaying is an essential climbing skill.

- The gym is an ideal venue to learn belaying since it's a safe and controlled environment.

- In the gym, the belayer keeps the rope snug on the climber, holds her if she falls, and lowers her to the ground.

- Belaying is serious business. Practice belaying so you can safeguard your partner.

tie into the harness belay loop.

Belaying, the process of securing the rope in a belay device and protecting a climber, is another essential skill you need to know. The gym is ideal to learn how to belay. Before you can belay at a gym, most require you to take a belay competency test. Most gyms also offer a skill class in belaying.

After you learn to belay, learn how to lower a climber from the top of the wall back to the base. Lowering, like belaying, is an essential skill. If you don't know how to lower your partner, you could drop her like a ton of bricks to the ground.

Lastly, learn climbing skills so you can look after yourself in the gym and at the cliff. That way you never have to rely on anyone else for your safety. Climbing safety is about taking personal responsibility. Learn all the basic skills to be safe at the gym and you'll have a lot more fun climbing.

Lowering

- Lowering is dangerous. Make sure your partner pays attention so he doesn't drop you.

- Let your belayer know that you are ready to lower. Don't assume he is ready to lower you.

- If you're lowering some-

one, feed the rope slowly through the belay device, don't let go of it, and make sure you're anchored if he weighs more than you.

- Don't lower the climber too fast. You could lose control and drop him to the ground, spraining an ankle or breaking a leg.

Look After Yourself

- Learn all the essential climbing skills so you can look after yourself on the rock and in the gym.

- Be responsible for your own safety at all times by tying into the rope and clipping into anchors.

- Don't rely on friends, spouses, or instructors to keep you safe climbing.

- What you learn in the gym will help you stay safe when you start climbing outside.

CLASSES & GUIDES

Take classes or hire a guide to learn the skills you need to climb safely

Not many years ago, most novices began climbing outside on rock, but now the easiest way to learn is indoors at a climbing gym. Artificial walls have become popular over the last couple decades, making them an easy and accessible place to start. Many gyms regularly run introductory climbing courses to acquaint beginners with skills as well as basic

movements. Take one of these classes so you understand the risks of climbing and how to avoid mistakes.

Most new climbers stumble around learning to climb, finding the best way by trial and error. This method takes a lot of time and mistakes to learn the right techniques. If you want to accelerate your progress as a climber, then learn from

Learn from Lessons

- If climbing is a sport that speaks to you, the best way to improve is to take classes and lessons with an instructor at your gym. Also take clinics on yoga, diet, and cross-training.

- Good instruction makes you climb better more quickly than learning on your own.

- Take classes in rope skills like belaying and lowering, as well as climbing movement.

- Many gyms arrange outdoor climbing trips to local crags through guide services, an ideal way to start climbing outside safely.

Take a Class

- Ask at your local climbing gym or outdoor shop where you can take introductory climbing lessons.

- Some colleges offer climbing classes for non-students.

- Climbing clubs like the Colorado Mountain Club and Appalachian Mountain Club hold regular how-to-climb classes.

- Look for specific women-only and kids climbing classes and clinics to have more fun.

lessons. Gyms offer lots of other classes and clinics besides those for beginners, including outdoor sessions to acquaint you with real climbing. You can hire a coach once a month to critique your technique and give you helpful tips on training and movement. You can also take affordable climbing classes from outing clubs or colleges.

If you want to climb outside and learn the important skills that keep you safe on real rock, then hire a climbing guide. Make sure they have insurance, permits, and certification before going out. Talk with your guide beforehand and make a plan about what you want to learn. Your guide can also lead you up exciting routes that would otherwise be beyond your skill level.

To start climbing outside, check if your gym does trips to local climbing areas. You can also hook up with more experienced climbers and serve an apprenticeship. Go climbing with someone better and you'll learn lots of new techniques and safety tips. Just remember not to climb outside until you're confident with your skills, because climbing outdoors is more dangerous than in the gym.

Hire a Guide

- Consider hiring a certified climbing guide and split the cost with friends for a customized outdoor lesson.

- If you don't live near a gym, travel to a climbing area and hire a rock guide for a day of outdoor climbing.

- Make sure the guide service has insurance and permits to guide on public land.

- If you hire a guide, make sure your trip is instructional rather than just a carnival ride. Use it as an opportunity to become better.

Climbing Outside

- Most climbers view gym climbing as training for the real thing—climbing outdoors on rock.

- The safest outdoor climbing for beginners is top-roping. Top-rope routes are found at all climbing areas.

- Become an apprentice to an experienced climber and follow her up lots of routes. You'll learn all kinds of tricks and become a safer climber.

- Don't go outside to climb unless you get proper instruction. A little bit of knowledge is a dangerous thing.

CLIMBING COMMUNICATION

Know climbing voice commands to be safe when you're climbing outside

Communication between climbers, especially between a belayer and leader, is essential for safe climbing. Miscommunication is a common cause of accidents, sometimes fatal ones. You need to learn all the climbing commands that allow a climbing team to function safely and smoothly. Climbing commands are simple standard phrases and single words used by climbers to ensure their safety when they're out of sight from each other.

Before starting to climb, talk to your partner. Review the basic commands if either one of you is unsure of what to yell while climbing or belaying. Also agree on commands if you can't hear each other because of wind, cliff topography, or a

Climbing Commands

- Climbing commands are standard phrases or words that let a climbing team safely communicate.

- Communication between a leader and belayer is very important. Bad communication causes accidents. Review basic commands before leaving the ground.

- If it's noisy or the weather is bad, agree on a system of rope tugs to communicate.

- Following are lists of basic commands. Listed first is the command; second who says the command; and third what the command means. Learn them all to be safe.

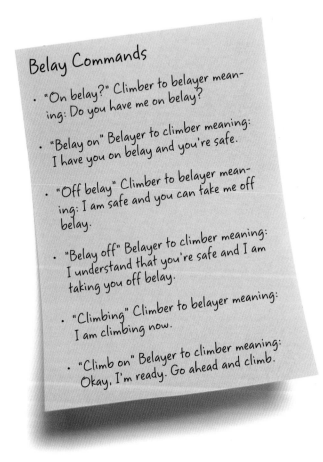

Belay Commands

- "On belay?" Climber to belayer meaning: Do you have me on belay?

- "Belay on" Belayer to climber meaning: I have you on belay and you're safe.

- "Off belay" Climber to belayer meaning: I am safe and you can take me off belay.

- "Belay off" Belayer to climber meaning: I understand that you're safe and I am taking you off belay.

- "Climbing" Climber to belayer meaning: I am climbing now.

- "Climb on" Belayer to climber meaning: Okay, I'm ready. Go ahead and climb.

loud river. Climbers usually use a system of prearranged tugs on the rope at those times.

If you learned to climb in an indoor gym, you might not value the necessity of using the same clear verbal commands outside. It's easy to communicate inside, although you might need to shout above the gym music. Outside is a different matter. Bad communication when you're climbing is a recipe for disaster. Good communication keeps you and your climbing partner safe on the rocks. Learn the basic commands and use them.

GREEN ● LIGHT

If words don't work, use rope tugs to communicate. Agree on signals before climbing. Use three sharp tugs for "Off belay" and then three more tugs for "On belay." After setting up the belay, pull the rope tight and the second climber will know it's safe to climb.

Climbing Commands

- "Slack" Climber to belayer meaning: Give me slack or loose rope and don't hold the rope tight.

- "Up rope" Climber (with a top-rope) to belayer meaning: Pull slack out of the rope.

- "Tension," "Take," or "Tight rope" Climber to belayer meaning: Pull the rope tight and hold me.

- "Watch me!" Climber to belayer meaning: Pay attention, this is hard and I might fall.

- "Falling!" Climber to belayer meaning: I'm falling and you need to hold me with the belay.

Descent Commands

- "Ready to lower" Climber to belayer meaning: I'm at the anchors and ready to lower down.

- "Got you!" Belayer to climber meaning: I feel your weight on the rope and am ready to lower when you give the next command.

- "Lowering" Belayer to climber meaning: Okay, I'm going to lower you now.

- "On rappel" Climber to anyone below meaning: I'm getting ready to rappel down now.

- "Off rappel" Climber to partner above meaning: I am disengaged from the rappel ropes, you can rappel now.

23

GYM CLIMBING BASICS

Learn climbing basics and safety in the gym, then take your skills to a cliff

Once you start climbing at an indoor gym, use it for more than merely clambering around on the walls. Most serious climbers go to the gym for learning techniques, practicing and getting better, and training for outdoor climbing.

Gyms are great for mastering climbing basics. Learn how to move across vertical terrain, use your hands and feet, keep in balance, and try new moves. Don't worry about lead climbing when starting out; do lots of top-ropes instead. Start with one wall and try to do all the routes. You'll probably fail, but you'll learn what you need to work on and you'll get better. Also practice belaying, lowering, and spotting a boulderer. Later, when you head outside, you'll bring all these skills and

Mastering the Basics

- Indoor walls are a great place to master basic climbing techniques and to become a competent belayer and spotter.

- Top-ropes are your best friend when starting out. Start with the easiest and work up to your limits.

- Climbing in the gym improves your movement and specialized techniques by doing them in a safe setting. Later transfer these skills to outdoor cliffs.

- Gyms are excellent for climbing instruction, fun and recreation, training for climbing, and socializing.

Keeping Safe

- *Stay aware, stay alive.* Every time you go climbing, make safety an absolute priority. Check your personal gear. Be aware of what's going on around you.

- Putting on your harness: Double-check that your harness is buckled correctly. Routinely inspect your harness for wear.

- Tying into the rope: Tie into the rope without distractions. Check your partner's knot as well.

- Belaying: Know and trust your belayer. Your life is in her hands. Be an attentive belayer.

won't feel like a total newbie on the cliff.

Also develop your safety sense and follow the mantra: Stay aware, stay alive. If something feels wrong in the gym, don't do it. If you need help or have a question about belaying, ask an experienced climber. Don't be afraid of feeling foolish. Safety is your number one priority. From the beginning, make a safety checklist that you follow every time you climb. Check your harness buckle, tie-in knot, the belay device and rope, and your belayer. Don't assume everything is always fine. It's not.

Besides climbing gym routes, go bouldering with a friend. Most gyms have bouldering areas with lots of problems. Push yourself to do harder sequences of moves. Climb traversing problems where you can link lots of moves. You can also boulder by yourself if you don't have a partner. Doing boulder problems is a great way to warm up and stretch your muscles. Just remember to learn how to spot or watch your climbing buddy to make sure she doesn't hurt herself if she falls.

Get Focused

- When you climb, treat it as time for relaxation and try to clear distractions like work and daily life from your head.

- When gearing up, take deep breaths and turn your focus to the climbing you are about to do.

- Staying focused keeps you safe. Climbing accidents occur when you don't pay attention.

- Develop pre-climb rituals like stretching and yoga to bring focus to your climbing session. Free your mind and you'll free your body to climb.

Gym Bouldering

- Gym bouldering is great training for strength and technique. Make bouldering meditative and relaxing or intense and focused.

- You can boulder alone or in a group. Bouldering is a good warm-up for climbing routes. Bouldering is always fun, no matter what your ability.

- Bouldering lets you push your climbing limits to the maximum by using and practicing difficult moves.

- Do gym wall traverses to practice footwork. Work on underclings, side pulls, gastons, backsteps, balance, and keeping your center over your feet.

GYM LEAD CLIMBING
Learn to clip bolts and lead routes in the gym and you'll climb safer

After climbing lots of top-ropes, try your hand at gym lead climbing. Most gyms require you to pass a lead test to show that you're competent at clipping the rope into quickdraws, which are two carabiners attached to a sewn sling, and following lead safety rules. Before leading a route, ask if there are any climbs you can do to practice clipping.

Master both the thumb clip and finger clip (see clipping in the Sport Climbing chapter) and then practice both techniques until they're automatic. Find good holds to clip from since you'll be hanging from one arm while pulling up slack. Also remember it's less strenuous to clip bolts when they're closer to your body than when they're overhead. Master clipping in the gym and you'll be thankful the next time you're climbing outside and trying to clip the rope.

Leading is dangerous, even in the gym, since you're climbing above protection and could fall and hurt yourself. Make

Gym Clipping

- At each bolt, find a good handhold that you can hang on to with one hand. Clip the rope with the other.

- If it's hard to pull up rope to reach a clip, pull a section of rope, hold it in your teeth, and then pull more rope to clip.

- Clip each quickdraw close to your waist so there's less slack if you fall. Excessive slack could mean injury.

- Find a secure position to clip the rope into each quickdraw. Make sure the carabiner gate faces opposite your direction of travel.

Leading Safely

- Don't let the rope run between or behind your leg and never let the rope twist around your ankles.

- Ask your belayer to pay attention to you and not get distracted.

- Never grab a bolt, quickdraw, or carabiner on a gym lead. If you slip grabbing gear, you can break a finger.

- Make sure you have a secure stance for clipping. "Blowing a clip" accounts for bad falls, including ground falls. It's okay to push your limits, but don't go too far and risk injury.

sure your belayer is competent and attentive. Don't let short gym falls turn into ground falls where you could get seriously injured. Also don't let the rope run between or behind your legs. If you fall it causes you to flip upside down.

Gym lead climbing is a step toward climbing outside. Train hard, practice leading, and you'll soon be rocking the vertical world.

Falling

- Learn how to take lead falls in the controlled gym environment. Practice short falls to build confidence.

- When you fall, keep your feet shoulder-width apart and arms in front to protect your head and torso from hitting the wall. Short gym falls can slam you into the wall.

- Stay aware of the rope to prevent becoming tangled if you fall.

- When traversing, run the rope over the front of your thigh. This keeps it from tangling and flipping you over if you fall.

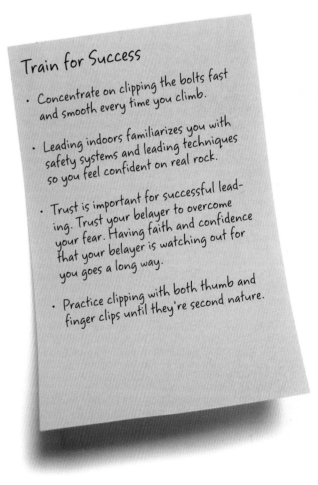

Train for Success

- Concentrate on clipping the bolts fast and smooth every time you climb.

- Leading indoors familiarizes you with safety systems and leading techniques so you feel confident on real rock.

- Trust is important for successful leading. Trust your belayer to overcome your fear. Having faith and confidence that your belayer is watching out for you goes a long way.

- Practice clipping with both thumb and finger clips until they're second nature.

INDOOR CLIMBING

BUILD A HOME WALL
Build and use a home wall and you'll climb stronger and better

If you don't have a nearby climbing gym, don't like the music they play, or just want your own training gym, then consider building a wall at home. Home walls are easy to build and don't break the piggy bank. Climbers around the world build and train in home gyms. Your wall's size and shape is limited only by your imagination. Some are small, simple, and efficient. Others are high, with complex angles and varied terrain. Consider how you're going to use it before building.

Erect one that you'll use, not one you'll leave idle because it doesn't fit your needs.

First, find a place to build a wall. A two-car garage is perfect; otherwise consider your basement or, if the weather is good, in the backyard. Ask yourself these questions: How much space do I have? How much do I have to spend? What difficulty will I train at? Should I build an indoor or outdoor wall? When building an inside wall, consider proper ventilation for

The Frame

- Purchase wood. Use 2x6s, 2x8s, or 2x10s for the support frame. Use ¾-inch plywood for paneling. Tools required: level, drill, pencil, chalk line, measuring tape, circular saw, and hammer.

- For a basic straight-angle wall, the frame is rectangular. The dimensions can be

8 feet wide by 12 feet high and fit three sheets of plywood. Use wood screws.

- For a self-standing wall, use either 4x4 or 6x6 posts.

- Screw the plywood sheets to the frame with wood screws, sinking the screws every 8 inches.

T-nut the Plywood

- To attach the holds, drill holes on each sheet of plywood and install T-nuts on the back. Feed bolts through each hold and tighten into the T-nut.

- Use a chalk line to mark out a pattern for T-nuts. Install bolt holes on 6- or 8-inch centers to maximize the

number of holds.

- To install a T-nut, drill an undersized hole and then hammer the T-nut flush to the back of the plywood.

- Make sure when installing T-nuts that you hammer each one straight and flush to the plywood.

chalk dust that gets stirred up. If you're not a carpenter, check with a professional to make sure that your home wall design is safe and sturdy.

The home gym is a secret training tool that most pro climbers use religiously. Customize your gym to meet specific training goals. Use colored tape to mark out various problems of different difficulties and create problems that strengthen your weaknesses. Consult a professional to check for safety.

ZOOM

Buying holds is the most expensive part of building a home gym. Starting out you'll need 200 to 300 holds for a small wall. Look online for close-out deals or check if you can get discounts for buying in bulk. Otherwise, buy some and make some from wood. Ask your buddies who will also use the wall to kick in bucks for holds.

INDOOR CLIMBING

Purchase Holds

- Look online or at your local mountain shop for the best deals. Many hold manufacturers offer discount combo packs.

- Which holds you use depends on the wall's angle, your ability, and desired training routine. Start with a selection of footholds—small, medium, and large. Then build a collection of handholds.

- If your budget is tight, make holds out of wood. Pieces of 2x4 lumber, trim boards, and other chunks can be cut, sanded, and fashioned into training holds that won't break the bank.

Start Training

- Once your wall is ready for climbing, clear the landing area of hazards.

- Use crash pads or old mattresses to cushion the landing below the wall. Good padding is important— you'll train harder if you're not afraid of falling.

- Be cautious of gaps in the padded landing area. Climbers can break arms and wrists when their hands fall between the pads.

- Use a spotter to avoid accidents and keep upright in a fall. A climber can be seriously injured even falling on a pad.

TRAINING TOOLS

Use hangboards and campus boards to build strong forearms and hands

Your fingers, hands, and forearms are perhaps your most important climbing muscles and appendages. If these are strong, you're going to get up a lot more routes than if they're weak. Muscle failure—that is, getting pumped—is the number one cause of falling off routes. Train your upper body using hangboards, campus boards, system walls, and other apparatus, and you'll be sending more difficult climbs.

Before training, however, remember that it's easy to get injured on any of these training tools. Don't be overenthusiastic and overtrain or attempt exercises that you're not ready to do. Also do exercises that are specific to climbing movements so you can apply your strength gains to climbing.

Hangboard Training

- Hangboards are an ideal training tool since they can be mounted anywhere. Most boards cost less than $100, allowing for affordable and effective training.

- A hangboard is shaped to include different-size grips. Hangboards are excellent for training muscles.

- Use a hangboard for warming up at home before climbing and for high-intensity hangs and lock-off sessions.

- Advanced climbers use many exercises. To avoid injury be cautious, warm up thoroughly, and don't push too hard.

Campus Boards

- A campus board is an overhanging wall with a ladder of wooden rungs. It is climbed or "campused" with only your arms and hands.

- Pieces of 2x4 lumber, wooden edges, and dowels can be fashioned into edges of many types and sizes. Some manufacturers sell prefab rungs to suit your needs.

- Campus training is high impact and can damage shoulders, elbows, and fingers. Warm up thoroughly before and after campusing. Consult advanced training books for campus exercises and advice.

Hangboards, mounted anywhere from your home gym to a doorway, are an efficient and easy way to train fingers and forearms. They have lots of grip positions. Try them all. Also do pullups on grips. If you're not strong enough to hang for long, use bungee cords to stand in to carry some of your weight.

Campus and system boards offer ideal training for advanced climbers, quickly improving contact strength and power. If you're just starting out, stay off these apparatus for a few years. You can seriously injure tendons in your fingers if you overdo it.

System Wall

- A system wall is designed for ladder-style training, except with feet on the grips. The climber places his feet and turns his body from side to side with each reach movement, which mimics climbing body movement.

- System walls are steeper than campus boards and feature a wider variety of grips. System walls are space-efficient and inexpensive to build.

- A system wall is a valuable training tool that builds power, endurance, and contact strength.

Ropes, Ladders, and Rings

- The Bacher Ladder is a rope ladder with plastic pipe rungs that hangs from a tree. Climb it and get strong.

- Hand-over-hand climbing up a thick rope is great training. Work up to holding your legs straight out in an L as you ascend to add a core workout.

- Gymnastic-style rings are a great upper body workout. Presses on the rings develop mantle strength.

- Since climbers are always looking for somewhere convenient and affordable to train, homemade versions of these devices are popular.

MORE TRAINING

Use calisthenics, weight training, and cross-training to become a better climber

While climbing takes balance and grace, you can improve your performance further by strengthening your bones and muscles with a cross-training program. Adopt an exercise regimen that supports your climbing efforts. A good routine works climbing muscles as well as opposing muscles to promote optimal performance and prevent injury. Calisthenics,

learned back in gym class, build endurance for climbing days, while weight training keeps you strong for power moves.

Base your routine on calisthenics. Pullups, dips, and pushups use your body weight to strengthen muscles. These exercises ensure a complete upper body workout, engaging the five main muscle groups: back, biceps, pecs, triceps, and delts.

Pullups

- Pullups are the standard arm and shoulder workout favored by rock climbers world-wide.

- The normal pullup position is palms facing forward with hands shoulder-width apart on the bar.

- Pyramid sets of pullups are great for training, staying in shape, or getting an occasional pump.

- Experiment with various grips, grip widths, number of reps, and amount of rest time between sets.

Pushups

- Pushups are a great exercise for your training-for-climbing routine. Do two sets of pushups twice a week to prevent shoulder injuries.

- Pushups strengthen chest, shoulder, and back muscles. These are often neglected by climbers during typical training sessions.

- Try various hand placements to work different muscles. Pushups with your hands close together work your triceps, while hands far apart work the shoulders and back.

- Pushups don't require any apparatus and you can do them anywhere.

Add weight training to work those muscles from different angles. Resist using heavy weights for training. Doing low reps with heavy weight builds bulky muscles that weigh you down on the rock. Instead, stay lean with high reps and light weight. Weight training also increases bone density and makes joints and tendons sturdy, keeping you strong and injury-free.

Don't neglect your core. Keep abdominal muscles strong with crunches and leg lifts, which improve balance and give you power on vertical and overhanging rock. Use proper form so you're working your core and not your hip flexors. Talk to a trainer to ensure you're performing exercises correctly.

Pay attention to your legs and calves, too. Running, hiking, and light weight training trims your lower body and keeps your upper body strong. Squats and lunges make a good leg workout. Again, resist the urge to use heavy weights. You'll find greater rewards with lighter weight and higher reps.

Your muscles and bones need food to grow and rest to recover. Take rest days. A healthy diet and a good night's sleep also help you build a fit body for climbing and life.

Weight Training

- Talk to a personal trainer about developing a weight routine for climbing.

- Weight training is useful to gain an all-around muscle base to prevent injury and serve as a foundation for climbing-specific training.

- The key to weight training is variety. Mix up exercises, weight, and number of reps regularly for the most effective results.

- Don't lift weights more than two or three days a week. Rest is critical to build muscle and prevent injury.

Core Exercises

- Situps and crunches are beneficial training exercises.

- Leg lifts and L-raises are a great way to work up to doing front levers. They strengthen your core abdominal muscles so you can lift your feet up to holds on overhangs and roofs.

- Use abdominal workout machines, too. A variety of exercises improves your strength and fitness.

- Climbing, especially overhanging routes and extremely difficult climbs, requires lots of core strength.

TRAINING GAMES

Training, drills, and games put more fun into gym climbing and improve all your skills

Gym climbing is about having fun moving across vertical terrain. It can, however, get boring if you do the same routine every time you hit the gym. Go for variety. Do different routes or reverse the order you climb them. Practice climbing and then downclimbing the same route. Try doing easy routes with one hand.

You can play games on the bouldering wall. An hour of intense game-playing with a buddy yields huge benefits to your strength and technique. By competing against a clock or each other, you'll bring a whole new level to the climbing game and have lots of fun.

Practice is at the heart of success for any sport. The best

Add-a-move

- "Add-a-move" is a game that builds power, endurance, technique, and route memory skills.

- To start, the first climber does a move then steps off. A second climber repeats the first move and adds a second. A third climber repeats the first two moves

and adds a third and so on.

- The game is best on a bouldering wall. Make it a long traversing problem.

- For a faster game, add two or three moves per turn. Add-a-move is a fun and exciting game that inspires competition.

One-arm Climbing

- One-arm climbing is a good game to improve balance, coordination, focus, and strength.

- Besides doing one-arm problems in the gym, do them outside on easy routes by climbing them first with the right arm and then the left.

- Traversing problems with one arm is great for training alone.

- Practice dynamic movements and body positioning for deadpoints with one-arm climbing. One-arm dynos increase your contact strength.

practice players are always the best players. The same is true with climbing. Use gym time as practice time. Practice rest positions like one-arm hangs, no-hands stems, and heel hooks. Also do drills to improve specific techniques. Identify weaknesses and work at strengthening them. The aim of training, games, and drills is to improve basic skills. Don't confuse gym climbing with real rock performance. Do it inside to take it outside.

GREEN ● LIGHT

Don't climb too much. It's easy to climb too much when you're having fun. It's a recipe, however, for getting injured. Climb three or four times a week at the most, especially if it's gym climbing, so you avoid overworking your muscles and tendons. Do cross-training instead. Go hiking, running, or swimming. A man cannot live by rock alone.

INDOOR CLIMBING

Pointing Game

- The pointing game is played with one climber getting on the wall and climbing. Another climber stands on the ground and points to the problem's next hold.

- Use either a laser pointer or a broom handle to point to the next hold in the sequence.

- The pointing game is a fun and effective training game that can be played by climbers of all abilities.

- Make the game more challenging by restricting footholds.

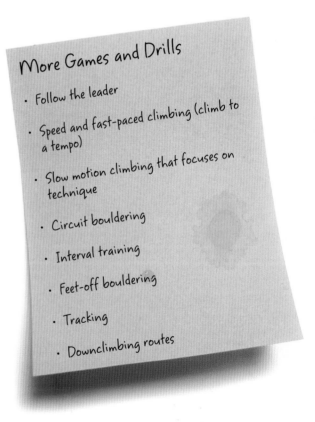

More Games and Drills

- Follow the leader
- Speed and fast-paced climbing (climb to a tempo)
- Slow motion climbing that focuses on technique
- Circuit bouldering
- Interval training
- Feet-off bouldering
- Tracking
- Downclimbing routes

ROCK SHOES

Get good rock shoes; they'll help you climb better, higher, and harder

What you wear on your feet when you climb is your most important equipment decision. You can wear sneakers or hiking boots when you start out, but if you want to improve and have more fun, then you will buy a pair of rock shoes.

Buy the wrong shoes and your feet will hurt and you'll probably give up climbing. But buy the right pair of shoes, ones

that mold to your feet like a second skin, and you'll be dancing up the cliffs.

Over one hundred different rock shoes are available, but most are for advanced climbers. Different climbing shoes behave differently, depending on the climbing you do. If you're a novice climber, it's an easy choice. You want an

What to Wear

- For granite, choose a stiff-soled, mid- to full-height shoe for edging and cracks.

- For sandstone, select a low-cut, soft shoe with a supple sole. This increases the flexibility of your forefoot, crucial for smearing on footholds.

- For limestone, choose a low- to mid-cut specialty shoe with a medium-stiff sole and pointy toe for standing in pockets and on edges.

- For volcanic and meta-morphic rock, choose an all-around, low- to mid-height shoe with a medium-stiff sole and pointed toe.

All-around Shoes

- All-around shoes are best for beginners and should always be your first shoe purchase.

- All-around shoes are versatile and are used for all types of climbing.

- They are best for multi-pitch climbing, where you face different types of climbing terrain.

- Don't size all-around shoes too tight. They shouldn't hurt your feet after several hours of wear.

all-around shoe for all the different climbing situations you'll encounter. You want a shoe that's comfortable, easy to put on and take off, and doesn't break the piggy bank.

When you're starting out, buy a stiff high-topped shoe that gives comfort and support around the ankle and arch. The stiff sole helps you stand on edges and develops your footwork. How you use your feet while climbing is important for success, and well-fitting, comfortable climbing shoes will help you be successful.

Later, as you improve, you can buy other shoes. Slippers are snug shoes that slip onto your foot. They're great for bouldering and gym climbing. High-performance rock shoes come in a huge variety of styles. Some are made for climbing limestone, with pointed toes for sticking in pockets, while others are great for hard sport routes where you might do lots of heel hooking.

You can also find lots of shoes made specifically for women and others for kids. Women's shoes, narrow with a low arch and smaller heel cup, generally fit women better than unisex shoes made for men, and are more comfortable.

Slippers

- Slippers are low-cut shoes with a soft sole and pointed toe box. The narrow toe excels in pockets and thin cracks.

- Slippers are great for gym climbing, slabs, and bouldering. They are easily taken off between routes.

- Size slippers snugly since most stretch after use. Ask your climbing shop about stretch when sizing them.

- Slippers dramatically improve your foot strength, since they don't provide the support of a lace-up shoe.

Specialty Shoes

- Many rock shoes are made specifically for kids and women.

- Women's shoes provide improved support, comfort, and performance for a woman's foot.

- Velcro slippers are stiffer and more supportive than regular slippers. They're the choice of many top climbers.

- Performance shoes usually have a down-cambered toe, making it easier to pull with the feet on steep rock.

MORE ROCK SHOES

Get the right shoes, snug yet comfortable, and you'll be dancing up the rock

Buy rock shoes at a reputable mountain shop with experienced salespeople who are climbers. There are shops that sell shoes but not the service and advice you need. Pick one by local reputation or ask other climbers which shop they like. As a beginning climber you have to rely and trust the shop staff to get the best shoes on you.

Buy a durable, comfortable rock shoe that fits well. As you learn to climb, you'll put them through the paces, so get a pair that stands up to abuse. Finding a good fit is essential, since learning to climb can be tough on your feet.

Get the right shoes for your feet. The wrong size will haunt you for a long time. If they're too wide or too small, you'll

Rock Shoe Parts

- The sole is the bottom of the shoe. It has sticky rubber for gripping the rock.

- The midsole is a strip between the inner sole and the outer sticky sole. It determines the stiffness of the shoe.

- The rand is a rubber strip around the toes and above the sole.

- The shoe's upper is made from either leather or synthetic leather and encases the foot and ankle, providing support and comfort. Some uppers are lined, which prevents stretch and gives extra support.

Fitting Rock Shoes

- Fit shoes from snug to tight, depending on your climbing ability and pain threshold. Your toes shouldn't slip or move in the toe box.

- Consider foot width when choosing shoes. Some manufacturers cater to either wide or narrow feet.

- All-around climbing shoes should be snug but comfortable. Performance shoes for hard climbing should always be tight.

- Fit shoes without socks. Most climbers don't wear socks for increased sensitivity to rock. For long routes, some prefer to wear thin socks.

end up tossing them in the garbage. Make sure they keep your foot flat and toes straight. If your toes are cramped or bent, they're too small. Look for shoes with a semi-rigid sole, one that bends with the resistance of a sneaker. That stiffness helps you stand on edges better.

Try on lots of different shoe styles and don't believe the sizes, which come in U.S., U.K., and European sizes. They all fit your feet differently. This makes it difficult to buy online, unless you're sure of your size or the retailer lets you send a scan of your feet.

Rock Shoe Care

- Air-dry shoes completely after use. This prevents mildew and bacteria and minimizes odor.

- Use odor-killing powder, baby powder, or deodorizing spray inside your shoes to avoid a certain funk.

- Never store shoes in sunlight, car trunks, or by excessive heat. Heat weakens glue, causes rubber to delaminate, and dries out the upper. Store in a cool dry place.

- Keep rubber soles clean and free of debris. Regularly clean the sole with soap and water.

Rock Shoe Buying Tips

- Rent a pair of shoes before buying.

- Buy shoes from a reputable outdoor retailer.

- Start out with an all-around shoe.

- New rock shoes stretch out after use.

- Size shoes carefully for a perfect fit.

- Try a few brands to see what fits best.

- Buy used for big savings. Check your gym's bulletin board.

- Buy online for great deals.

- Check for last year's models and close-out deals to save big bucks.

PERSONAL EQUIPMENT

CLIMBING HARNESS

Buy the right type of harness for years of climbing comfort and safety

The harness is another important piece of personal equipment. A harness, composed of a waist belt and leg loops constructed of nylon webbing, connects you to the rope, anchor points on cliffs, and to your climbing partner.

The harness waist belt rides above your hips while the leg loops fit snugly around your upper thighs. The waist belt and leg loops attach you to the climbing rope with a tie-in knot. If you fall or hang, the harness transfers the energy and force of a fall onto your pelvis. It also provides a comfortable seat for lowering and rappelling.

Before the invention of modern harnesses, climbers tied the rope around their waists. This was not only uncomfortable

Harness Types

- There are five harness styles—all-around, gym, big wall, alpine, and body.

- The best for novice climbers is the all-around, multipurpose harness.

- Lightweight gym and alpine harnesses are made for speed and ease of movement. They have little padding and can be uncomfortable. Big wall harnesses are made for comfort.

- Body harnesses are recommended for children and adults with narrow hips. They have a high tie-in point, reducing the chances of flipping upside down.

Parts of the Harness

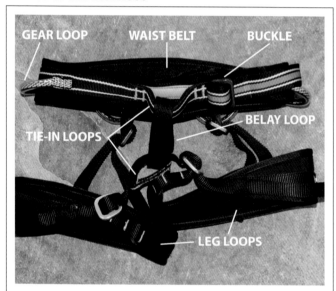

GEAR LOOP   WAIST BELT   BUCKLE

TIE-IN LOOPS   BELAY LOOP

LEG LOOPS

- A harness has lots of straps, buckles, and loops. Study the photo above so you understand the parts before buying a harness.

- The waist belt and leg loops are the most important parts.

- Harnesses have either one or two buckles on the front of the waist belt. Always double back a single buckle so it doesn't come undone.

- Tie the rope into the tie-in loop. Use the belay loop for belaying and rappelling. Gear loops support only gear, not body weight.

but also dangerous if the climber hung from the rope since it tightened around the waist and could lead to suffocation. Climbers began making crude harnesses from webbing, tying leg loops in a long length of webbing, wrapping it around the waist, and then tying the rope into it. Sewn harnesses similar to today's harnesses appeared in the early 1970s. Since then harnesses have evolved for comfort, safety, and durability.

Harnesses are made for different types of climbing—gym, alpine, big wall, and general climbing. Specific harnesses are made for women and children. Before you buy a harness, think about your experience level, how you will use it, the type of climbing you do, and what features are important to you.

While unpadded, no-frills harnesses are fine when you start out, if you're serious about climbing then buy a comfortable harness with padded leg loops and waistband. Your body will thank you for it.

Fitting a Harness

- Make sure the harness fits snugly around your waist and legs. It shouldn't slip, pinch, or restrict movement.

- The waist belt should be above your hip bones. You shouldn't ever be able to pull it below your hips. If you can, it's too big and you could slip out of it. Make sure the waistband is large enough. Be sure you have 3 inches of extra webbing after you've doubled it back through the buckle.

- Get adjustable leg loops if you're going to be wearing bulky clothes.

Harness Care

- Harnesses don't last forever. Even if you rarely wear it, the nylon webbing degrades and weakens over time.

- Protect your harness by not storing it in direct sunlight or near gasoline or chemicals.

- Check your harness regularly for abnormal wear and frayed seams. Pay special attention to the belay loop and make sure it is not damaged before rappelling.

- Regular climbing wears your harness out. Repeated sport climbing falls weaken the tie-in points. Retire your harness at any sign of unusual wear or after a couple years.

CHALK & CHALK BAGS

Chalk keeps your hands dry, but use it carefully to avoid damaging the rock

Many climbers use chalk on their hands to keep them dry and secure on handholds. If you're climbing on small edges on a hot day, you'll quickly grasp that using chalk keeps your hands from greasing off holds. Chalk absorbs moisture, including sweat, and improves your grip. John Gill, the father of bouldering and a former gymnast, introduced chalk to

climbing in the 1950s. You can buy chalk in blocks, loose in sandwich bags, or in chalk-filled fabric balls. Some chalk is specifically made for climbing. Most chalk is white, although you can buy colored chalk to match the rock for less visual impact.

If you use chalk, you need to buy a chalk bag. It's best to

Chalk

- Climbers use nontoxic chalk (magnesium carbonate) to keep their hands dry and secure on handholds. Chalk improves your grip on the rock in heat and comes in blocks, loose powder, and chalk-filled fabric balls.

- Block chalk, used by gymnasts, is absorbent

and cheap.

- Loose powdered chalk is mixed with drying agents for better grip. It's more expensive than blocks.

- Chalk balls are porous sacks filled with loose chalk. They keep you from spilling chalk.

Chalk Bags

- A chalk bag is simply a fabric sack that holds chalk as you climb. It's usually attached to a nylon belt around your waist or clipped to your harness with a carabiner.

- Chalk bags are cylindrical and come in various

sizes and colors. The most versatile are medium-size bags with a drawstring top. Make sure your hand slips in and out easily before buying one.

- Most bags have a stiff rim, fleece lining, and tooth-brush loop.

purchase a mid- to large-size, fleece-lined chalk bag. Make sure you can easily dip your hand inside. Chalk bags come in lots of different shapes, sizes, and fabric patterns. Pick something wild if you want to make a fun fashion statement. Also get a nylon belt to hang the bag on your waist.

Chalk use is controversial. It creates an eyesore on cliffs and boulders. It cakes onto handholds, requiring a toothbrush to scrub off the build-up. Some climbing areas require the use of colored chalk or ban it altogether. When using chalk, it's best to be mindful and restrict its use.

Using Chalk and Chalk Bags

- Wear the chalk bag on a belt around your waist in the middle of your back so either hand can reach it. Keep it loose enough so you can pull it to either side as you climb.

- Don't overchalk your hands. You usually don't need much unless it's hot outside and you sweat a lot.

- Always bring extra chalk. Have plenty in your bag for longer climbs that take all day.

- A toothbrush is handy for scrubbing old chalk off slimy handholds. Most chalk bags have a toothbrush loop.

Environmental Concerns

- The use of chalk is controversial. It's outlawed at some climbing areas because its long-term use damages the rock surface.

- Use chalk sparingly in dry climates. Chalk on overhanging faces that rarely get wet can linger for years.

- The build-up of chalk creates a slippery surface, especially on limestone. Also avoid ticking or marking holds with chalk marks unless you wash them off when you're done.

- Chalk stains are unsightly and can cause land managers to close bouldering areas.

PERSONAL EQUIPMENT

BELAY & RAPPEL DEVICES

These devices keep you and your partner safe

Belaying, the technique for safeguarding a climber with a rope, is an essential skill, and the belay device that you use makes it happen. Belay devices, also used for rappelling or sliding down a rope, come in an array of shapes and sizes. It's hard deciding which device is best for you. The good news is that most are easy to use and safe.

Belay devices are designed to let the belayer control the rope by creating friction and drag when it's loaded through the device. The most common devices are manual tubular ones, which require the belayer to lock the rope down with their brake hand. Experienced climbers often use auto-locking, self-braking devices that lock the rope without belayer action if the climber falls. These are fairly foolproof but require a learning curve and are expensive.

The invention of modern belay devices revolutionized climbing safety. In the old days, climbers belayed with a hip

Tube Devices

- Use a tube by pushing a bight of rope through the device and clipping the rope and device into a locking carabiner on your harness. When the brake hand locks in a downward position, the friction controls the belay or rappel.

- Lighter climbers complain

about difficulty rappelling, having to feed the rope through until body weight overtakes friction.

- Tube devices are popular and suitable for all types of climbing. They are the lightest, most compact, reliable, and easy-to-use belay devices.

Self-locking Devices

- Self-locking devices lock the rope in the event of a sharp tug, fall, or rope tension.

- Benefits include being able to hold the rope locked with little effort; the device remaining locked if the belayer lets go; and a smooth and easy feed of the rope through the device.

- Self-locking devices are recommended for use with ropes between 10mm and 11mm. Only use one rope at a time.

- Self-locking devices are best for sport and gym climbing. They are fairly foolproof but require expert training.

belay, where the rope was simply wrapped around a climber's waist. If a climber fell, the belayer held the rope with his hands and its friction around his body. This led to rope burns or worse since if the belayer's grip slipped, the climber dropped. That's still the case—belayer inattention and error leads to belaying accidents. Get proper instruction before belaying.

Figure-8 Devices

- The figure-8 rappel device takes its name from its shape, with a large hole and a small hole. A bight of rope passes through the large hole, then wraps around the neck beneath the small hole, which is clipped to the harness with a carabiner.

- Figure 8s work great for rappelling, since they accommodate any size rope and they dissipate heat quickly.

- Unlike other belay devices, the figure 8 works poorly for belaying. They provide less friction and kink or twist the rope.

Buying Tips

- After shoes and harness, your next climbing purchase is a belay/rappel device.

- Tubular belay devices are ideal. They're inexpensive, lightweight, and the most versatile for every climbing situation.

- Look for beginner package deals in stores or on the Internet that include a belay device, harness, and locking carabiner.

- If you climb a lot, consider using a self-locking device for sport climbing.

PERSONAL EQUIPMENT

HELMETS

Always wear a helmet to protect your head from falling rocks and head injuries

Always wear a helmet. That's a climbing safety mantra. Helmets save your life at the cliff if you get hit in the head by a falling rock or hit your head if you fall. Get in the habit of always wearing a helmet from your first day of climbing.

Climbing outside is not like climbing in a gym where there are few dangers. Potential problems can occur at every cliff we visit. No matter how safe a climbing area seems, lots of things can go wrong. We fall off and land upside down, hitting our head. Loose blocks fall off a ledge and hit us below. The rock doesn't care if we get hurt. Wear a helmet and you'll be safer.

Lots of helmets are available. They're stylish, modern, and

Helmet Types

- There are three types of climbing helmets.

- Suspension helmets, the most common helmets, have a hard outer plastic shell and an inner suspension system that allows the helmet to float on the head.

- Foam helmets, sit directly on your head. They're lighter and less durable than suspension helmets.

- Hybrid helmets combine the best of suspension and foam helmets with a suspended shell and thick foam cap.

Buying a Helmet

- Get a comfortable helmet; you'll be more likely to wear it.

- Place the helmet on your head with the front edge in the middle of your forehead. Don't tilt it back leaving your forehead exposed.

- Adjust the sizing before buckling the chin strap, then shake your head. The helmet should not feel loose or fall off.

- Buckle the chin strap and make sure there is no slack and that the helmet doesn't shift to either side.

light. Before you buy, try several on and find one that not only fits you well but looks good. If it's comfortable and stylish, you'll be more likely to take it to the crag every day you go climbing.

Just remember the consequences of not wearing a helmet and getting banged in the head with a rock. Head injuries are usually severe and have life-changing consequences. Wear a helmet—your head will thank you for it.

Wearing a Helmet

- Foam helmets, rather than suspension helmets, usually offer the best all-around protection, especially in absorbing energy from off-center and side impacts.

- Don't put stickers on your helmet. Solvents in the adhesive can damage the helmet shell.

- Helmets don't last forever. Retire it after a bad fall or no later than five years. Sunlight damages the plastic, so retire it sooner if you climb frequently.

- Look after your helmet by checking the chin strap and buckle before use.

Why Wear a Helmet

- Always wear a helmet. The rock is hard and your skull is soft.

- Statistics indicate that many climbing fatalities occur as a result of head injuries, most of which are preventable by wearing a helmet.

- Most head injuries in climbing are from falling and hitting your head rather than from rockfall.

- Wear a helmet when you're standing at a cliff-base and belaying.

- Wear a helmet on cliffs with loose rock.

- Wear a helmet if you're climbing below any other party. They might knock rocks off.

PERSONAL EQUIPMENT

WARM WEATHER CLOTHES

Wear lightweight clothes, sunscreen, and a hat to be prepared for hot weather

It gets hot when you're climbing in summer so you need to bring the right clothes to stay cool. Wear lightweight synthetic clothing, which protects your skin from the sun and is loose enough to allow airflow to cool you. Synthetic fabrics are great because they dry fast and don't chafe, although lots of climbers still wear cotton for comfort. Remember that

light colors deflect the sun's rays and are cooler than dark colors, which absorb them.

A good climbing outfit is shorts along with a t-shirt, tank top, or sports bra. If you're in mountains, bring long pants and rain gear. It's always a balancing act in summer—should you wear less if it's hot or more for sun protection. Wear what's

Dressing for Warm Weather

- You'll often climb in warm weather. Wear light, comfortable clothes that allow complete movement. Light colors absorb less heat.

- Clothes made of nylon or other synthetic fabrics wick perspiration away and dry quickly.

- If you're in mountains, bring extra pants, a long-sleeved shirt, and rain parka even on warm days.

- Shorts are best for summer climbing, but remember to apply sunscreen on your legs.

Sun Protection

- Prevent sunburn and skin cancer by using generous amounts of sunscreen on all exposed skin. Use at least SPF 30 or higher.

- Wear a hat to protect your face and top of your head from the sun and to shade your eyes.

- Sunglasses protect your eyes in mountains and deserts and reduce glare.

- Carry lip balm with an SPF rating to protect your lips from sun damage.

comfortable but use sunscreen to mitigate sun damage.

Sunscreen provides essential summer protection. Bring sunscreen with a sun protection factor (SPF) of at least 30. Lather it on exposed skin, including arms, legs, face, and the back of your neck and reapply later in the day. Get a sport sunscreen so it doesn't burn if sweat drips into your eyes. Also carry lip balm with an SPF rating to protect your lips.

If you're climbing in mountains, summer weather can quickly change. Be prepared by bringing a rain parka and rain pants in your pack. If you stay dry in rain, you won't get hypothermia.

Rain Protection

- If you're climbing in mountains during summer, bring a raincoat and rain pants to stay dry.

- Get lightweight raingear that rolls up small and can be stashed in the bottom of your climbing pack.

- A raincoat doubles as a windbreaker, providing extra protection from the elements.

- Always bring your rain parka. Heavy thunderstorms can leave you soaked and chilled.

Tips for Summer Sun

- Dehydration: Drink plenty of water and sports drinks. Bring at least three quarts per person in summer.

- Follow the shade: Look for cool shady cliffs. Avoid climbing in direct sun if you can.

- Sun exposure: Use sunscreen and lip balm. Wear a hat. Wear sunglasses.

- Watch for overheating: Pay attention to how you feel. If you're nauseous, have a headache, are flushed and red, have leg cramps, or are sweating heavily, then take time for a break. Find shade, drink fluids, and relax. A wet cloth on your forehead helps, too.

COLD WEATHER CLOTHES

Dress in layers when you're climbing to keep out the rain, snow, and cold

If you're climbing in the mountains or in winter, the weather quickly changes. It's essential that you bring extra clothing to provide insulation from wind, rain, and snow. If you prepare for the worst, you'll survive whatever weather you're out in. Just remember the old saying: There's no bad weather, only bad clothes.

When you go climbing, consider the weather and dress accordingly. Bring plenty of warm clothes and dress in layers so you can shed as you warm up. Your base layer should be lightweight and breathable to wick moisture away from your skin. The best garments are made of nylon, polypropylene, or other synthetics. The middle layer needs to insulate

Keeping Warm

- Cool weather is ideal for climbing hard routes since you don't sweat as much.

- Dress for temperature and weather conditions and pack plenty of warm clothes.

- Bring synthetic, fleece, and wool garments rather than cotton, which absorbs water and robs heat from your body.

- Put a stocking cap and light gloves in your pack for cool weather.

Dress in Layers

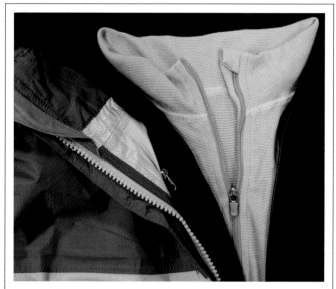

- Dress like an onion by wearing several thin layers of clothing rather than one thick layer.

- An inner layer of synthetic material moves moisture away from your body, keeping you dry and warm.

- Wear a middle layer of

insulating fleece or wool. Synthetic garments are best because they're light and compact.

- Choose an outer layer to ward off wind, rain, snow, and cold. A zipped rain parka does the trick. Get one that breathes so body moisture passes through.

and warm. Use fleece, pile, or wool to keep toasty. The outer layer protects you from weather. Bring waterproof or water-resistant fabrics that let perspiration out.

Wet cotton kills—avoid it for cool weather clothes. Cotton absorbs water, sucks heat from your body when wet, and is slow to dry. Save cotton clothes for summer climbing.

A warm stocking cap is important for cold weather climbing. You lose lots of body heat through your head. Remember that if critical body parts, like your head, are warm then more blood flows to your feet and hands. Wear a hat and stay warmer.

ZOOM

Bring these essential clothes—raincoat, rain pants, long pants, synthetic shirt, fleece pullover sweater, hat, and gloves. Extras include long underwear, wool socks, and a fleece jacket. Don't wear blue jeans or hoodies.

Outerwear

- Wear an insulating layer on your upper body when climbing in cool weather.

- Synthetic clothing like a vest, pullover fleece sweater, and fleece jacket are ideal. They absorb little water and dry quickly. On cold days, bring a down jacket for belaying.

- Bring an outer shell layer for rain, wind, and snow. A light wind shirt is compact, weighs nothing, and keeps you warm.

- Bring a hooded rain jacket with large pockets and rain pants with half-leg zippers. If it starts raining, you'll stay toasty and dry.

Cold Climbing Tips

- Rock shoes are thin. Keep your feet insulated on cold ground. Bring a carpet patch to stand on to keep feet dry and warm.

- Keep your hands warm. Avoid routes with pockets and cracks. Stick a chemical hand warmer in your chalk bag to toast your fingers.

- Warm your shoes before you climb by keeping them inside your coat between routes.

- If your body's core is warm, you'll be warm. Wear a coat if belaying or sitting around.

- Warm cold fingers by putting them on the nape of your neck at rest stances.

MORE PERSONAL EQUIPMENT

CLIMBING PACKS
Pick a climbing pack that's light, fits right, and carries all your gear

When you go climbing, you need a pack. The type you carry is determined by what you're climbing, how much gear you need to tote, and if you're carrying the pack up the route.

If you're climbing for the day and not planning on wearing a pack up your route, then you need an all-around pack with 2,400 to 3,000 cubic inches of capacity. You can put everything you need for a day's climbing in there, including rock shoes, harness, rack of gear and quickdraws, rain parka, extra clothes, food, and water. The rope can fit either inside the pack or tied under the lid.

A versatile pack used for both climbing and mountaineering is ideal. These packs have removable frame sheets or stays (used as stiffeners), attachments for gear outside, compression straps, reinforced gear loops on the waist belt, and floating top lids that can be used as fanny packs. Make sure the pack allows you to easily reach overhead for a hold when

Day Pack

- Climbing takes lots of gear. You need a roomy day pack to carry personal equipment and haul gear.

- Small day packs just aren't big enough to carry gear plus water, food, and clothes. Get one with 1,000 to 2,000 cubic inches of capacity.

- Top-loading packs are better than panel ones. Get one with a floating top lid to increase capacity. A top pocket is good for keys, wallet, and first-aid kit.

- Outside straps are handy for tying down a rope and attaching a helmet and ice axe.

Mountain Pack

- If you're climbing in mountains, then you need a big pack. Look for one with 2,400 to 3,000 cubic inches of capacity to carry gear and extra clothes.

- Choose a pack with a narrow profile, padded back, internal frame, and hip belt.

- Make sure it has a sturdy haul loop, ice axe loop, built-in daisy chain, and external pockets.

- Test it out in the store before buying. You want a pack that's stable and doesn't shift when you scramble on steep terrain or climb mountain rock.

you're wearing it, has helmet clearance, and fits above your harness. A good suspension system makes long approaches tolerable. Keep the unloaded pack weight under five pounds.

If you're carrying the pack up a route, use one with a narrow profile so it doesn't catch on rock and doesn't sag when loaded. Make sure it has a sturdy haul loop for hauling and a hydration pocket for a bladder, which saves digging for water bottles and collapses as it drains.

Fast and Light

- Get an ultra-light day pack if you're going to be climbing long routes. Make sure it has a small profile, haul loop, outside mesh pockets, and at least one zipped pocket.

- Fanny packs are handy for climbing multi-pitch routes. Keep it small with a low profile. Pack it with water, snacks, and compact raincoats.

- During summer, bring a pack with a built-in water bladder to stay hydrated all day. Make sure it's made of sturdy nylon to avoid tears.

Rope Bag

- You don't have to carry a pack if you've got a rope bag, which is basically a fancy tarp your rope lies on at the base of a route.

- They are usually big enough to stash your rock shoes, a rack of quickdraws, and a water bottle.

- Get one with a zipper, buckled straps to tighten down, and a shoulder strap.

- Spread the rope bag's tarp at the cliff-base to keep your rope out of the dirt or sand and your shoes clean.

MORE PERSONAL EQUIPMENT

FOOD & WATER

Bring nutritious snacks and water to stay energized and hydrated when you're out climbing

When you're climbing all day, bring plenty of food and drinks. Food keeps you fueled, energized, and alert. Water and energy drinks keep you hydrated, especially if it's hot.

If you're climbing, you're going to get thirsty. Carry plenty of water for the day as well as a way to disinfect water you might find. Try to anticipate how much water you'll need for a day trip.

If it's hot, plan on drinking four quarts in a day. Drink before you feel thirsty. Take small sips throughout the day to stay hydrated. This gives your body plenty of time to absorb fluids.

If you're sweating, you're losing essential salts and minerals. Bring electrolyte replacement powder or tablets, or energy drinks to replace lost electrolytes. Water doesn't replace

Water

- Bring plenty of water, at least four quarts per person in summer.

- Use durable water bottles (BPA free) with screw lids that are easy to carry and pack. Make sure they don't leak.

- On longer trips, bring water purification tablets like iodine (aqua tablets) or chlorine (Halazone). Don't drink untreated water to avoid water-based illnesses.

- Drink plenty when it's hot to stay hydrated and don't wait until you're thirsty. Drink between sixteen and thirty-two ounces hourly.

Sports Drinks

- If you're climbing and it's hot, you'll be sweating and losing essential salts and minerals. Replace these to maintain performance, especially at the end of the day to also replace carbohydrate stores.

- Good sports drinks containing electrolytes, like Gatorade and Powerade, replace lost salts.

- Electrolyte pills or mixes like Emergen-C can be added to water and are easily carried.

- Avoid taking salt pills unless prescribed by a doctor. Salty snacks like chips help replace salt.

electrolytes, so if you have cramps, nausea, or fuzzy thinking, then swallow an energy drink. Easily carried gel packets contain carbohydrates and give a quick shot of energy.

You need nutrition when you're hiking and climbing. Bring plenty of items that have easily digested carbohydrates like energy bars, gorp, nuts, and dried fruit. Energy bars are ideal since they're easy to carry. Pack four to six for a day of climbing. For a long day at the cliffs, bring real food, too. Ideal snacks include beef jerky, salami, cheese, tuna, carrot and celery sticks, peanut butter, and crackers.

•••••••••••••••••• RED ● LIGHT ••••••••••••••
Never drink untreated water because of waterborne diseases. Bring iodine or chlorine tablets, a stove and pot for boiling, or a water filter to disinfect backcountry water. Otherwise plan on some nasty intestinal bugs.

Energy Bars and Food

- Energy bars are compact, easy to carry, and provide fast fuel. Look for high carbs, low protein, and good sugars.

- Easy snack foods are good, too. Gorp or trail mix are great and easy to carry.

- Bring real food for a long day at the cliffs. Beef jerky, pepperoni or salami, cheese, tuna, carrot and celery sticks, and crackers are tasty and easy to pack.

- For a quick boost, squeeze energy gel into your mouth. These concentrated doses of carbohydrates are easily carried in a pocket.

Nutrition Tips

- If you're a climber, you're an athlete. Eat a balanced diet with complex carbohydrates, fruits, veggies, and lean protein.

- Before climbing, eat simple, easy-to-digest carbs like rice, oatmeal, and bananas for energy. Protein won't give you energy today.

- Munch on snacks throughout the day to keep alert, aware, and energetic. Small snacks keep your blood sugar stable and muscles nourished for action.

- Bring snacks and drinks in a cooler in your car for nutrition after climbing. Salty snacks like tortilla chips, pickles, and peanuts help recovery.

MORE PERSONAL EQUIPMENT

FIRST-AID KIT

Bring a first-aid kit and know how to use it so you're prepared if an accident happens

When you're climbing, there's always the possibility of injury to yourself or your partners. Always bring a basic first-aid kit, and know how to assess injuries and use first-aid supplies. It could make a big difference in case of an accident. Lots of things happen when you're climbing. You could trip and break a leg, get hit with a loose rock, or sprain an ankle. If you have a first-aid kit, you can patch these injuries up and survive until you get medical help.

It doesn't matter what first-aid supplies you carry if you don't know how to use them. Take a course in first aid and CPR and learn how to deal with life-threatening emergencies. The Red Cross regularly offers classes in most cities or

Personal First-Aid Kit

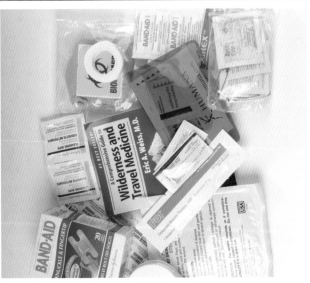

- Carry a small, lightweight personal first-aid kit in your pack. Make it from six to eight ounces and store in a waterproof ziplock bag or plastic container.

- Your first-aid kit should include: Gauze pads or rolls/sterile dressings, medical tape/duct tape, moleskin, butterfly bandages, triangular bandages, disinfecting ointment/Neosporin, over-the-counter pain medication /ibuprofen, tweezers, small scissors, safety pins, medical gloves, anti-diarrheal medication, Aloksak bag or ziplock bag, and a compact first-aid book.

Group First-Aid Kit

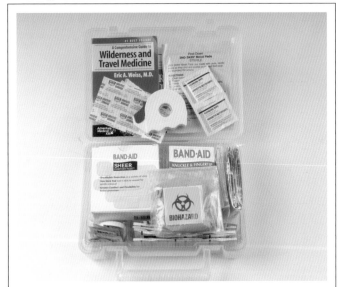

- For multi-day climbing trips or a large group, bring a group first-aid kit.

- Consider buying a prepackaged first-aid kit and adding extra items to make it complete.

- Extra items include inflatable splints for fractures, bandage scissors, space blanket, EpiPen, fingertip bandages, and duct tape.

- Make sure the person with the most first-aid training, preferably a Wilderness First Responder, knows where the first-aid kit is and what it contains.

online. If you once took a class, get a refresher every year to stay up to date.

Climbing accidents are usually either minor inconveniences or major emergencies. Your first-aid kit should cover the in-between injuries. As you fill your kit, think about common injuries and buy supplies to treat those. Some of the usual injuries are sprains, wounds, bleeding, headaches, blisters, pain, broken bones, and head injuries.

Try to find a balance between what supplies you need and how big and heavy the kit will be. You can buy a prepackaged first-aid kit and then personalize it with extra items. For day trips, keep the kit to six ounces. For long trips, carry a bigger kit since you'll be farther from help. Also bring a cell phone. If you need to call for rescue, you may be able to get service. It's best to keep your kit simple, but know how to use everything in it to save a life.

First-Aid Extras

- Know the most common climbing injuries and how to treat them. Carry extra bandages and an inflatable splint if you're climbing in the backcountry.

- Know your climbing partners' medical history and drug allergies, and what drugs they currently take.

- If you're in an emergency situation, first take a deep breath and then assess injuries.

- Keep your first-aid kit simple and know how to use everything in it—otherwise it won't do any good.

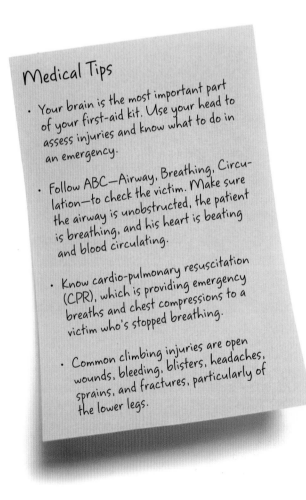

Medical Tips

- Your brain is the most important part of your first-aid kit. Use your head to assess injuries and know what to do in an emergency.

- Follow ABC—Airway, Breathing, Circulation—to check the victim. Make sure the airway is unobstructed, the patient is breathing, and his heart is beating and blood circulating.

- Know cardio-pulmonary resuscitation (CPR), which is providing emergency breaths and chest compressions to a victim who's stopped breathing.

- Common climbing injuries are open wounds, bleeding, blisters, headaches, sprains, and fractures, particularly of the lower legs.

ACCESSORIES

Additional items that can be a luxury or a necessity, depending on your situation

It's good to bring some extras in your climbing pack, especially if you have a couple pockets in the lid.

Carry a lightweight headlamp in case you get caught out after sunset and have to walk in the dark. You can easily pack a three-ounce headlamp with bright light-emitting diodes (LEDs) along with an extra battery. These lights use little power, give lots of light, and free your hands.

Sunglasses are another piece of critical gear. Get ones that block 100 percent of ultraviolet light (both UVA and UVB) and offer wraparound protection to protect your eyes from wind. Make sure they have sturdy frames. Keep them in a hard case in your pack.

Headlamp

- Carry a small headlamp in your pack in case you get lost or have to finish a climb and hike out in the dark.

- Get a headlamp with high and low beams, high and low settings to conserve power, a strobe setting for emergencies, and a built-in battery indicator.

- Look for one under five ounces with light-emitting diodes (LEDs) and a headband. Make sure your helmet has headlamp clips.

- If you're climbing with a headlamp, you need a range of 60 feet. For hiking, get one with a range up to 300 feet.

Sunglasses

- Protection from the sun is essential to the health of your eyes.

- Get sunglasses that block 100 percent of ultra-violet light (both UVA and UVB). UVB rays can cause cataracts.

- Wraparound sunglasses offer protection from the wind.

- For mountaineering or climbing on snow, get glacier glasses with extra-dark lenses to avoid getting snow blindness.

It's great to carry a camera to record your vertical adventures. Look for a compact point-and-shoot digital camera that you can stash in a case clipped to your harness. Make sure you have a long leash so you don't drop it from a high ledge.

There are other items you can take if you have room. A climbing guidebook is worth its weight since you can figure out what you're climbing. Bring athletic tape for taping your hands for crack climbs or repairing cuts. A tube of sunscreen, at least SPF 30, protects exposed skin. Bring something to start a fire. Waterproof matches are a good bet. Bring a knife for cutting slices of cheese or old rappel slings as well as a multi-tool device with blades, screwdrivers, and awls for making repairs.

On a multi-day trip, bring an emergency shelter, like a lightweight camping tarp, as well as a map and compass so you don't get lost. Also toss a cell phone in your pack. If you have an accident or emergency, you just may get cell service and can call for help.

Camera

- You'll want to bring a camera to record your vertical adventures and the good times.

- The best climbing camera is a light, sturdy, point-and-shoot digital camera. You should be able to use it one-handed. More expensive models have image stabilization. Pack extra batteries.

- Use a 30-inch leash made from thin accessory cord to attach the camera to you. Clip it to your harness with a small carabiner, then put it in your pocket or use a small padded case.

Climbing Extras

- Athletic tape for taping hands for crack climbing.

- A climbing guidebook helps you find the right routes.

- Sunscreen keeps you from getting sunburned.

- Matches, preferably waterproof, are a lifesaver if you get benighted.

- A knife is essential for cutting rappel slings and has other uses. Look for one with a carabiner hole.

- A multi-tool device with scissors, awl, and blades for repair jobs.

59

CLIMBING ROPES

Your rope is your lifeline; treat it with respect and it will take care of you

Many different ropes are used for climbing. Ropes come in various lengths, diameters, and types to cater to every climber's needs. The rope you use depends on the climbing you do. Veteran climbers often keep extra ropes in the closet for different climbing adventures.

The two basic rope types are static and dynamic. Static ropes don't stretch and are best used for rappelling, caving, big walls, and rescue work. Never lead climb on a static rope—it will break your neck or back if you fall. Dynamic ropes, on the other hand, are a climber's best friend. Like a bungee cord, they stretch significantly when weighted by a fall. This dynamic quality effectively saves the climber by

Types of Rope

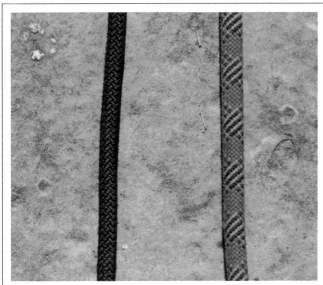

- Dynamic rope is climbing rope. It stretches to absorb forces during a fall, lessening the impact on a climber.

- Never use a static rope for lead climbing. If you fall, the rope won't stretch and absorb the impact load. Static ropes are fine for top-roping and rappelling.

- Dry ropes are treated not to absorb moisture, improving the rope's strength and life. Dry ropes are used for mountain climbing.

- Half-ropes are used on wandering routes. The climber clips different ropes into alternating pieces of protection, lessening rope drag.

Choosing a Rope

- How long? A 200-foot (60-meter) single rope is today's standard rope, although a 165-foot (50-meter) works fine.

- How thick? The standard diameter is 10mm to 10.5mm. Use thicker ropes for top-roping and heavy use. Use a thin rope when

- weight is a consideration on hard routes.

- An all-around rope is best for most situations.

- All-around ropes aren't heavy, so unless you're humping it into the high mountains, think safety and strength over weight.

reducing the stress impact of a fall on the climber and the protection system used.

Dry ropes are specially treated so they don't absorb water. They're perfect for ice climbing, mountaineering, or climbing in inclement weather. Half-ropes are basically two ropes of small diameters that are used together as a system to prevent rope drag and for making double-rope rappels.

The best rope to buy is a 200-foot (60-meter), 10.5mm, all-around dynamic rope. This versatile rope lets you climb long pitches or sport climbs up to 100 feet long and is thick enough to feel sturdy and strong. As your climbing skills improve, you can purchase specialty ropes that are either longer or thinner.

Treat your rope with care and respect—it's your lifeline. Your rope protects your vertical adventures and keeps you safe on the rocks. Coil your rope when you're not using it and store it in a rope bag. Most rope bags include a fold-out tarp, which keeps dirt and sand from weakening the rope. Regularly inspect your rope for abnormal wear or frays. Store it away from heat, dirt, sunlight, and chemicals.

Coiling a Rope

- Grab the ends of the rope together and pull four arm-lengths of slack onto the ground. Place two strands together behind your neck.

- Loop the rope back and forth on each side of your neck until the rope is gone. Lift the coil from your neck. Wrap them tightly around the middle for five coils. Pass a double bight of rope through the hole. Feed the ends through and pull tight.

- Carry a rope by splitting the ends and looping each over opposite shoulders. Crisscross the ends behind the back and tie a square knot in front.

Take Care of Your Rope:

- Use a rope bag that unfolds into a tarp to protect your rope from dust, dirt, and debris.

- Don't step on your rope. This grinds dirt into the sheath and core.

- Make sure the rope runs free and doesn't cross sharp edges. Friction wears through the sheath or can cut the rope.

- Wash your rope when it's dirty. Regular washing keeps dirt off the sheath and core and extends its life.

- Retire your rope after a long fall.

- Regularly inspect your rope. Feel with your fingers and look for wear spots, including damaged sheath; soft, mushy, and hard spots; frays and wear.

CARABINERS

A small yet strong device, the mighty carabiner serves many crucial roles in safe climbing

Carabiners, sometimes called "biners" and "crabs," are essential gear that links other equipment like ropes, cams, nuts, and slings into a working safety system. They are strong, lightweight metal links, made from either steel or aluminum, with a spring-tensioned gate that opens so that you can attach climbing gear.

Climbers use light aluminum carabiners most of the time, although steel ones, which are stronger but heavier, are often used on top-rope anchors. Some carabiners have a locking gate, which is crucial for climbing safety and essential gear. Carabiners with a key-lock or wire gate are stronger and less likely to come unclipped. Wire gates are lightweight yet strong

Carabiner Shapes

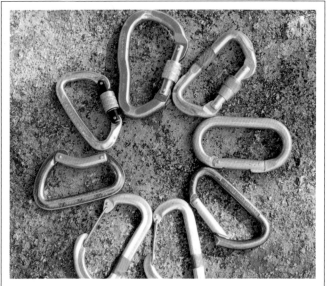

- Carabiners come in four basic shapes: oval, D-shaped, asymmetrical D-shaped, and pear-shaped.

- Oval carabiners, the original style, are affordable and versatile for all kinds of climbing. The rounded bottom limits shifting when it's loaded.

- The D-shaped carabiner, the workhorse biner, is the strongest and lightest carabiner. It shifts weight away from the gate to the stronger spine.

- Asymmetrical D-shaped and pear-shaped biners are like regular Ds, except the top end is narrower. They have larger gates for easy clipping.

Carabiner Gates

- Straight-gate carabiners are the most common and least expensive biners.

- Bent-gate carabiners have a concave or curved gate to make it easier to clip the rope into it.

- Bent-gates are used in sport climbing when the leader

- often needs to be able to quickly clip the rope for protection.

- Wire-gate carabiners, with a loop of stainless steel wire for the gate, are strong, lightweight, and open wider than other gates.

carabiners, which are important when weight is a factor.

The four types of carabiners are oval, D-shaped, asymmetrical D-shaped, and pear-shaped. Oval carabiners are popular, affordable, and versatile for all types of climbing. Asymmetrical D-shaped carabiners, available with straight and bent gates, are standard for sport climbing. Bent-gate carabiners are light and shaped so it's easy to clip the rope into them while leading.

Locking carabiners are extremely safe since the gate won't open, and they keep you attached to anchors and gear. Use locking carabiners for tying into your safety system.

Locking Carabiners

- Locking carabiners have gates that lock closed to prevent the gate from accidently opening.

- There are two types of locking carabiners: screw-gate and auto-locking gate. Auto-lockers are safer, since they will not come undone.

- Locking biners are very important for your climbing safety.

- Always use a locking carabiner when you have to rely on one carabiner, such as when rappelling, belaying, on your first piece of protection, or at anchors.

Carabiner Care

- If your carabiner gates get sticky or won't close properly, give a few squirts of compressed air and see if that cleans any dirt.

- If not, wash them in soapy water and scrub with a toothbrush.

- Thoroughly dry the carabiners and spray the gates with a lubricant.

- Retire any carabiner that exhibits excessive wear, has grooves in the base, has hairline cracks, or has been dropped more than 20 feet.

SLINGS & QUICKDRAWS

Use slings and quickdraws to reduce rope drag and link together your safety system

Slings and quickdraws are crucial pieces of gear that work together with carabiners and your rope to make a safe climbing system.

A quickdraw is a specially designed piece of sewn webbing with carabiners attached to its top and bottom. The top carabiner is clipped into a bolt or piece of gear, while the rope is clipped into the bottom carabiner. This reduces stress on the anchor and reduces the load on each carabiner since the sling absorbs energy from a fall.

Slings are lengths of $1/2$-inch or 1-inch webbing that are tied or sewn together in 1-, 2-, and 4-foot lengths. Sewn slings are stronger than tied ones. Slings are used to clip into gear like

Choosing Quickdraws

- A quickdraw is two carabiners attached to each other with a sewn sling. Most quickdraws have a straight-gate carabiner at the top and bent-gate at the bottom.

- Always clip the rope to the bent-gate carabiner.

- Buy ten to fifteen quick-

draws to climb sport routes. Get a couple quickdraws with a locking carabiner at the top for clipping into anchors and for the first bolt.

- Use mostly short 4-inch quickdraws. Longer draws from 6 to 12 inches are handy for reducing rope drag.

Using Quickdraws

- Quickdraws reduce rope drag when they are clipped into various protection points.

- Clip the rope into the bottom carabiner of the quickdraw. Make sure the spine, the strongest part of the carabiner, faces your direction of travel.

- Orient the gates on each carabiner so they open opposite each other. This keeps the gates from accidently opening under load at the same time.

- For safety, put a locking carabiner at each end of a draw to attach the rope to belay anchors or top-rope anchors.

cams and nuts to reduce rope drag, for equalizing belay and protection anchors, for attaching yourself to anchors, and for tying off natural anchors. Two-foot slings, the most common, fit over your shoulder and are usually used to reduce rope drag.

Always carry untied 1-inch webbing in your gear cache. This flat or tubular tape is used for many tasks, like rappel anchors or an emergency harness. Bring a knife to cut it.

ZOOM

As you build your rack of climbing gear, purchase twelve to fifteen quickdraws, a couple 2-foot slings, a 4-foot sling, four to six short slings, and 40 feet of webbing. Use quickdraws with a rubber or tight-fitting bottom to keep the bottom bent-gate carabiner from turning and crossloading.

Slings

- Slings are either ½-inch or 1-inch-wide webbing with their ends either sewn or tied together with a water knot. They usually come in 2-foot or 4-foot lengths. Sewn slings are stronger than knotted ones.

- Carry a few sewn 2-foot slings, each with two carabiners, for clipping into gear to reduce rope drag.

- Slings do lots of work—tying off blocks and flakes, extending anchors, and equalizing belay, top-rope, and rappel anchors. Some slings are made from ultra-light, super-strong polyethylene material like Spectra.

Webbing

- Webbing is a strong tape, usually made of nylon, which is either flat or tubular. It comes in widths of ½ inch, 1 inch, and 3 inches.

- Webbing is used to make harnesses, quickdraws, slings, pack straps, and chalk bag belts.

- A 30- to 40-foot length of webbing can be used to make a climbing harness called a Swiss seat.

- Buy webbing in whatever length you want to make slings or to leave for rappel anchors. Tie the webbing together with a water knot.

NUTS

Inexpensive, lightweight, and easy to use, nuts are an economical addition to your gear rack

Nuts, a type of passive protection, are metal anchors of various shapes and sizes that are used to protect cracks. These wedge- and hexentric-shaped devices are placed and locked into constrictions and bottlenecks in cracks on a rock face. Nuts are slung with either a wire cable or tied piece of webbing, which a carabiner and the rope are then clipped onto.

When a nut is placed in a constriction, it's seated in place by being weighted or pulled. When placed correctly, nuts offer incredibly strong and reliable anchors for both lead climbing and for belay anchors. Nuts are clean climbing tools, meaning they don't damage the rock with their placement and removal. They're also very affordable.

Hexentrics

- Hexentrics are six-sided aluminum nuts with a sling for clipping a carabiner.

- Hexes, when wedged inside tapered cracks, are held in place by friction.

- They're a useful addition to any rack since Hexes are cheap and fit a wide variety of cracks. They're often ideal for wider cracks.

- Hexes are lightweight compared to cams, making your rack lighter overall than if you carry a set of cams.

Wired Nuts

- Wired nuts, also called tapers, have wedge-shaped aluminum heads that are placed in constrictions in a crack. A strong wire cable is threaded through the nut, allowing a carabiner to be clipped onto it.

- Skilled climbers carry a variety of wired nuts for different climbing situations.

- Micro-nuts are the smallest nuts available. Their strength depends on the cable strength, the head, and the rock. Use only when no alternate protection is available. Leader falls on micros are not recommended.

The three main nut types are Hexentrics, wired nuts or tapers, and Tri-Cams. Hexentrics are six-sided aluminum nuts in small to large sizes. They're a great alternative to expensive cams, discussed in the next section. Wired nuts, also called tapers, are four-sided, wedge-shaped heads threaded with a wire cable for clipping a carabiner. Wired nuts are ideal for protecting thin cracks. Tri-Cams are specialty nuts used in pockets and weird-shaped cracks. Don't forget to bring a nut tool to remove stuck gear.

Tri-Cams

- Tri-Cams are tapers that combine the benefits of cams and nuts. They are curved across the back with a fulcrum point on the opposite side.

- Placed as a nut, Tri-Cams perform well in cracks and pockets.

- Their camming action protects difficult placements in pockets and parallel-sided cracks. Round pockets are protected by Tri-Cams.

- Place the Tri-Cam with its sling along the curved side. This leverages the point on the opposite side, which cams into the rock.

Nut Tool

- These blade-shaped metal devices pry, push, pull, and tap on stuck nuts. Every rack needs one.

- When a nut is wedged tight and can't be jerked out by hand, use the nut tool.

- Use the tool as a chisel to tap a stuck nut loose. Take care not to damage the nut's wire.

- Nut tools can also clean stuck cams. When a cam walks back into a crack beyond reach, use the nut tool to pull the trigger and release it.

CAMMING DEVICES

To make anchors and provide lead protection, camming devices are your best friends

Spring-loaded camming devices are the modern safety net for traditional climbing. In the days before cams, climbers protected routes with various types of nuts that were wedged into cracks. In the late 1970s, climber Ray Jardine revolutionized the sport with the invention of the "Friend," the first camming device. Suddenly, parallel-sided cracks at

places like Indian Creek in Utah, which until then were not protectable, opened to climbers.

A cam is a specialized device that expands and retracts to fit inside cracks of almost any size, giving secure protection to leaders and as belay anchors. Using a trigger, the cam is retracted to a smaller size and placed inside a crack. When

Spring-loaded Cams

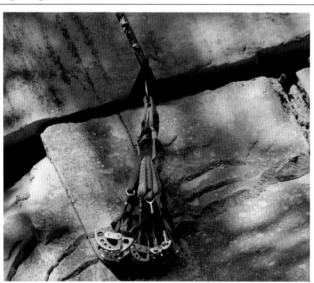

Specialized Cams

- Spring-loaded camming devices use movable parts to provide protection in cracks where nuts won't hold.

- Using a trigger, the cam is retracted to fit inside a crack. When the trigger is released, the cam expands to fit the crack.

- Rigid or flexible cams? Rigid cams are stronger and used in vertical cracks. Flexible cams, though weaker, are used in horizontal cracks.

- Cams have a larger range of expansion. One cam fits different-size cracks, making them versatile.

- TCUs are cams with three lobes. TCUs work in small, narrow, or constricted cracks. Their narrow head makes them ideal for pin scars, thin cracks and seams, and aid climbing.

- Link cams offer an increased range of motion over regular cams, making one piece

- fit inside a wide range of cracks. The disadvantage is increased weight.

- Large cams protect off-width cracks. Large cams are heavy and rarely carried.

- Spring-loaded tube chocks are telescoping tubes used in wide cracks.

the trigger is released, the cam expands to fit perfectly inside the crack. Cams are popular with climbers because they're quick and easy to place in cracks and offer a lot of security. A well-placed cam will almost never pull out of a crack.

There are many types and brands of camming devices available at your local climbing shop, catering to every crack size you'll find. There are rigid cams and flexible cams, very large cams for off-width cracks, link cams, which fit many crack sizes, and TCUs for thin cracks.

With all the cams available, which ones should you buy first for your rack? If you're starting out, buy a basic set of standard cams. These complement sets of nuts and protect most moderate routes for novices. After that you can expand your rack and buy specialized cams for very wide and very thin cracks.

Your cams are expensive so take good care of them. Inspect regularly for wear and tear, especially checking the trigger wires, and keep them clean and free from dust and dirt. Clean cams will keep you safe and last for a lot of great climbs.

Buying Cams

- Try out different types and decide which ones feel best in your hand. Also consider the type of rock and routes you climb.

- Build your rack of cams with a combination of flexible- and rigid-stem cams. Rigid cams are cheaper.

- Double-axle cams have a wider range of expansion than single-axle cams.

- Improvements are made to cams every year. Ask your local mountain shop about the latest innovations.

Cam Care

- Inspect cams regularly. Look for hairline cracks, inspect cam teeth and cables, axle movement, and integrity of the sling.

- Keep cams dry, clean, and away from dirt, sunlight, and corrosives.

- To clean cams, mix cam cleaner and water. Rinse cams in the solution to work out dirt. Use a toothbrush to scrub it. Rinse in hot water and air dry. When dry, apply a cam lubricant to moving parts including the cam head, axle pivots, and trigger. Work the trigger until smooth motion is restored.

OTHER GEAR

Special features, including off-width cracks and steep blank faces, require specialty climbing gear

Modern technology has spawned lots of ingenious climbing equipment, engineered to protect a climber on difficult faces. Beyond the usual gear, there is specialized climbing gear for almost any situation. This variety makes cutting-edge ascents possible. Climbing gear you might eventually have on your rack includes off-width protection, bolts, ascenders, and aid

climbing equipment. Almost every long multi-pitch route has an off-width crack, so it's crucial to know what off-width gear is available and how to use it. The primary protection for off-widths are large cams and spring-loaded tube chocks.

To protect faces devoid of cracks, climbers use bolts, which are placed in drilled holes. A bolt hanger with an eye to clip a

Off-width Protection

- Spring-loaded tube chocks, called Big Bros, are used to protect cracks wider than 6 inches.

- Big cams fit cracks up to 7 inches wide.

- Inspect off-width cracks and chimneys for cracks inside walls that might offer protection with smaller gear.

- Find natural pro in wide cracks. Look for chockstones to tie off with slings and threads.

Bolts

- Bolts are mechanical metal anchors that are permanently placed in a hole drilled in rock. A carabiner is clipped into a bolt hanger attached to the bolt.

- Bolts are used on sport climbs. They protect a lead climber where no gear can be placed or as belay and

- rappel anchors.

- Bolts should only be placed by expert climbers since they damage the rock surface.

- Bolts should never be placed next to cracks where removable protection can be placed.

carabiner and rope is attached to the bolt. Bolts are common fixed protection on sport climbs. *Bolts should only be placed by experienced climbers since they damage the rock.*

Mechanical ascenders are used to climb fixed ropes safely. Used in pairs, they clamp onto the rope when downward force is applied, but when unweighted, slide freely up. Using slings with footsteps, the climber can ascend a rope with relative ease.

Aid climbing requires tools that make steep faces climbable. Gear includes aiders to stand in, hooks, and pitons.

Ascenders

- Ascenders are mechanical devices with handles that attach to a rope and are used to ascend it. A spring-loaded plate of metal teeth bites the rope when downward force is applied.

- They are used for big-wall climbing, rescue, and climbing fixed ropes.

- A climber attaches slings with foot loops to his harness and the ascenders. He stands in the slings, allowing him to transfer weight between ascenders and climb the rope.

- It takes time to learn how to use ascenders. Practice at a local cliff with a top-rope.

Aid Gear

- Aid climbing requires lots of equipment, including nuts, cams, pitons, hooks, and specialized gear. You also need aiders or four-step webbing ladders to stand in.

- Pitons are metal pegs of many shapes and sizes that are hammered into cracks where cams and nuts won't work. Using pitons damages the rock.

- Specialized aid gear includes copperheads, RURPS, and hooks, used to cling to blank faces.

- Experienced climbers can tell you what you need to start aid climbing.

71

KNOTS FOR CLIMBING

You don't need to learn a lot of knots; you just need to learn a few knots well

Climbing knots are tools that allow you to safely use the rope and protect yourself from the effects of gravity. Climbers use knots for lots of different situations, including tying into anchors, tying into the rope, tying ropes together, for belaying, and in emergency situations.

Knots are one of the most important aspects of your

climbing safety system, which begins with your climbing rope. Your rope is your lifeline. Your knot is your life preserver. They are the basis of your safety when you're climbing. Learn them. Practice them. Tie them right. Your life depends on them.

You don't need a lot of knots to go climbing. While there are over 4,000 knots, all the ones you need to know are in this

Learn Your Knots

- The climbing knots you use are essential to your personal safety while climbing.

- Every climber needs to know how to tie into the end of a climbing rope and how to tie into an anchor on the cliff.

- If your knot is tied incor-

rectly or comes undone, you can suffer severe injuries or death.

- Learn how to tie all the recommended climbing knots until you have them memorized and can tie them in all kinds of weather and at night. Practice makes perfect.

Knot Strength

- Climbers always use the strongest knots when they climb.

- Knots reduce the strength of a climbing rope, which is strongest when it is straight and without bends, kinks, and knots.

- How well a knot is tied is

reflected by its holding power. A properly tied knot is stronger than a sloppy one.

- Take your time when tying knots. Always make sure you finish the knot—your life depends on it. Ask your partner to double-check your knots.

book. As your climbing career progresses, you will learn other specialized knots, but these everyday knots are the ones you need to know backwards, forwards, and in the dark.

Some knots are stronger than others, and those are the ones that climbers use. A knot, however, is only as strong as the rope it's tied into. Knots reduce a rope's strength, so it's important to tie the strongest knots for important safety tasks. How a knot is tied affects its strength, although even sloppy knots still retain most of their strength. Also remember that even though knots reduce a rope's strength, modern climbing ropes are incredibly strong so safety is never compromised.

There are three types of knots—bends, loops, and hitches. The end of the rope used to tie a knot is the working end, while the opposite end is the standing end. When rope is bent into a U-shape, it's called a bight of rope. A piece of rope that crosses itself is a loop. Learn the types of knots and know the rope parts and it will be easier to learn your knots.

Knot Terms

- A bend knot has opposite ends of the rope coming out opposite sides of the knot.

- A loop knot is tied in the rope's middle.

- A hitch is an adjustable knot with a loop of rope wrapped around something.

- The working end is the end used to tie a knot. The standing part is the rest of the rope. The tail or standing end is the opposite end. A loop is a piece of rope that crosses over itself. A bight is an open U-shaped bend in rope.

Best Climbing Knots

- You don't need to learn a lot of knots. You only need to learn the right knots for different situations. Learn these six knots and climb safe:

- Figure-8 follow-through knot is the best knot for tying yourself into a rope.

- Figure-8-on-a-bight knot is ideal for tying your rope into belay anchors.

- Clove hitch works great for tying into belay anchors.

- Double figure-8 fisherman's knot is the best knot for tying two ropes together.

- Prusik knot is a rescue knot for ascending a fixed rope in an emergency.

- Münter hitch is used for belaying and rappelling in an emergency.

USES OF KNOTS
Knots have specific duties; learn each one's use and tie the right knot every time

Climbers use knots for many tasks including tying into the rope, tying into belay anchors, joining two ropes together, tying lengths of webbing and cord into loops, ascending a fixed rope, rescue and escaping a belay, belaying and rappelling, and as a safety backup. Knots put the rope to work and keep you safe.

Your most important knot is the one that ties your harness into the climbing rope. You want to use a knot that's strong and won't come untied. The knot that fits the bill is the figure-8 follow-through. Some sport climbers use a double bowline, but this is not recommended since it can come undone and it's more difficult to tie than the figure-8 follow-through.

Tying into the Rope

- The most important knot you will learn is the knot that ties the rope into your climbing harness. Tie the wrong knot or tie it wrong and you could die.

- The figure-8-follow-through knot is the best knot

- for tying into a harness because it's strong, easy to check, and easy to untie. If it's weighted, it gets tighter.

- Always use the same tie-in knot. Practice it often and learn to tie it in rain, sun, and at night.

Tying into Anchors

- Climbers use loop knots and hitches to attach to belay anchors or other cliff anchor points.

- The clove hitch is a basic knot used to tie into carabiners on belay anchors. It's easy to tie, easily adjustable, and easy to untie.

- The figure-8-on-a-bight knot, also called figure-8 loop, is a strong knot to attach the rope and yourself into anchors.

- Learn the equalizing figure-8-on-a-bight to tie into two or three anchor points.

You also use knots to attach the rope and yourself to belay anchors on ledges. The clove hitch is ideal for this duty. It's easy and quick to tie and can be easily adjusted. Also learn the figure-8-on-a-bight since it's super strong and easy to tie.

There are several great knots for tying two ropes together for rappelling or top-roping. The best is the double figure-8 fisherman's knot since it's strong and won't come untied. Other common knots are the double overhand knot, double fisherman's knot, and square fisherman's knot.

Every climber needs to know essential rescue and safety knots for emergency situations. The Münter hitch doubles as both a rappel and belay knot in case you lose your belay device. Use a Prusik, Bachmann, or Klemheist knot to climb a fixed rope to an injured leader or if you've fallen below an overhang. Use an autoblock as a safety backup knot when you're rappelling, especially on steep cliffs, and always tie stopper knots in the ends of the rappel ropes so you don't fall off the ends.

Tying Ropes Together

- Climbers use bend knots for tying two ropes together for top-roping and rappelling. You need a strong knot that won't come untied and will support your weight.

- The double figure-8 fisherman's knot is recommended for tying ropes together. It's easy to tie and strong.

- The double overhand knot is also popular. It's easy to tie and has a low profile so it doesn't snag or get stuck.

- The double fisherman's knot and square fisherman's knot are also good choices to tie ropes together.

Safety and Rescue Knots

- Climbers need to know several knots that are used in rescue and emergency situations, like ascending a rope, tying off an injured climber, or escaping a belay.

- The Münter or Italian hitch is tied onto a carabiner for an improvised belay, for rappelling, and for rescue.

- The Prusik, Bachmann, and Klemheist knots are friction knots used for ascending a fixed rope.

- Autoblock and stopper knots are used as safety backup knots when rappelling to control the rappel and to avoid going off the end of the rope.

TIE & UNTIE KNOTS

Follow basic knot rules to ensure that your knots are tied correctly and keep you safe

Properly tied knots not only look better, but they're stronger than careless knots, easier to check, and untie readily. Take your time tying a knot. Don't let anyone distract you. Remember that your life depends on that knot. Make sure you always finish tying it before doing any other task.

After you've tied the knot, dress it neatly. This simply means

finishing the knot in its most secure orientation. Make sure the separate strands lie next to each other, are not crossed over, and are free of twists and kinks. Knots with crossed strands are bulky, can jam, and risk coming loose and untied. After dressing, firmly pull the knot tight. It's best to tug on each side of the knot to make sure it cinches down.

Dress the Knot

- After you've tied a knot, always dress it—that is, neaten the separate rope strands so they lie free of kinks and twists and are not crossed over each other.

- Knots with crossed strands can work loose and come untied.

- Next, cinch the knot tight by pulling on each of the separate strands. With a figure-8 follow-through knot, that means four pulls.

- Finally, make a visual inspection to ensure the knot is tied correctly.

Leave a Tail

- Before you do the final tightening of your knot, make sure the tail or loose end of the rope is long enough.

- A short tail, usually less than 4 inches, can work up into a knot, loosen it, and cause it to fail.

- The tail should be 8 to 12 inches long if you aren't tying a backup knot.

- On your tie-in knot, usually the figure-8 follow-through knot, keep the tail between 18 and 24 inches long and tie a couple fisherman's knots as backup knots.

Before tightening the knot, leave a tail of rope at least 8 to 12 inches long if you're not tying a backup knot, or 18 to 24 inches long if you do tie a backup.

When you're climbing, you'll have to untie knots. When you load a rope by falling on it or weighting it, knots can get tight and are difficult to untie. If you have problems, grab the long end of the rope and work it loose in the knot.

Untying Knots

- If you fall or hang on a knot, it gets tighter under the weight load and can be difficult to untie.

- A properly dressed knot is easier to untie than a messy undressed one.

- For hard-to-untie knots, grab one or both strands of rope and wiggle and push them into the knot to loosen it up.

- Practice untying each knot you use to understand how the knot tightens. It'll make it easier to untie it when you're climbing.

Practice Your Knots

- Knots are essential to your climbing safety. Learn how to tie them. Then practice until you can do each without thinking or looking.

- Check and double-check your climbing knots, especially when you're a beginner, when the weather's bad, or if you're in a hurry.

Tie them right and be safe.

- Practice your tie-in knot. It's the most important. And use the buddy system—check your partner's knot before she climbs.

- Knots are not difficult to learn, but your life depends on them.

FRICTION KNOTS

These knots rescue you from sticky situations; learn and practice them to stay safe

Every climber needs to know at least one of these friction knots for self-rescue, as well as the autoblock knot for a safety backup on a rappel. Friction knots are simply hitch knots wrapped around a rope, which tighten and lock when they're loaded with weight.

Friction knots are very useful, particularly in an emergency situation. You can use the knots to ascend a rope if you fall below an overhang, escape a belay for self-rescue, or tie off an injured climber. The knots are easy to learn, quick to tie, and don't damage the rope like a mechanical ascender, which uses teeth to grip the rope.

Tie the knots with a length of 5mm or 6mm cord that is tied

Prusik Knot

- The Prusik knot or hitch is the most common friction knot used to ascend a fixed climbing rope.

- The knot is easy to tie and very secure when loaded with weight. It won't slip on the rope.

- Prusik knots are used in pairs with an aider or sling attached to each one for your feet to sit in.

- Its main disadvantage is that the Prusik is difficult to release and slide up the rope after it's been weighted.

Klemheist Knot

- The Klemheist is an ideal friction knot or hitch for ascending a rope or for self-rescue.

- The knot slides easily on a fixed rope, but catches when it's weighted.

- The Klemheist is better than a Prusik knot because it releases its grip on the rope easily, works in one direction, is faster to tie, and can be tied with webbing.

- Use two knots in tandem to ascend a fixed rope. Attach them to your harness or to aiders for your feet.

into a loop from 18 to 24 inches long with a double fisherman's knot. The thicker the cord in relation to the diameter of your climbing rope, the less holding power or friction the knot will have. Use webbing in a pinch, but thin cord is best. Carry a couple of the cords attached to a carabiner on your harness and you'll always be ready.

To ascend a rope, always tie two friction knots. After the knots are tied, attach them to your climbing harness. You ascend the rope by sliding the knot up and then weighting it, a technique called Prusiking. The knot, using friction when loaded with your weight, grabs the rope and holds you. When using the knots to ascend a rope, always use two knots and make sure you're tied into the rope's end—never trust your life to a single friction knot.

The autoblock knot, an essential safety knot, is used as a safety backup knot on a rappel rope. Tie the knot on the rope below your rappel device and attach it to your leg loop with a carabiner.

Bachmann Knot

- The Bachmann knot is a friction knot or hitch that uses a carabiner as a handle, making it easy to slide the knot up a fixed rope.

- The Bachmann can slip on the rope because the smooth surface of the carabiner doesn't grip it.

- The knot is ideal for rescues and as a safety backup because it easily releases and slides on a rope.

- The Bachmann is also ideal for hanging loads from a rope, such as a climbing pack or a food bag.

Autoblock Knot

- The autoblock knot, also called a French Prusik, is an essential safety knot or hitch that every climber needs to learn.

- The autoblock is used as a safety backup knot on a rappel rope. The knot adds friction to a rappel, allowing a climber to stop mid-rap- pel and to stay in control.

- The easy-to-tie knot is attached on the rappel ropes below the harness and clipped into the leg loops.

- Never use an autoblock to ascend a rope since it easily slips.

RAPPELLING KNOTS

Rappelling is dangerous; make it safer by using the right knots for the job

When you reach the top of a route, you often need to tie two ropes together and rappel down. Rappelling is a dangerous part of climbing because you rely solely on your equipment for safety. Besides needing secure anchors, you need to tie your ropes together with a strong knot that will support your weight and won't come untied. The double figure-8

fisherman's knot, double overhand knot, and double fisherman's knot are the best knots to tie the ropes together.

The double figure-8 fisherman's knot is extremely strong, won't come untied, and is easy to check visually. It's the best knot to use for ropes of different diameters. Bulk is its biggest disadvantage. Watch that it doesn't jam in a crack or flake

Double Figure-8 Fisherman's Knot

- This is the recommended knot to tie two ropes together for rappelling and top-roping. It will never come undone if tied properly.

- Use it for tying ropes of unequal diameters—a thin rope and a thick rope—together.

- The knot's big disadvantage is its bulk; it may jam in a crack or behind a flake when you pull your rappel ropes.

- It's easy to check if the knot is tied properly. Finish with single fisherman's knots on each loose tail.

Double Overhand Knot

- The double overhand knot is popular because it is easy to tie.

- Make sure the tails are 12 inches long after tying the knot. Finish by tying another overhand knot in a loose tail.

- It is the least bulky rappel

knot, which makes it less likely to get stuck when you pull the rappel ropes.

- Do not use this knot with ropes of unequal diameters, new ropes, and large-diameter ropes, since it can come undone. Never use this knot except for body-weight situations like rappelling.

80

while pulling the ropes.

The double overhand knot is popular. It's the fastest and easiest knot to tie and is the least bulky, so it's less likely that your rope will snag while being pulled. Don't use it with ropes of different diameters, since accidents have occurred from it coming untied.

The double fisherman's knot is tricky to tie and is difficult to untie after being weighted, especially if the ropes are wet. Also use it for tying thin pieces of cord together for Prusik slings or on threaded nuts.

A stopper knot, usually a double fisherman's knot, is tied in both ends of a rappel rope so you don't rappel off the ends—a cause of climbing fatalities. Always tie stopper knots if you're unsure if your rope reaches the ground.

Practice tying and using all the knots on the ground until you know how to tie them right. Then choose one that you like and use it every time you tie ropes together. By using one knot, you become familiar with it and are less likely to improperly tie it. Remember, your life depends on the knot being properly tied.

Double Fisherman's Knot

- The double fisherman's knot is the traditional knot for tying two ropes together since it is extremely strong and secure.

- After being weighted, the two double fisherman's knots bond together, mak-ing it ideal for making slings from thin accessory cord.

- The knot is difficult to check visually and can be difficult to untie, especially if your ropes are wet.

- Only use this knot on ropes of the same diameter.

Stopper Knot

- Stopper knots are tied in both ends of rappel ropes so that a climber doesn't rappel off the ropes.

- Rappelling off the ends of the ropes is a common cause of climbing accidents and fatalities. Use a stopper knot and save your life.

- The best stopper knot is a double fisherman's knot tied in each rope end.

- Tie a stopper knot in the rope's end when you belay sport routes. This ensures that the rope doesn't slip through the belay device and drop the climber to the ground.

TIE-IN & ANCHOR KNOTS

To stay attached to the rope and your anchors, these knots never let you down

The tie-in knot you use to attach the rope to your harness and to clip yourself into anchors is the most important safety knot you will learn. If you tie it correctly, you'll live long and prosper. If you tie it wrong, however, you could be injured or die if it comes untied. Learn these knots and practice them until you can tie them without looking. Always use the same

knot for tying into the rope and you'll be less likely to tie it improperly.

The figure-8 follow-through knot is the best knot to tie the rope into your harness. It's strong, secure, and if tied right, it won't come undone but only gets tighter when the rope is weighted. It's also easy to check. If it's tied properly, then

Figure-8 Follow-through Knot

- Use the figure-8 follow-through knot as the main tie-in knot, connecting the rope to your harness.

- Practice tying the knot until you can tie it blindfolded and in the dark. Your safety depends on the tie-in knot being properly tied.

- When tying into the rope at the base of a route, make sure that you always finishing tying the knot. Avoid being distracted and not completing it.

- Tie the knot close to your body and leave an 18-inch tail, which you tie with a fisherman's backup knot.

Double Bowline Knot

- The double bowline knot is often used as a tie-in knot by sport climbers who take lots of falls.

- The knot's main advantage over a figure-8 follow-through is that it's easier to untie after a fall or after the knot's been weighted.

- The knot is less secure than a figure-8 follow-through.

- The double bowline knot is tricky to tie and hard to check if it's tied correctly.

each side of the figure-8 knot is a clone of the other. If it looks wrong, it probably is wrong.

The double bowline is sometimes used as a tie-in knot but it can come untied. Better to use it for tying the rope around a tree.

The figure-8-on-a-bight is ideal for clipping into anchors since it's easy to tie and very strong. You can also use it for tying a haul line on the back of the leader or clipping the middle of the rope to a carabiner on a second climber. Also learn the equalizing figure-8, which is great for clipping into three anchors and spreading the load equally between them.

The clove hitch is a fundamental climbing knot. You need to know this knot because it's useful, easy to tie and untie, can be tied with one hand, is easy to adjust, and uses little rope. It's perfect for tying into anchors. Always use a locking carabiner and make sure the load strand is by the carabiner's spine for maximum strength.

Figure-8-on-a-bight Knot

- The figure-8-on-a-bight is the easiest and most common knot used to tie a climber into belay anchors.

- It's a strong, secure knot that is easy to tie and then untie after being weighted.

- Use this knot for clipping a climber into the middle of a rope or for attaching a haul line to a lead climber.

- Learn the equalizing figure-8, a variation of this knot, to make three loops for equalizing anchors.

Clove Hitch

- The clove hitch is an essential knot to learn for clipping yourself into anchors. Practice so you can tie it with one hand if necessary.

- The hitch is easy to tie, quickly adjusted, uses little rope, and is easy to untie.

- Tie a clove hitch into a locking carabiner whenever possible.

- The clove hitch has been used by humans for over 10,000 years. It's got to be good!

FIGURE-8 FOLLOW-THROUGH KNOT

For tying into the rope, use the best and strongest knot for this important task

The figure-8 follow-through knot is the best knot to tie a climbing rope to your harness. This knot is extremely critical for your safety. If you tie it properly, you'll be safe and secure. If you tie it wrong, then you could die if the knot comes undone. The knot is also the strongest one used in climbing. If tied properly, it will never come undone but instead cinches tighter as the knot is loaded with your weight.

The knot is also easy to check if it's tied right since each of the two figure-8 knots are clones of each other. Make sure the knot is well-dressed with each of the strands lying next to each other and not crossed, and then cinch it down snugly.

When you tie the knot, make sure you thread the rope

Figure-8 Follow-through: Step 1

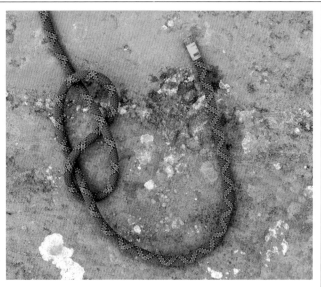

- Start with the loose working end of the climbing rope.

- Tie a single figure-8 knot between 2 and 3 feet from the end of the rope according to the following description:

- Form a loop in the working end of a rope. Twist the end of the loop to form a second loop. Bring the working end of the rope up through the second loop.

- Tighten the knot by pulling on both the working end and the standing part.

Figure-8 Follow-through: Step 2

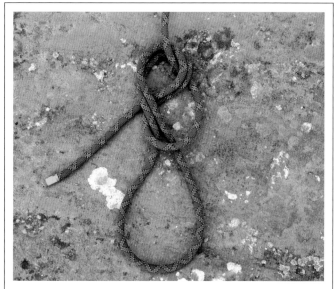

- Thread the free end of the rope above the knot through the harness tie-in points—the leg loops and the waist loop on the waist belt (same loop that the top of the belay loop is attached to).

- Pull the knot snug against the harness.

- Check harness instructions for exact tie-in points.

through both leg loops and the tie-in loop on the front of the waist belt on your harness. Pull the first figure-8 knot close to your harness before rethreading it to complete the knot. This keeps the knot close to your body.

Do not ever use the belay loop on the harness as your tie-in point. Nor should you tie a figure-8-on-a-bight and clip it into a carabiner on your harness.

After tying the knot, have your partner double-check it to make sure it's tied right.

Figure-8 Follow-through: Step 3

- Retrace the original figure-8 knot with the free end of the rope.

- Follow each bend of the original knot.

- Dress the knot by making sure the separate parallel rope strands don't cross each other.

- Leave a tail about 18 inches long and tie a fisherman's backup knot.

Completed Knot

- A fisherman's backup knot is best because it cinches tight.

- To tie, wrap the tail twice around the rope then pass the free end through the coil and tighten.

- If you don't tie a backup knot, make sure the tail is 12 inches long.

- Double-check your knot and you're ready to climb.

CLOVE HITCH

Fast, secure, and adjustable, the clove hitch is ideal for tying into anchors

The clove hitch is a simple, quick hitch knot that is used for tying yourself into anchors on a belay ledge with the climbing rope. The beauty of the knot is that it's easy to tie and untie and is easy to adjust so you can lengthen or shorten your tie-in point to the anchors without untying or unclipping the knot.

The clove hitch is not, however, as strong as the figure-8-on-a-bight knot for clipping into anchors. It also loses some of its strength if it's not tied tightly or is tied with a stiff, wet, or frozen rope since it can slip when loaded with your weight. If the knot slips, the rope's sheath can be abraded and damaged.

Clove Hitch: Step 1

- Twist two loops into the climbing rope, one in the right hand and one in the left hand.
- Pass the right-hand loop over the top of the left-hand loop.

Clove Hitch: Step 2

- Clip both loops into a carabiner on an anchor and tighten down.
- Make sure the load-bearing strand of rope is next to the carabiner's spine, the strongest part of the carabiner. If it's near the gate, you lose about 35 percent of the carabiner's strength when it's loaded.

After tying a clove hitch, immediately cinch it down tight and load it. This will keep it from slipping or climbing onto the side of the carabiner it's attached to. Always tie the hitch on a locking carabiner because you run the risk of an unloaded carabiner opening when loaded and the rope popping out.

Make sure you tie the knot correctly with the load strand of rope near the spine of the carabiner, its strongest part. If the strand is in the middle, you run the risk of carabiner failure.

· · · · · · · · · · · · · GREEN ● LIGHT · · · · · · · · · · · · ·

Learn how to tie a clove hitch with one hand so that you can quickly and efficiently tie yourself or your partner into an anchor while still keeping the rope on belay with your other hand.

Completed Clove Hitch

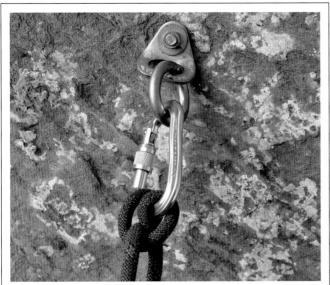

- Snug the clove hitch tight for maximum holding power.

- Clove hitches are not the strongest knot. They slip at 1,000 pounds of load.

- Clove hitches have a tendency to work loose, especially if the rope is stiff.

- The hitch can be tied anywhere on the rope and is easy to adjust. Also there's no need to untie it—just take it off the carabiner and it's gone.

How to Use Knot

- The clove hitch is useful when constructing an anchor since it's easy to tie off lots of strands.

- Don't use a clove hitch as your single anchor tie-in knot. It could loosen or shift. Always use a figure-8 somewhere in the anchor system.

- Always use a locking carabiner with a clove hitch to reduce the risk of the knot popping open the gate if it loosens.

- Try to keep the pull of the rope at a right angle to the point of attachment on the carabiner.

TWO FIGURE-8 KNOTS

Learn these two figure-8 variation knots for tying into and equalizing anchors

It's important to use good solid knots to tie yourself into anchors with a climbing rope; then you don't have to worry about coming untied from the anchors. These two knots are ideal for this climbing task.

The figure-8-on-a-bight knot is a loop knot tied on a bight or bend of rope. The knot is an excellent choice for tying

yourself into anchors because it's super strong, won't come untied, and is easy to untie after being weighted. Make it a habit to always clip the knot into a locking carabiner and you will never be disconnected from the anchor by the carabiner gate accidently opening.

You can also use the knot for tying a haul line to a carabiner

Figure-8-on-a-bight: Step 1

- Take a bight or open loop of rope anywhere on the rope's length.

- Tie a single figure-8 knot (see page 84) with both strands of rope by twisting the ropes over, under, and then through the top coiled loop.

Figure-8-on-a-bight: Step 2

- Tighten the knot down and make sure the strands are properly dressed.

- The knot will look exactly like the figure-8 follow-through knot used for tying into your harness.

- Use the knot for tying your-self into anchors, for tying a

climber into the middle of a rope, for clipping a haul line to a lead climber, or for clipping a carabiner onto a pack for hauling.

- Undo and loosen the knot by pushing both strands up from the bottom of the knot.

on the back of the leader's harness, for hauling a pack at the end of a rope up to a ledge, and for tying a climber into the middle of a rope. If you tie a climber in mid-rope, you'll need to attach the knot to him with a couple locking carabiners clipped to his harness tie-in points.

The equalizing figure-8 knot is another great climbing knot that is used to equalize two or three different anchors or pieces of gear to the rope, maximizing the overall strength of your anchors by transferring the load equally on all the anchors. An advantage to using this knot is that you don't have to equalize with slings or a cordelette. Either two or three loops can be formed from the knot, depending on how many anchors you're clipping into. The knot is easy to learn, especially if you already know how to tie a figure-8-on-a-bight.

Equalizing Figure-8: Step 1

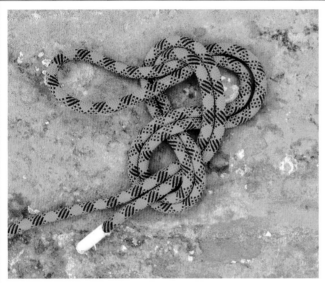

- Follow the same first step as for a figure-8-on-a-bight but tie the first figure-8 knot with a long loop of rope.

- After tying the knot, bring the long loop of rope through the top of the doubled figure-8 knot but don't pull the loop through.

- This creates three separate rope loops.

Equalizing Figure-8: Step 2

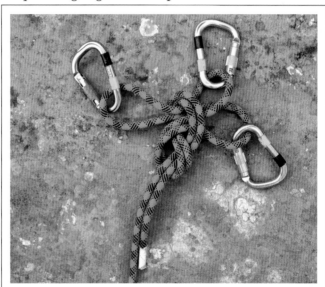

- Finish the knot by tightening it down, leaving the three loops.

- If you have two anchors, clip two loops into one carabiner and one loop in the other. Equalize and tighten. Or collapse one loop and use two on the anchors.

- With three anchors, clip separate loops in each, equalize, and tighten.

- This great knot is handy for equalizing anchors and spreading the load equally.

DOUBLE FIGURE-8 FISHERMAN'S
Need to tie two ropes together? Use the best knot to rappel safely

If you're at the top of a route and need to rappel back to the cliff-base, you're going to have to tie two ropes together so they reach the next set of anchors. The best and strongest knot for rappel ropes is the double figure-8 fisherman's knot.

There are several knots you can use to join rappel ropes, but the double figure-8 fisherman's knot is recommended not only because it's very strong and won't come untied, but also because you already know how to tie the figure-8 follow-through knot, so learning it is a cinch. It's also the best knot for tying ropes of unequal diameters together and for tying two ropes together for top-roping. Be careful when you pull your ropes after rappelling to ensure that the knot doesn't snag on flakes or edges since it has a bulky profile.

Practice tying the knot on the ground before you attempt to use it on a climb at the rappel anchors, because your life depends on it being properly tied. Remember to leave

Double Figure-8 Knot: Step 1

- Find the ends of the climbing ropes.

- Begin by making a figure-8 in one of the rope's working ends. Leave a tail about 18 inches long between the knot and the rope end.

- Tails are left in the working end to ensure that the knot doesn't work loose and slip apart.

Double Figure-8 Knot: Step 2

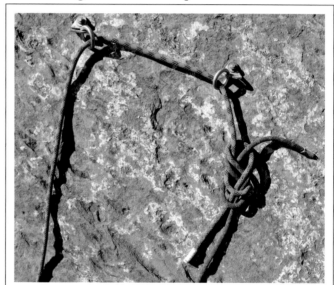

- Thread the working end of the other climbing rope into the first figure-8 knot.

- Retrace the original figure-8 knot the same way as you do a figure-8 follow-through knot.

- After retracing, the second knot is a clone of the first. Make sure the tails are at least 18 inches long.

- Tighten the knot. Keep the standing part or tail end of each rope on the outside of the knot for greatest strength.

enough tail after tying the knot to back it up with fisherman's knots for safety. Also when rappelling, always tie a stopper knot at the ends of both ropes so you don't accidently rappel off the loose ends.

It's best to always use the same knot for tying ropes together for rappelling and top-roping. If you use the same knot, you'll become very familiar with it and have less chance of not tying it right. Practice tying the knot and rappelling at a small, safe cliff before trying it on a big wall.

Completed Knot

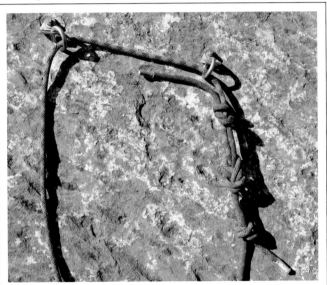

- Tie a fisherman's backup knot with each free tail of rope.

- Tie it by coiling the free end twice around the rope with the second coil closest to the main knot.

- Pass the free end back through the coils and cinch tight.

- The fisherman's backup knot is the best backup since it remains tied after tightening.

How to Use Knot

- Use the double figure-8 with fisherman's backup knots for tying two rope ends together for rappelling or top-roping.

- There are other good knots, including the grapevine, square fisherman's knot, and double overhand knot, but this knot will never come apart and is easy to tie and check.

- Practice tying this knot with backups before using it on the rocks.

- The knot can become wedged, stuck, or snagged in cracks and flakes when you pull the rope.

AUTOBLOCK KNOT
Stay safe on rappel with an autoblock knot; it keeps you in control

The autoblock knot is an essential friction hitch that is tied around your climbing rope with thin cord as a safety backup knot when you're rappelling. The knot, tied below your rappel device, slides down the rope as you rappel, but if you stop or lose control, then the knot cinches onto the rope and stops you. The autoblock is a knot that every climber should know how to tie and use. It could save your life.

Besides stopping you in an emergency, the autoblock knot

lets you hang mid-rappel to clean rope snags, free twists in the rope, or toss it farther down the cliff. The knot lets you rappel slowly and in control, so it's invaluable if you're making a rappel down overhanging rock and aren't able to touch the cliff.

Tie the knot with a thin piece of cord that is 24 inches long. Tie the cord ends together with a double fisherman's knot to form an 18-inch loop. Remember that the thinner the cord,

Autoblock Knot: Step 1

- To tie the knot, you need an 18- to 24-inch-long length of 6mm cord or a sewn ½-inch sling.

- First clip a locking carabiner onto your harness leg loop. Clip it on the side where your brake hand will be. Clip one end of the loop into the caribiner.

- Now wrap the cord or sling from four to six times around the rappel ropes. Make sure the cord's knot or sewn overlap on the sling is not in the wraps.

- Use up most of the cord on the wraps. The more wraps you have, the more friction.

Autoblock Knot: Step 2

- Clip the loose end of the cord or sling into the locking carabiner attached to the leg loop.

- Lock the carabiner so it won't open.

- Dress the knot by arranging all the wraps so they're neat and not crossed.

- Do not tighten the knot.

the more it will grab the rope. You can also use a 2-foot sling instead of cord. Also carry a locking carabiner to attach the knot to a harness leg loop. Make sure your sling isn't too long because it can jam in the rappel device.

Before rappelling, make sure the knot is loose on the rope and slides easily. Place your brake hand below the auto-block and grasp the rope. Put your guide hand atop the knot and begin rappelling. Or you can put your brake hand on the knot and guide hand above the rappel device. Try both and see what works for you. As you rappel, let the knot slide down the rope. If you want to stop, simply let go of the knot and let it lock.

Completed Knot

- Check the knot before using and make sure that the cord is not too long after being tied to the ropes. If it is, it will jam in your rappel device.

- If it's too long, use a shorter cord or extend the rappel device from your harness with a sling.

- Make sure the knot slides up and down on the rope and cinches when it's weighted.

- Always tie the autoblock knot below your rappel device.

How to Use Knot

- To rappel with the auto-block safety knot, hold the loose autoblock knot in your brake hand, lean back, and start rappelling.

- If you stop and let go with the brake hand, the auto-block cinches on the rope and holds you in place.

- To resume rappelling, loosen the autoblock and continue.

- Pay attention so that the knot and cord doesn't get caught in your rappel device. If it does—you're going to have an epic .

PRUSIK KNOT
Learn how to Prusik and you'll be able to save yourself

The Prusik knot is an essential climbing knot used to ascend a fixed rope in an emergency. The knot is easy to tie and very secure. After the knot is attached to a rope and your harness, ascend the rope by sliding the knot up. This technique is called "Prusiking."

The knot is simply a piece of thin cord wrapped around a climbing rope, forming a hitch knot. To make the knot, you need two Prusik slings or lengths of thin cord, 5mm to 6mm in diameter, and 2 feet long. To make a Prusik cord, use a 5-foot length of cord, made for climbing, with its ends tied together with a double fisherman's knot and forming a closed loop. The thinner the cord compared to the rope's diameter, the more it will grip the rope.

The biggest problem with Prusik knots is that they grab the rope so tightly that they are difficult to release. If this happens, loosen the knot by pushing the center loop in the knot

Prusik Knot: Step 1

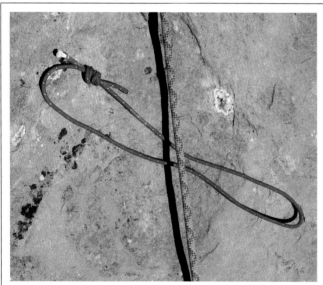

- The first step to tie a Prusik knot is to take a loop of cord, the ends tied with a double fisherman's knot, and place it behind the climbing rope.

- Bring half of the cord loop through the other half of

the loop and form a girth hitch, which is a basic hitch knot for attaching a sling to any object.

- Keep the knot in the cord on the outside of the hitch.

Prusik Knot: Step 2

- Bring the loop of rope back through the girth hitch on the rope two or three more times, forming a rope barrel with the free end of the cord hanging from the middle of the hitch.

- Do this by wrapping the cord through the inside of each previous wrap.

- Next, dress the knot by straightening the cord wraps so they lie next to each other and are not crossed.

- Finally, tighten the knot and you're ready to ascend the rope.

to release the wraps on the rope. The knot is sometimes used as a rappel backup knot, but because it cinches so tightly it is advisable to use an autoblock knot instead.

After you learn to tie and use Prusik knots, carry a couple Prusik slings on your harness for emergency use when you do long routes. You can use them to hold an injured climber's weight on your belay anchor, freeing yourself to render assistance or you can ascend the rope if you fall below an overhang and are dangling in space.

Completed Knot

- The more wraps you put on the Prusik knot, the more it will grip the rope. Usually three wraps is enough for good friction.

- If you're unsure how many wraps to use, test the knot by weighting it. If it slips, add another wrap.

- If the knot cinches too tight, is hard to loosen, and is difficult to slide up the rope, take away a wrap and see if it slides better.

- When the knot is loose, it's easier to slide up the rope.

How to Use Knot

- Use two Prusik knots in tandem to ascend a rope in an emergency.

- Attach the top knot with a sling to your harness belay loop. The bottom knot has a long sling for a foot.

- Weight the bottom knot by standing in the sling.

- Slide the barrel of the top knot up the rope until it's tight on your harness. Sit in your harness, let the knot tighten, then slide the bottom knot up.

- Practice first and learn how long the slings to your harness and foot should be.

WHAT IS BELAYING?

Learn how to belay and protect your buddy with the climbing rope

Belaying is the process of holding and managing the rope, which loops through a belay device attached to your harness, for another climber. Belaying, a cornerstone of climbing safety, is simply how we use a rope as a safety device. It's an essential skill that every climber must master. As a belayer, you are responsible for the safety of your climbing partner. His life is in your hands if he falls.

The belayer and the climber form a team and partnership.

When you belay, you look out for your buddy. You need to take belaying seriously, give it your full attention, and always watch the climber above. Your buddy does the same for you. Signals between belayer and climber are used so that both understand each other. It's important for the belayer to let the climber know when she's ready to belay and give full attention.

To set up the belay, thread the rope through a belay device

Belaying Makes a Team

- The climbing rope connects a climber to a belay device and belayer, making a team. This is the basic safety system for climbing.

- A good belayer stops your fall. A bad belayer can injure you.

- When you belay, you either pay out rope for the lead climber or you pull rope in for a top-rope climber or a seconding climber.

- Belaying requires your total attention. Don't belay on auto-pilot. Watch the climber and always be prepared to hold a fall.

Learn in a Gym

- It's best to learn how to belay in an indoor gym, since it's a safe, controlled setting and help from the gym staff is available.

- Start with a basic belaying class and learn the fundamentals. You'll need to take a belay test to belay on your own at most gyms.

- Gym routes are short so you not only climb a lot of routes, but you also get a lot of belay practice.

- After belaying a lot of gym routes, you'll understand what kind of mistakes to avoid.

and clip it to a locking carabiner attached to the belay loop on your harness. When belaying, you feed out or take in rope, keeping the climber safe. If the climber falls, you lock the rope in the belay device, and the friction of the rope through the device and your brake hand holds the rope and stops the fall. You also use a belay to lower a climber back to the ground on sport routes.

An indoor gym is a great place to learn how to belay. You can take a beginning belay class and learn the necessary skills to be a good belayer. Once you know those skills, the gym will give you a belay test before letting you do it solo. You also get lots of practice belaying at the gym since the routes are short and you regularly trade belays with your partner.

You need a belay device, locking carabiner, and harness to belay. The device is a piece of hardware with two slots. Thread the rope through a slot, clip it to the carabiner, and attach it to the belay loop on the harness. You're on belay!

Rigging the Device

- The rope runs through the belay device creating friction that allows you to control the rope.

- First, pass a loop or bight of rope through one of the two slots in the device.

Next, clip the device and rope to a locking carabiner, which you clip to the belay loop on your harness.

- The top rope should go to the climber and the bottom rope to your brake hand.

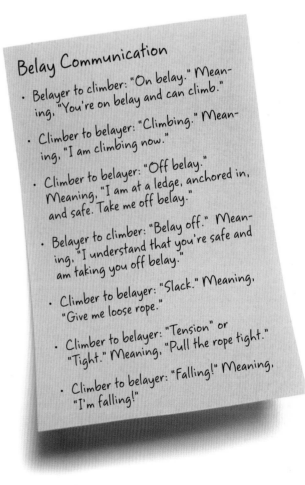

Belay Communication

- Belayer to climber: "On belay." Meaning, "You're on belay and can climb."

- Climber to belayer: "Climbing." Meaning, "I am climbing now."

- Climber to belayer: "Off belay." Meaning, "I am at a ledge, anchored in, and safe. Take me off belay."

- Belayer to climber: "Belay off." Meaning, "I understand that you're safe and am taking you off belay."

- Climber to belayer: "Slack." Meaning, "Give me loose rope."

- Climber to belayer: "Tension" or "Tight." Meaning, "Pull the rope tight."

- Climber to belayer: "Falling!" Meaning, "I'm falling!"

HOW TO BELAY
Proper belay technique takes time and practice in the gym before going outside

Belaying is a fundamental climbing skill. You'll learn to belay as you learn to climb since belaying and looking after your partner are as important as moving up stone. It's easy to think of climbing as an individual sport, but, unless you're a boulderer, you're part of a team linked together by the rope. When you climb, your buddy is your belayer. When she climbs, you're the belay slave.

The belayer's primary duties are to take up or give out rope to the climber and to hold his falls. Both are serious tasks that take lots of practice. Strive to become a great belayer, which in turn makes you a great climbing partner. Do that and you're going to have a beautiful friendship with your partner.

Learn to Belay

- Two climbers tie into opposite ends of a rope. One climbs and the other belays.

- The belayer protects the climber by holding the rope, which is threaded through a belay device.

- The belayer gives or takes rope using her guide hand above the belay device and her brake hand below it.

- The vertical distance between belays is called a pitch. A place to belay is called a belay ledge or belay stance.

Your Brake Hand

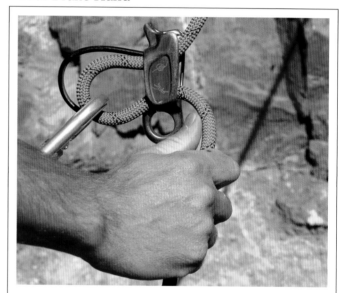

- Never let go with your brake hand. It should always be below the belay device and on the same side as the anchor.

- Always keep your brake hand in the braking, locked-off position unless you're taking in rope or feeding it out.

- It's difficult to keep your brake hand on the rope when you learn belaying. Practice until you're smooth and coordinated.

- Some belayers wear a glove on the brake hand to hold the rope and avoid possible rope burns.

To belay, first thread the rope through a belay device and clip it to your harness's belay loop with a locking carabiner. As the climber ascends, pay out or take in rope by feeding it through the device. Keep the rope slack. If it's tight, you'll pull the climber off the wall. Always keep your brake hand below the device, firmly gripping the rope.

If the climber falls, pull the rope across the device and let the friction of rope through metal stop him. It doesn't take much strength, just a steady brake hand. Pay attention to the climber, don't be distracted. Falls happen quickly and unexpectedly. If you're not ready, rope runs through the device and the climber could be injured.

Learn belaying mechanics in a gym. It's a safe environment so you can learn to belay, lower, and hold falls. Before belaying on your own in a gym, you're required to take a belay test proving competence. Gyms are great places to learn to belay and then practice until it's second nature.

Giving and Taking Rope

- The belayer gives or pays out rope to a lead climber as they move upward.

- As the climber moves away from you, feed the rope out so there's always slack in the rope between the climber and you.

- The belayer takes in or pulls up rope from a top-rope climber.

- Most top-rope climbers like the rope kept tight on them so they feel secure. As they climb, pull the rope so that you can always feel them at the end of it.

Holding a Fall

- A belayer's primary duties are to catch a falling climber and to manage the rope.

- When your brake hand locks the rope in the belay device, the friction of rope in device holds the fall.

- Falls happen unexpectedly. Always be ready for a fall with your brake hand. Pay attention to the climber all the time.

- Learn to hold top-rope falls with a backup belay in case you panic and let go of your brake hand. Practice in the gym.

BELAY ANCHORS

Take an anchor building class; it's a skill that must be done right every time

Your anchors are the foundation of climbing safety and a secure belay. Anchoring is attaching yourself to fixed points of protection on a cliff, usually a combination of natural and gear anchors. These include cams, nuts, pitons, bolts, trees, and boulders that are tied off with slings and rope. The anchors are then equalized to a master point so the weight

load of at least two climbers and the forces of a fall are evenly distributed on the anchors. Use at least three anchors at a belay unless there are two solid bolts.

After building your anchor on a belay ledge, tie yourself into it. It's best to clip in with the rope and a daisy chain or sling. The best knots to use are the figure-8-on-a-bight and

Backbone Anchors

- Anchors are the foundation of secure belays. A great anchor is essential for your safety and long life.

- A belay anchor needs to support the weight of two climbers as well as the forces generated by a long fall.

- Natural anchors include

trees and boulders. Tie off at least two for a strong anchor.

- Gear anchors are constructed from cams, nuts, pitons, and bolts. Use at least three gear anchors whenever possible. Build with redundancy. Never trust one piece of gear for an anchor.

Anchor Yourself

- The first step in belaying is to build a solid and secure anchor that you tie yourself into with the rope and a daisy chain.

- It's best to clip yourself into a belay anchor with locking carabiners that won't accidently open when loaded.

- Tie a figure-8-on-a-bight knot or an equalizing figure-8 knot to clip onto your belay anchors.

- Anchor yourself at the cliff-base when you're lowering a climber off a sport route so you aren't lifted off the ground.

equalizing figure-8 knots. Also use clove hitches for easy adjustment. Just make sure that you're clipped tight against the anchor so you can't be pulled off the stance by a fall.

If you're sport climbing, you'll belay on the ground. Your best belay position is close to the cliff and directly below the leader's first piece of protection, usually a bolt. From this preferred position, you don't necessarily need an anchor unless the leader weighs more than you. If you're belaying away from the cliff, always tie in to an anchor. A fall could drag you against the cliff and you could lose control of the belay rope.

Top-rope anchors are protection points atop a cliff that are equalized to a master point where the rope threads through a couple locking carabiners. This anchor needs to be bomb-proof. If it fails, the climber could fall to the ground. Extend the anchor with slings over the cliff edge to avoid rope damage. Take an anchor class or learn from an experienced climber before rigging your own belay anchors.

Cliff-base Anchors

- If you're doing a top-rope slingshot belay at the bottom of a cliff, anchor yourself. One solid piece, like a tree, is usually enough.

- Always anchor yourself when you belay at the cliff-base if the climber weighs more than you do.

- Position yourself in line with your anchor and the direction that a fall will pull you.

- Always stand and belay below a leader. Don't stand away from the cliff unless you're anchored. If the leader falls, you'll be pulled into the cliff.

Top-rope Anchors

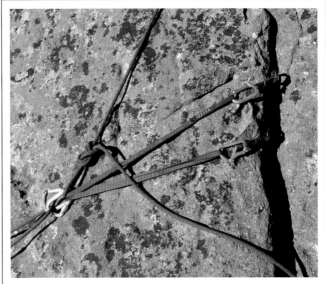

- Top-rope anchors are the anchor points atop a cliff that secure a rope, which is attached to the anchors with carabiners.

- If the top-rope anchor fails, the climber will fall to the cliff-base. Make your anchor absolutely secure.

- Let an experienced climber set up your top-rope anchors until you learn the skills and judgment to do it yourself.

- Take an anchors class from a climbing guide to learn how to choose and rig a safe top-rope anchor.

SLINGSHOT BELAY

A good belayer never lets you down until you're ready to come down

The slingshot belay is the best way to belay a climber with a top-rope. The rope runs up the cliff from the belayer to an anchor and then back down to the climber on the ground. The belayer, anchored at the cliff-base, pulls the rope through the top-rope anchor above while the climber works up the wall to the anchor. Then the belayer lowers the climber back to the base.

The beauty of this arrangement is that the climber is protected with the rope above him, and the belayer can watch the climber, keeping the rope snug on him. This is good for belaying beginners who might be tentative and afraid.

The cliff-top anchor needs to be totally solid and secure.

Belay Anchors

- Use two bolts, at least three pieces of gear, or natural anchors equalized with slings or rope for your sling-shot belay anchor on the cliff-top. Always use at least two anchors.

- Extend the anchor slings and carabiners over the cliff edge so the rope doesn't rub and abrade.

- Always run the rope through two locking steel carabiners at the anchor.

- The belayer, especially if she weighs less than the climber, needs to anchor into a tree or piece of gear. A fall could jerk her off her feet.

Ready Position

- When slingshot belaying, you'll pull in rope as the climber ascends and let out rope as you lower him.

- To start, place your guide hand an arm's length above the belay device. Now you're ready to pull in rope as the climber moves up.

- Place your brake hand just below the belay device. Angle the rope across the device so you're ready for a fall.

- Now pull the rope toward the device with the guide hand. At the same time, pull the rope through the device with the brake hand.

It's best to use existing bolt anchors, like those on a sport route. In this situation, just clip a couple slings to the bolts with locking carabiners. Make a sliding-X twist (see page 116) and clip a couple more locking biners for the rope to run through. Always use two locking carabiners, preferably steel ones, gates opposed, for the rope. Some climbers run the rope through quickdraws, but you run the risk of them opening and the rope popping out unless you use locking biners to prevent the rope from coming out.

After the climber reaches the cliff-top, it's time to lower to the ground. Lowering is one of climbing's most dangerous situations—miscommunication between climber and belayer causes fatalities. The basic rule is never take the climber off-belay until you are certain that they're safe. If they're lowering, there is no reason to ever take them off belay.

Before lowering the climber, make sure he's ready. Let him know you're ready to lower. Let the rope run slowly and smoothly through the belay device. You shouldn't have to feed it unless he's a lightweight. Let gravity do the work. Keep both hands on the brake side of the device.

Pull, Grab, and Slide

- After pulling the rope through the belay device with the brake hand, release your guide hand. Bring it down and place it next to the device in a brake position.

- Slide your brake hand up so it's next to the guide hand and belay device.

- Next, remove your guide hand from the brake position and move it back above the device in the ready-to-pull position.

- Repeat the three-step process—*pull* with guide and brake hands, release and *grab* with guide hand, *slide* the brake hand.

Slingshot Belay Tips

- It takes practice to feel comfortable with top-rope slingshot belaying. Practice in the gym until you're coordinated and smooth.

- Grab the rope with the guide and brake hands in either an overhand or underhand position. Experiment and see what feels best.

- Try to match the speed of the climber's ascent with the pace of your belaying. Get into a steady rhythm.

- Don't keep too much slack in the rope or keep it too tight. Aim for snug.

BELAYING THE LEADER
When belaying a leader, give him enough rope and be ready to catch falls

Belaying the leader is a sober responsibility. A lead climber, working up the wall, assumes a lot of the risk of climbing since the rope is not above but hanging down to the belayer. As the leader climbs, he clips bolts or places gear in the rock and attaches the rope so that if he falls, he only falls twice the distance that he's above his last piece of protection.

Leader falls generate tremendous forces that are transferred onto the rope, gear, belay anchors, and belayer. The belayer needs to stand always vigilant and ready to hold a fall so that the lead climber doesn't get seriously injured by hitting the ground or a ledge. Pay attention. Falls are part of leading. If your partner falls, don't panic. Keep your brake hand on the

Belaying Is Serious

- Belaying a lead climber is much more serious than belaying a top-rope climber.

- A leader fall generates huge forces that directly impact on the belayer, the belay system, and the belay anchor.

- For a lead climber, give rope by paying out small amounts through the belay device as he climbs. Keep both hands on the rope.

- The belayer needs to pay close attention to the leader, even if she is out of sight above. Try to feel what the climber is doing through rope movement.

How to Belay

- Get your hands in the ready position. Place your guide hand above the belay device on the live end of the rope to the leader. The brake hand grips the rope below the device.

- As the climber leads, your guide hand feeds the leader rope by pulling it through

- the device.

- Keep your brake hand on the rope but let it run through your hand as the guide hand pulls.

- Slide your brake hand up the brake end to pull slack into the system. Just don't let go!

rope and stop him. He'll thank you for that.

Belaying a lead climber is easier than belaying a top-rope climber. The mechanics of the belay are similar but reversed. Instead of pulling rope in, you give rope out as the climber works upward. It's important to always keep your brake hand on the rope on the braking side of the belay device. Never let go with the brake hand—your buddy's health depends on it.

Leader Falls

- If the leader falls, don't panic and let go of the rope. Hold the rope with the brake hand below the belay device.

- Some rope may slip through the belay device during a leader fall. This is fine; just make sure that the slippage doesn't cause the climber to hit a ledge.

- The lead climber should always place a piece of protection within 10 feet of your belay so that the force of a fall will come on that gear rather than on the anchor.

Leader Belay Tips

- Always keep slack rope between you and the leader so she has freedom to move and doesn't feel tension.

- Don't keep the rope tight. It can pull the climber off.

- Try to anticipate the leader's movements like making a quick high step or pulling up rope to clip into a bolt. The leader shouldn't have to yank on the rope for slack.

- The belayer needs to be in a solid stance and tied tight against the belay anchor.

BELAYING TIPS
Belay often—you'll become an expert and a better climbing partner

Belaying is an essential skill that takes practice to become competent and safe. It's not always obvious what to do, and reading about belaying in a book doesn't give experience. Learn belaying in a gym where you can master it under a watchful instructor. Then practice and you'll get better and understand the nuances of belaying technique. You'll also learn lots about belaying if you become a belay slave for a few days to a better climber.

The two most important rules of belaying are *Pay Attention* and *Don't Let Go*. If you always watch the climber and pay attention to what they're doing and how you're belaying, then you'll be prepared to catch a fall. If your partner does fall, hang onto the rope with your brake hand and don't let go. You follow those two bits of advice and you'll be a solid belayer.

Also remember that three important factors make the belay work. First, you need a skilled belayer to manage the

Belaying Rules

- Double-check harness buckles, all knots, anchors, rope, and belay device before climber leaves ground.

- Stack rope so it feeds properly without kinks and snarls.

- Never take your brake hand off the rope.

- Use bombproof belay anchors and tie tight into them.

- Keep a secure stance in line with possible direction of a fall.

- Tie into end of the rope or tie a stopper knot.

- Insist that leader put in solid protection within 10 feet of leaving the belay.

Pay Attention

- Belaying, while relatively simple, is a serious climbing task. Always pay attention to your climbing partner so the belay is safe.

- Don't visit with other climbers, talk on a cell phone, look for snacks, or do anything that jeopardizes your belay.

- Watch the climber. Try to anticipate his movements by either pulling up rope or giving rope out.

- If you can't see the climber, then feel her movements through the rope. But be ready to catch her if she suddenly falls.

rope and apply friction in case a climber falls. Second, you need an anchor to secure the belayer to the cliff and absorb some of a fall's energy. And third, you need a belay device to amplify the friction that you apply on the rope.

Never Let Go

- The most important rule for belaying is to never let go with your brake hand.

- Stop falls by bending the rope across the belay device, creating friction and locking the climber off.

- With an auto-locking device like a GriGri, practice using it in the gym until you're competent. Also keep your brake hand on the rope.

- Accidents occur when lowering. Lower the climber slow and steady. Keep both hands as brakes on the rope below the device. Let the rope run through your palms.

Belaying Sport Routes

- Stack the rope neatly below a route so it uncoils without snags, snarls, and knots.

- Be prepared for the leader to quickly pull rope to clip a bolt. If you're too slow to feed rope, the climber might fall.

- When you lower a climber, always have both hands on the brake side of the device so you won't lose control.

- Tie a stopper knot in the rope's end before lowering a climber so it doesn't whiz through the device and drop him to the ground.

BELAYING BASICS

NATURAL ANCHORS

Before you set an anchor, see what natural features are already available for you

Natural anchors are anchor points that the cliff and environment provide, including trees, boulders, blocks, horns, spikes, chickenheads, chockstones, and tunnels. They were the first anchors used by early rock climbers, who looped ropes over spikes for belays or horns for protection. They're still excellent anchors because you find them on most cliffs and they're usually quick and easy to sling. Natural anchors are often stronger and more secure than gear you might place. Test every natural anchor to make sure it's safe and secure.

Natural anchors aren't fancy; you only need simple climbing tools—slings and carabiners—to tie them off. Slings, the basic gear for natural anchors, are very useful. You can tie off

Trees

- Trees are one of the best and strongest natural anchors you will find. Not all trees, however, are created equal.

- Use a live tree, the thicker the better. Make sure it's rooted in deep soil or with roots in cracks.

- Use a long sling to girth-hitch the tree. Wrap the sling around the tree and slip one end through the other. Clip in with a carabiner.

- Tie the tree off as low as possible. Back up with gear or other anchors if possible.

Boulders and Blocks

- Boulders and blocks make great anchors, but only if they're big and won't move.

- You shouldn't be able to budge or rock the boulder.

- Tie it off with slings, not with the rope. Place the slings where they won't shift or slip. It's best to

- girth-hitch them and clip in with carabiners. Sometimes you might have to thread two or three slings together.

- Look for places where the boulder pinches against the cliff. You can thread a sling on the pinch and tie it off.

trees and chockstones or boulders wedged in cracks, loop them around big boulders, and thread them through holes. Carry a few 2-foot slings, a couple 4-foot ones, and some 6mm or 7mm cord slings for flakes and horns.

Trees make great anchors, as long as they're at least 4 inches thick and have stout roots. Use live trees, not dead ones. The best trees are often on cliff-tops rather than ledges. Look at the root system and the soil it grows in. Don't trust trees in sandy or shallow soil. Make sure they're rooted in deep cracks. Give the tree a good shake to evaluate its strength. If

it passes the shake test, sling the tree at its base.

Boulders and blocks make great anchors, as long as they're stable and aren't going to fall off. Pick a big one, make sure it doesn't move or rock, and tie it off with slings. Ditto for knobs, spikes, horns, chickenheads, and other rock protrusions. Thump on them to make sure they're secure. Make sure the rock is quality and not rotten. Girth-hitch slings through tunnels and around chockstones wedged in cracks.

Rock Features

- Look for any rock feature that you can tie off or thread with slings and cord. These features include flakes, chickenheads, horns, spikes, and bollards.

- Make sure flakes are attached to the face. Wrap a sling over and tie with a girth hitch or slip knot.

- Chickenheads and horns are protruding features you can loop a sling over and tighten down.

- Spikes and bollards are large pointed or rounded blocks you can drape a sling over. Make sure they're not detached from the main cliff.

Threads and Chockstones

- A rock wedged inside a crack is a chockstone. These are great for protection. Make sure the stone is securely lodged and won't shift, rotate, or break. If it does, don't use it.

- Thread a sling around the chockstone with a girth hitch and attach a carabiner

and the rope.

- Look for tunnels, arches, and points where two rocks contact each other. Make sure it's strong and doesn't have fracture cracks.

- Girth-hitch a threaded sling through the hole and clip a carabiner onto it.

GEAR ANCHORS

Specialized anchor equipment fits specific rock features found on cliff faces and ledges

Climbing equipment is used for anchors in two ways—as single anchor points that climbers place for protection, and as complex anchors that are multiple anchor points united and equalized by slings and rope into a solid anchor for rappelling or belaying. Gear anchors are broken into two categories: passive gear and active gear.

Passive gear, such as chocks or nuts, are anchor tools that wedge in a crack and hold a climber by friction. Commonly used chocks are tapers, Hexentrics, Tri-Cams, and Big Bros. Before nuts, climbers used pitons or metal spikes that were hammered into cracks, but rock damage led to the development of nuts. Nuts are clean climbing tools since they don't

Tapers and Hexentrics

- Nuts are simple, secure, inexpensive, and easy to place. They're basic gear every climber needs.

- Carry wired taper nuts for small cracks. Small- to medium-size tapers are useful.

- Hexentric nuts fit finger- to fist-size cracks. They're light, fit lots of placements, and are cheaper than cams.

- After placing nuts, give a hard yank to seat the nut and test its security. Make sure a lot of the nut surface touches the rock surface. Use quickdraws to clip the rope to the nut.

Camming Devices

- Cams are essential. Carry cams and wired nuts to protect most climbs.

- Cams are fast to place and work where nothing else does. Practice before using them on a climb.

- Study the crack before placing a cam. Make sure the stem points down, not outward. Good spots are where the crack constricts below the cam.

- Make sure cams are in the middle expansion range. Cams in too wide or narrow a crack are weak placements. Clip with a quickdraw to keep it from "walking."

damage the rock with repeated placement and removal. They work by wedging in crack constrictions. Nuts are simple, useful anchors that are standard on every climber's rack. Easy to place and remove, they're inexpensive and fit a huge variety of cracks from thin seams to off-width cracks. A well-placed nut makes a solid anchor.

Active gear anchors are complex mechanical devices with moving parts, like camming units, which have either three or four spring-loaded cams that oppose each other on an axle. A trigger retracts the cams for placement and removal.

Cams work great, especially in parallel-sided cracks, and can be placed in a wide variety of cracks. The invention of cams in the late 1970s revolutionized climbing anchors and protection and let climbers pursue difficult routes that were impossible to safely protect before.

As you grow as a climber, you'll build a rack of gear. When starting out, all you need is passive gear. Buy sets of wired nuts and Hexentrics. Later you can slowly add pricey cams from small three-cam units to 4-inch cams for big cracks.

Fixed Gear

- Never trust fixed gear. Always back up fixed gear with your own, especially at belay and rappel stations.

- Bolts: Inspect bolts for age and rust. If a bolt is a ¼-incher, it's no good and could break, even under body weight.

- Pitons: Don't trust fixed pitons. Freeze-thaw cycles loosen them.

- Webbing: Never trust fixed webbing on anchors. While strong when new, webbing ages and weakens, especially from exposure to weather. Replace old webbing with your own stuff.

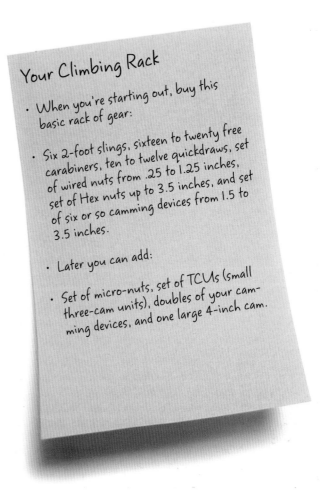

Your Climbing Rack

- When you're starting out, buy this basic rack of gear:

- Six 2-foot slings, sixteen to twenty free carabiners, ten to twelve quickdraws, set of wired nuts from .25 to 1.25 inches, set of Hex nuts up to 3.5 inches, and set of six or so camming devices from 1.5 to 3.5 inches.

- Later you can add:

- Set of micro-nuts, set of TCUs (small three-cam units), doubles of your camming devices, and one large 4-inch cam.

SINGLE ANCHORS
Protection anchors attach you to the cliff as you climb and shorten possible falls

Single anchors are exactly that—single anchor points or gear that you place as you lead a pitch. These placements, also called pro, protect the leader and keep him from long falls by attaching the rope to the cliff. It's relatively simple to place single anchors. Find a section of crack as you're climbing, analyze it for gear possibilities, place gear in the crack, clip

your rope to it, and continue climbing. If there are no cracks, find natural anchors like trees or chockstones.

It takes experience to develop the judgment to decide that a piece of pro is secure. Do lots of climbing, preferably following experienced leaders, to learn to safely place gear. Practice at a cliff-base and test each placement. Don't trust your life to

Placing Single Anchors

- When leading a pitch, place single pieces of gear to protect yourself rather than multiple anchors at belays.

- While climbing, look for cracks for nut and cam placements. When you find a good spot, pick the right-size gear and anchor it in the crack.

- Always look for the easiest, most obvious placement.

- The last anchor you place is the most important one since it's at the top of the belay chain. If you fall, it absorbs the greatest force. Make each piece as secure as possible.

When to Place Pro

- Place protection when you need it. If you're at a good crack, place an anchor. The placements might not be as good up higher. Place gear at least every 10 feet.

- Anticipate where you might fall and place gear accordingly, especially on routes you've never climbed.

- Be aware of ledges or features you might hit if you fall and place gear to keep from impacting.

- Place gear immediately after leaving a belay ledge. This puts a fall's load on the gear, rather than on the belay.

gear on a route until you're competent. Remember that you not only have to judge the placement's quality, but you have to be able to select and place gear quickly while leading.

Put in lots of gear when climbing, at least every 10 feet. Pay attention to rock quality. Gear in bad rock is usually bad and a leading cause of accidents. Use slings on gear to avoid rope drag and keep pieces from lifting out. Make sure all your gear is bomber (a term for secure) and you'll come home safe.

Direction of Pull

- Routes don't follow straight lines. Imagine if you fall how the rope will pull on your gear. If there are upward or sideways pulls, gear can get yanked out.

- Make the rope follow as straight a line as possible. Use 2-foot slings to extend the pro to an imaginary midline. Quickdraws are usually too short.

- Slings lessen rope drag or friction from zigzags in the rope, letting the rope run easier from belayer to climber.

Single Anchor Tips

- The anchors you place are only as good as the rock you put them in. If it's rotten or loose, watch out!

- Find solid rock to place nuts and cams. Gear holds better in good rock. Adjust to make it secure.

- Practice placing gear on the ground. Find a crack and fill it with anchors. Have an experienced climber critique your placements. Also follow lots of pitches and see how a good climber places gear.

- Learn to place gear quickly and safely.

CLIMBING ANCHORS

ANCHOR SYSTEMS
Complex anchors are a science and an art

A complex anchor is a system of single anchor points that are connected together with slings, rope, and carabiners to form a multi-directional and redundant anchor for top-ropes, belays, and rappels. Complex anchors are all about redundancy so that if one component fails, the anchor itself does not.

Always follow this rule when you build a complex anchor: The anchor system must be able to withstand the greatest

possible force and still remain intact. Complex anchors take work and experience for maximum strength. If you're at all unsure about the strength of the gear you're placing, then use lots. Two pieces of gear is good. Three is better. Better to be safe than sorry.

When you do a multi-pitch climb, placing gear as you ascend, stop and build belay anchors on ledges. These complex anchors are extremely important since failure is

Complex Anchors

- Use different anchor components—natural, nuts, cams, and fixed.

- The various pieces are connected and equalized with slings to form a strong multi-directional anchor for belays, top-ropes, and rappels. Anchor systems are about redundancy so if one piece

fails, the anchor does not.

- The anchor system must be able to withstand the greatest possible force and still remain intact. If complex anchors fail, you may die. Practice on the ground before attempting to build any anchor mid-cliff.

Creating an Anchor System

- If there are no fixed anchors where you need them, create your own anchor system.

- Find a place with enough anchor placements. This is often an established belay ledge that others use.

- Analyze the site and look for

good cracks and features for gear. Keep upward and downward directions of pull in mind for both leading and following: upward for leaders, downward for followers.

- Set a primary piece first and tie yourself into it before shouting "Off belay!" to your belayer.

catastrophic. The good news is that most climbers are very careful and serious about complex anchors, so they rarely fail completely. Climbers gain experience and judgment and then apply it every time they climb. You do the same. Be an apprentice to an experienced climber or hire a guide to teach you anchor skills.

The first step to build a complex belay anchor is to place primary anchors. These are your strongest pieces. They must be absolutely secure. Use three if possible. Clip yourself into the best one as soon as you place it and go off belay. Now look for secondary anchors. These back up the primary ones. Next equalize all of them with a cordelette, slings, or rope. Tie a master point to clip into.

Building a rappel anchor is simpler. Use three primary anchors if possible, although two will do. Rap anchors only need to hold 500 pounds. Equalize with webbing and you're rappelling.

Primary and Secondary Anchors

- First look for primary anchor placements. These are the best gear you can place. Get at least two pieces. Three is better.

- Use secondary placements to back up primary ones. In bad rock, spread placements around and use lots of gear.

- Connect and equalize all anchors with slings and rope so they become one multi-directional anchor system that works as a single unit.

- Make the system simple. Find the strongest anchors, set and equalize them, and start belaying. Use the least amount of gear to be safe.

Use E.R.N.E.S.T.

- Use ERNEST to analyze anchors.

- Equalized. The load should be distributed equally on all anchors in the system.

- Redundant. Use two to four primary anchors. Never use a single anchor. All system components are backed up.

- No Extension. If one anchor fails, the system should not shock-load any of the other anchors, causing failure.

- Solid. Each anchor and the whole system must be rock solid and totally bombproof.

- Timely. Don't spend lots of time on your system. Build your anchor, equalize it, and get climbing.

115

EQUALIZING ANCHORS
Equalization spreads the same load on each anchor point and prevents anchor disaster

After building a multi-directional, complex anchor, the final step is to equalize all the anchor points and make it a single safe and functioning anchor system. Do that by tying all the anchors together with slings, the rope, or a cordelette to a master point. Equalizing the anchors makes them stronger since the force of a fall is divided equally between the various anchor points. It's not always easy to rig and equalize complex anchors. You might have four or five pieces of gear in a couple different cracks. Before equalizing an anchor, consider the main direction of pull on the anchor. Belay anchors should be multi-directional—that is, resist both downward and upward pulls. Top-rope and rappel anchors primarily pull downward.

Use a Sliding X

- The self-equalizing sliding X equalizes the anchors when the load changes direction. It's good because it's simple.

- Use a couple 2-foot slings for redundancy and two carabiners. Clip the carabiners and slings to each bolt, leaving an open loop.

- Bring the top loop between the two bolts down and make a single 180-degree twist. Clip a carabiner into the X formed by the twist and the bottom loop.

- The carabiner is the master point for your tie-in knot or for top-roping on a sport route.

Use Slings

- Use slings and carabiners to equalize anchor points.

- For a two-bolt anchor, clip a sling into each bolt and a locking carabiner into each sling for a master point.

- Or rig a two-bolt anchor with a long sling and carabiners. Clip the sling into carabiners on each anchor. Pull down both loops and tie an overhand knot in the sling for a master point.

- Using slings doesn't provide total equalization, but they work well for connecting bolt anchors together.

Equalizing anchors is an art. It's not something you'll pick up overnight, especially since every one is different. The components are never in the same place, so you have to study first and then equalize.

The easiest anchor to equalize is a multi-directional two-bolt anchor, usually on a sport route or rappel station. It's easy to make a sliding X by clipping two slings to the bolts, giving a 180-degree twist to the top loop, and clipping into the middle of the X. You can also use two slings, clipped separately to two bolts, and tie them together with an overhand knot to create a master point. Tie into master points with a daisy chain and the rope.

For more complex anchors, it's simple to use a cordelette to rig three or more anchors to a master point for clipping. A cordelette is easily adjusted and spreads the load among all the anchors. It's difficult and time-consuming to rig complex anchors with slings. For three anchors, use an equalizing figure-8 knot. It's quick, easy, and adjustable.

Use a Cordelette

- It's easy and fast to rig and equalize two or more anchors to a master point with a cordelette.

- A cordelette is a 20-foot length of 7mm cord tied into a loop. It spreads the load between anchors, creating a static system that works best if each loop is the same length.

- Clip the cordelette into a carabiner on each anchor point. Pull the loops down until even. Tie an overhand knot with the cords. The resulting small loop is the master point; clip into it with the climbing rope.

Tying into Master Points

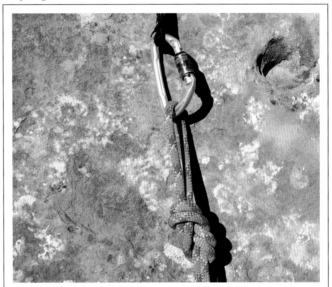

- Tie clove hitches or an equalizing figure-8 knot and clip into the individual anchors.

- Equalizing with rope only works if you're switching leads with your partner; otherwise you have to dismantle the anchor to lead.

- Use a daisy chain to clip into anchor master points but don't let it be your primary tie-in. It's not a full-strength anchor and can fail if you're clipped into more than one loop.

- Use locking carabiners or two regular biners with gates opposed to clip into master points.

117

ANCHOR SAFETY

Build solid, redundant, equalized anchors every time—it's a matter of life or death

Anchors allow climbers to safely ascend steep faces, set up belays, rappel down, bivouac on a wall, and top-rope up a short cliff. Solid equalized anchors coupled with rope management prevent climbing falls from being fatal. They're a technical skill we use every day that we go climbing. We rely on them for our safety, sometimes exclusively. Learn to place

safe anchors and you'll avoid catastrophe.

Strive to make your anchors as safe and as simple as possible. Make them easy to rig and dismantle. Use redundant primary and secondary anchors at belay stations. Equalize the gear so all the pieces share the load in a fall. Make sure there is no extension in the system that shock-loads other pieces, causing them

Practice Building Anchors

- It's an art to build anchors. Take an anchors class and practice before making any anchor system that your life depends on.

- Learn to place nuts and cams for protection expertly and efficiently. You won't hang around trying to find the right piece and

  you'll climb faster.

- Follow an experienced climber up lots of routes. Notice what gear he uses and where he places it.

- On the ground, test practice placements by clipping a sling on one and jerking it or standing in it.

The KISS Principle

- Anchors are the basis of safe climbing.

- Most of the anchors you place and build will be straightforward, simple, and easy to rig. Try to keep it that way and follow the KISS principle—Keep It Simple, Stupid!

- Belay anchors can be subjected to loads as great as 4,000 pounds. Rappel anchors need only hold a few hundred pounds. Build accordingly.

- Don't take shortcuts when building anchors. Look at and analyze the site before building the anchor.

to fail. When you place gear for protection, check that each placement is stable, solid, and in line with the direction of force.

Anchors are only as good as the climber who creates them. Practice building anchors on the ground before taking your skills high on a cliff. Learn to place protection by being an apprentice to a good climber. Look at his placements and ask questions. Take an anchors class from a certified guide to get a complete education in anchor placement and creation. Only then will you be ready to begin placing anchors and assuming that awesome responsibility.

••••••••••• GREEN ● LIGHT ••••••••••••

Build an anchor system on the ground. Find a cliff-base with cracks. Use cams, nuts, and natural pro to create different anchors. Place the gear then rig it with a cordelette, slings or webbing, and the climbing rope. See what works best for the situation and have an experienced climber evaluate your efforts.

Anchor Organization

- When you reach a ledge, analyze the site and decide the best anchor system to construct.

- Try for four anchors—three with downward pull and one opposing with upward pull. Anything less is risky.

- Visualize the direction of pull if your partner falls. Consider where you will stand while your partner leads and the direction of pull above.

- If you have lots of anchors, your belay stance can be crowded. Keep it simple so you can quickly find your primary tie-in point.

Anchor Safety Checklist

- If you have doubts about the integrity and security of any anchor point, back it up.

- Three anchors are sufficient for a belay, but if the rock is poor then use as many as possible.

- Avoid cams for top-rope anchors since loading and unloading the rope causes them to walk or move.

- Find great primary placements and the rest of your anchor system will be sound.

- If you're climbing a thin crack, use more gear than for a wide one.

- Place a cam every body length in sandstone jam cracks.

119

WHAT IS RAPPELLING?

Rappelling is an advanced climbing technique for descending down cliffs

Rappelling is a specialized climbing technique used to descend from cliffs by sliding down a rope fixed to anchors. Rappelling requires lots of climbing skills: making anchors; tying knots; managing the ropes; rigging the rappel device; using safety backup systems and knots; and retrieving the rope.

Rappelling is one of the most dangerous climbing activities and causes many accidents. The ugly truth is that when you lean back on the rope and begin to rappel, you're totally dependent on the safety of your equipment. The good news is that most accidents are due to climber error rather than equipment failure. Learn the essential rappel skills and you'll

The Rappel System

- Rappelling is descending a cliff by making a controlled slide down a rope to the ground or a ledge.

- The rappeller threads the rope through a friction rappel device to control his descent. After reaching the bottom, the climber retrieves the rope by pull-

ing it through the anchors.

- Rappel ropes are anchored with artificial and natural anchors.

- Rappelling is one of the most dangerous climbing activities since the climber relies solely on equipment and anchors for safety.

Tying Ropes Together

- Sometimes you need to tie two ropes together to rappel to the next anchors or the ground.

- The double figure-8 fisherman's knot is best for tying two rappel ropes. It's strong and won't come untied. It's also best for ropes of different diameters.

- Always use the same knot to tie ropes together. With practice you'll always tie it right.

- Practice tying the knot at home before using it at rappel anchors—your life depends on it.

be safe on all your rappels.

You've climbed to the cliff-top and need to get back down. You can scramble down easy terrain or you can rappel back down your route. To rappel, secure the rope to the cliff with anchors like bolts, pitons, and nuts or natural anchors like trees and boulders. The rope is doubled at its midpoint or two ropes are tied together, depending on how far you need to rappel. You then use a rappel device. Thread the ropes through the device and a locking carabiner, clip it to your harness, and begin rappelling. The friction of the rope running through the device allows you to control your descent as you slide down the rope to the bottom.

After you get to the base of the rappel, retrieve your ropes by pulling them through the anchor and letting them drop down. The word rappel comes from the French word *rappel*, which means "to recall" since the climber recalls his rope. In the United States, climbers often shorten the words rappel and rappelling to "rap" and "rapping." In Europe the technique is called abseiling from the German word *abseilen*, meaning "to rope down."

Tossing Rappel Ropes

- Make sure the rope is loose and neatly stacked before you throw it.

- Hand-coil each end of the rope separately. Toss one end first, then the other.

- Ropes can get snagged on flakes and cracks or can be blown around a corner.

- Don't rappel past snagged ropes or with the rope above you. Always pull the rope down to you and toss it down the cliff.

- If the rope snags on flakes, rappel down and free the snag. Then toss the rope farther down.

Pulling Rappel Ropes

- Keep the ropes separate as you rappel. Twisted ropes can be impossible to pull.

- Untie stopper knots and start pulling the rope. Sometimes standing away from the cliff-base makes it easier to pull.

- Before the rope falls, pull it hard so it falls away from the cliff. Watch for rocks dislodged by the rope. Call "Rope!" when it falls to alert others.

- Watch that the knot doesn't jam as you pull. The last rappeller should make sure the knot is below the rappel ledge to avoid a stuck rope.

121

RAPPELLING GEAR

Don't skimp on rappelling equipment; you trust your life to it every time you climb

Rappelling is gear intensive. When you rappel, use the same equipment that you used to climb up. Use good equipment—you must completely trust your gear since you rely on it exclusively for personal safety.

Buy a good rappel device. With the rope threaded through the device, your descent is controlled with rope friction.

There are three basic rappel devices: tubular, figure-8, and self-locking devices. While all three do the job, the best one is a tubular device since it not only works great but also doubles as your belay device, so you carry one piece of gear for two jobs. Use an auto-locking carabiner to attach the device to your harness.

Rappel Devices

- There are three basic rappel devices: tubular, figure-8 descenders, and self-locking devices.

- Tubular rappel devices are the best choice because the climber has more control over the friction of the rope through the device and it can also be used as a belay device.

- Figure-8 descenders are often used but can kink the rope and offer less control.

- Self-locking devices are good for single-line rappels but are complicated to use with double ropes.

Ropes

- The rope is one of the most important pieces of equipment used in rappelling. Use either one or two ropes up to 200 feet long, depending on the rappel length.

- Make sure the rope doesn't rest on sharp edges, which can cut or damage the rope sheath.

- Thicker ropes (10mm to 11mm in diameter) offer more friction when rappelling than thin ropes.

- Do not tie thin ropes (7mm to 9mm) together with a thick rope because the joining knot can work loose.

You need a rope or ropes for rappelling, depending on rappel length. For most rappels, a single 200-foot (60-meter) cord is fine. When doubled you can make a 100-foot rappel. Use your dynamic climbing rope; just watch for sharp edges that damage the sheath. Thick ropes from 10mm to 11mm in diameter give more friction and are less likely to cut than thin ones. For long rappels, tie two ropes together to reach the next anchors.

Rappel anchors are fixed with permanent metal hardware including bolts and chains on many descents so you don't need to carry additional anchor material. Sometimes you have to leave gear for a rappel anchor or to beef up an existing station. Don't be a cheapskate and skimp on leaving gear—your life depends on a solid anchor. Bring extra webbing, a knife, and rappel rings to replace worn rap slings.

You need personal equipment to rappel, including a climbing harness. Make sure it's snug and the waist belt is doubled back. Leather gloves are handy, allowing for control on steep rappels. Bring a short cord and locking carabiner to rig an autoblock knot.

Anchor Equipment

- Rappel anchors are a combination of trees, rock features, bolts, nuts, and cams.

- Bring 10 to 20 feet of webbing to use for rappel anchors. Webbing weakens from sun exposure and needs to be replaced. Don't forget a knife to cut it to the right length.

- Nuts make excellent rappel anchors. They're cheap and are bomber if properly placed. Cams are not recommended.

- The best bolts are ⅜-inch or ½-inch stainless steel bolts. Don't think about placing bolts for rap anchors. Leave that to expert climbers.

Personal Gear

- Always wear a climbing harness when you rappel. Make sure it's comfortable, fits snugly around your waist and legs, and has a belay loop in front.

- Always use a locking carabiner, preferably one that is auto-locking, to attach the rappel device and rope to your harness belay loop.

- Gloves allow you to maintain control and keep from getting rope burns.

- Carry an 18-inch length of cord or a 2-foot sling and locking carabiner to tie an autoblock knot on your harness and the rope.

BASIC RAPPEL SKILLS

There's no room for error when you rappel; learn all the skills to stay safe

Rappelling appears simple, but it requires particular skills and techniques. Before attempting any rappel on your own, learn the needed skills and take a class from a certified guide to ensure your safety. Lots of accidents occur rappelling, and most are the result of climber error and bad judgment. Learn the essential rappelling skills and you'll be safe on all your rappels.

Rappelling requires six basic climbing skills: making anchors, tying knots, managing ropes, rigging the rappel device, using safety backup systems, and retrieving the ropes afterwards.

Learn to rig the rappel ropes by evaluating the anchor and updating it if necessary. Check the anchors, look at the webbing slings, and make sure the rap rings aren't worn. Note the

6 Basic Rappelling Skills

- **Anchors:** Know how to evaluate anchors and place two or three secure anchor points.

- **Ropes:** Know rope management including how to rig the rope and retrieve it.

- **Knots:** Know the stopper and autoblock knots and how to tie ropes together.

- **Rappel device:** Know how to rig a rappel device and tie and use a Münter hitch as a backup.

- **Autoblock knot:** Know how to tie and use an autoblock knot as a backup.

- **Retrieving ropes:** Know how to pull rappel ropes and avoid problems like knot jams and too much friction.

Rig the Rappel

- You're on a ledge with your partner. Make sure you're both tied into the anchors.

- Thread one rope through the rappel master point, tie both ropes together, and tie a stopper knot in each rope. Yell "Rope" and toss each rope down separately.

- Push the ropes through both slots of your rappel device, clip them into a locking carabiner, and attach it to your belay loop. Tie an autoblock knot.

- Yell "On rappel" to alert anyone below to watch out in case loose rocks get knocked off.

length of the rappel and, if needed, tie two ropes together with the right knot. Tie stopper knots in the ends so you don't rappel off them. Now rig your rappel device and clip it to your harness with a locking carabiner. You're ready to rappel!

Put your hands in the ready position. The guide hand holds the rope above the device. Put a finger between the rope strands to keep them separated so they're not tangled when you get to the bottom. It makes them easier to pull. Your brake hand goes below the device. If you're using an autoblock, place your hand on top of the knot. The cardinal rule of rappelling is to never let go with your brake hand. Always keep it on the ropes below the device.

After stepping off the ledge, weight the ropes and assume the rappel stance. Keep feet shoulder-width apart, knees slightly bent, torso upright, and butt sitting in the harness. As the rock steepens, let gravity and your body weight carry you down. Don't rappel too fast. Go slow and enjoy the ride.

The Brake Hand

- Rappelling Rule #1: Never let go of the rope with your brake hand while rappelling.

- Keep your brake hand below the device and next to your hip. Let the rope slowly slide through your hand as you rappel.

- Place your guide hand above the rappel device. Let the rope slide through your hand. To keep the ropes separated, put your index finger between the two ropes.

- You can also place your guide hand below the device so you have two brake hands.

Rappel Stance

- Keep your feet shoulder-width apart, legs perpendicular to the rock, knees almost straight, and upper body bent at the waist so your torso is upright.

- Sit down in your harness. It feels uncomfortable at first but it keeps your feet pressed against the rock.

- If your knees bend too much, if you lean into the rock, or don't keep your torso erect, your feet will slip and you'll feel unsteady.

- As you feed rope through the device, walk slowly and smoothly down the cliff. Don't bounce; it stresses the anchors.

125

RAPPEL ANCHORS

Take an anchors class from a climbing pro—don't trust your beginner skills to make an anchor

Established rappel routes have fixed anchors, making it easy to rig your ropes and rappel. Don't assume, however, that the rap station and all anchor points, including bolts, pitons, nuts, and tied-off trees and chockstones, are good. Some are excellent, but others are unsafe and dangerous. You need to inspect the anchors, slings, and chains and decide for yourself if they're safe. Back them up with your own gear or re-rig if necessary. Don't trust what's there—that's a recipe for disaster. If the anchors fail, you'll probably die.

Rappel anchors don't need to hold a truck like a belay anchor. They just need to hold body weight plus a bit more since they're not subject to big loads. Use at least two but

Fixed Anchors

- Most rappel stations have fixed anchors already in place. Double-check all anchors. Never trust that the anchors are bombproof.

- Rappel anchors are a combination of bolts, pitons, tied-off trees, and rock features.

- Many rappel stations have two or three bolts that are equalized with chain or webbing. These are usually very strong.

- Check any webbing and replace if it's weathered or damaged. All piton anchors are suspect. Don't trust them unless they appear new and solidly placed.

Trees and Features

- Trees make great rappel anchors. Pick a tree at least 4 inches in diameter and sling with webbing and a rap ring. Tie off close to the ground for leverage.

- Inspect trees carefully before rappelling. Make sure they have strong roots in cracks and not just in shallow soil.

- Rock features, including boulders, flakes, chockstones, horns, and tunnels, can be tied off with webbing for a solid rap anchor.

- Make sure the feature and surrounding rock is solid. Back up with a nut if necessary.

preferably three solid anchors for rappelling. Thick trees make good anchors. Make sure their roots are deep. You can also use webbing on boulders, chockstones, and threads. Rig all anchors to an equalized master point and attach beefy metal rings for your rope. Lots of rappel stations use bolts and chains. These are great but double-check them.

Don't build rappel anchors until you're experienced. Bad anchors fail and kill. Take an anchors class from a certified guide to get first-hand knowledge from an expert.

Chains and Slings

- Many rappel stations on busy cliffs have bolt anchors that are permanently fixed with chains or thick rings. Check the hardware for excessive wear.

- Chains and rings are easy to use—just thread and rappel.

- Webbing, slings, and cord are often used to rig and equalize rap anchors. Bring extra webbing to re-rig if needed. Equalize your new rigging to a master point.

- Always use two metal links—rapid links, quick links, carabiners, or rap rings—at the master point for threading your rope.

Build an Anchor

- Don't build an anchor unless you're an expert. Take an anchor class from a certified guide. Bad anchors fail and kill.

- If you make an anchor, use at least two solid pieces of gear and equalize them with new webbing to a master point.

- If you make an anchor to retreat, then make it good. Use plenty of gear. Don't be a cheapskate and get by with a minimum anchor.

RAPPEL SAFETY KNOTS

Rappel knots keep you safe; learn to tie them correctly and practice them at home

Climbers use a handful of knots for rappelling. Several knots are used to tie two rappel ropes together. The recommended knot here is the double figure-8 fisherman's knot. It's easy to tie, super strong, won't come untied, and easy to learn. Learn how to tie it in the Essential Knots chapter.

The autoblock knot is an important rappel safety knot that

every climber needs to know and use. It's a friction hitch tied around your rappel ropes with a thin cord and attached to a harness leg loop. The knot, tied below your rappel device, slides down the rope, but if you lose control or stop, it locks onto the ropes and holds you. The autoblock lets you hang on the rope to clear rope snags and kinks, and also stops you

Autoblock Knot

- The autoblock knot is a friction hitch tied around a climbing rope with a thin cord. It's used as a safety backup.

- The knot slides on the rope below your belay device. If you lose control, the knot cinches on the rope and stops you.

- Every climber should know how to tie and use an autoblock knot—it could save your life.

- The knot lets you hang on the rope mid-rappel to free twists and kinks, unsnag the rope, and toss it down the cliff.

Using the Autoblock

- The autoblock lets you rappel slowly so you don't lose control. Use it on free or overhanging rappels where you aren't in contact with the rock.

- Make sure the knot is loose on the rope and easily slides down.

- Put your brake hand below the knot on the rope and your guide hand on the knot, or your brake hand on the knot and guide hand above the rappel device.

- Slide the knot with your hand as you rappel. To stop, just let go and it locks.

in an emergency situation. Use the knot to rappel slowly and in control, which is important if you're rappelling down an overhanging face.

Stopper knots are another important safety knot used in rappelling. Always tie stopper knots in the ends of your rappel ropes so you don't accidently rappel off the loose ends, which is a leading cause of climbing accidents. Remember to untie the knots before pulling the ropes.

Stopper Knot

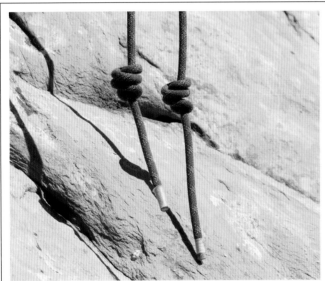

- A stopper knot is tied in the end of a rappel rope so that a climber doesn't rappel off the end but stops at the knot.

- Rappelling off the ends of the ropes is a common cause of accidents and fatalities.

- The best stopper knot is a double fisherman's knot tied in each rope end.

- Untie your stopper knot before you pull your rappel ropes or it will get caught in the anchor and you will have to climb back up to free it—a dangerous task.

Tying the Knot

- A stopper knot is a double fisherman's knot tied on a single rope. It's easy to tie but takes practice to get it right.

- Start by taking the loose rope end and coiling it three or four times around the rope about 12 inches from the end.

- Pass the loose end down through the coils and pull the knot tight. Leave at least 4 inches of tail.

- Now tie another stopper knot in the other end of the rappel rope.

129

RAPPELLING SAFETY

Rappelling is dangerous; learn what can go wrong and how to prevent accidents

Rappelling is one of the most dangerous parts of climbing since you're relying exclusively on your equipment and the anchors for safety. When you rappel, you don't have a lot of redundancy in the system. You're trusting your life to an anchor setup and your rope; both have to be secure for you to be safe.

Rappelling accounts for many climbing accidents and fatalities, making it one of the most dangerous climbing activities you will learn and do. The good thing is that most accidents result from climber error rather than equipment failure and can be avoided. Lots of things can go wrong when you rappel. Go over the tips below before trusting your life to the

What Can Go Wrong

- The knot tying ropes together can come undone.

- The rope is rigged wrong through the rappel device.

- Your hair or shirt gets caught in rappel device.

- You lose control by rappelling too fast or letting go with your brake hand.

- The rappel rope cuts on a sharp edge.

- Your rope gets stuck in a crack or flake when you pull it.

- Most rappel accidents are from misjudgment rather than equipment failure.

Use Buddy System

- Use the buddy system, like in swimming, with your climbing partner.

- Check and double-check the rappel anchors, the knot tying the rappel ropes together, and the rope threaded through each other's rappel device.

- Pay attention to each other in bad weather or if you're tired at the end of a long day.

- Check your buddy even if he doesn't ask you to. Better to be safe than sorry.

anchors and the rope.

Many times you're rappelling at the end of a long day when you're tired and it's getting dark. At those times you're most vulnerable to mistakes and accidents. You need to double-check all your safety systems—your knots, your anchors, and your rappel device. Remember at those times that we climb as a team. Use the buddy system and check each other's harness and rappel setup. Also eyeball the anchors, the anchor slings, and the knot tying your two ropes together. Be a buddy and be safer.

Leaving the Anchor

- Double-check your system, harness, ropes, rappel device, and knot before rappelling.

- Weight the rope before unclipping from the anchor.

- Stepping off a ledge can be tricky. Lean over the edge and walk your feet onto the face below. Keep your torso upright.

- Make sure hair and clothing is tucked in so it doesn't jam in the rappel device. Remember which rope to pull so the knot doesn't stick in the anchor.

Belaying Rappels

- Belay novice rappellers from a top-belay at the rappel anchors. They need the extra security and safety of a belay.

- Tie the rope into the rappeller's harness and put them on belay. Keep it loose while they descend.

- A fireman's belay is good at the bottom of a rappel. Simply hold the rope with both hands and pull it tight if the rappeller loses control.

- As the climber rappels, hold the ropes with both hands. If she loses control, pull the rope tight and it will lock in the rappel device.

131

SLAB CLIMBING

Learn to climb friction slabs and you'll learn how to effectively use your feet

Slab climbing is fun and an important part of the climbing game. Slabs, the best terrain for novice climbers, are rock faces inclined at an angle below vertical, usually between 45 and 75 degrees. Slab routes often have indistinct handholds and sparse footholds, making balance and footwork important. Climb slabs and you'll learn to trust your feet.

To climb a slab, position your body so your weight sits directly on your feet. Keep your butt away from the rock and your torso upright. Strive to keep your body at a 90-degree perpendicular angle to the earth. The natural tendency for beginners is to lean into or "hug" the rock. Leaning, however, takes weight off your feet, makes you feel out of balance,

About Slabs

- Slabs generally range from 45 to 75 degrees; anything steeper is a vertical face.

- Climb slabs keeping all of your weight on your feet. Use your hands primarily for balance. Most slab climbs have very small handholds.

- Slabs are an invaluable

school of rock for beginners, teaching balance, footwork, hand placement, finesse, and body positioning.

- If slabs are used to learn the fundamentals of face climbing, beginners will progress faster to steeper, more demanding climbs.

Slab Footwork

- Foot technique involves smearing on tiny holds or frictioning on the rock itself. Use flexible shoes and keep your toes square to the rock for maximum contact.

- Slabs require small steps to unlock a sequence. To move a hand, you may make several foot moves first.

- Look around to see which foothold feels best for your body position. Select the best one, test it, and then move.

- Keep your center of gravity over your feet and your butt out from the cliff. Keep your heels lower than your toes.

and causes your feet to slip. All these make the novice feel unsteady and scared. Keep erect, stand on your feet, and move.

To climb slabs, find your center of gravity, stand with hands and feet shoulder-width apart for stability, and keep your heels low, transferring weight to the balls and toes of your feet. Most slab footholds are dime-size edges or slight undulations. Look for subtleties in the rock like dimples, dips, crystals, and pebbles to place your foot on, especially as the angle steepens. Smear your shoes on holds, get rubber against the

rock, and avoid making big steps.

Slabs rarely have good handholds. Scan for finger holds, including thin edges and flakes to crimp and indentations to palm and press. Try to keep your hands low to stay in balance. If a good handhold is above, don't make a big reach but rather small moves until you latch it.

Climbing slabs requires a calm mind and precise movement. Climb carefully and deliberately. Look ahead, plan your moves. And remember your footwork.

Slab Handholds

- Slab handholds are usually small edges, sloping dimples or dishes, or micro-features.

- Keep your hands below shoulder level. High reaches force your body into the rock and take weight off your feet. Make small moves.

- Take advantage of palms and mantles, using your hands to "smear" when better handholds are sparse.

- Test each handhold for the best position before applying weight. Your hands are primarily used for balance.

Slab Climbing Tips

- Get rubber on the rock. Smear the toe and ball of your shoe on the rock. Place your shoe squarely on each hold.

- Climb with your heels as low as possible. This places weight on your feet, gets shoe rubber on smears, and keeps your calves from burning out.

- Constantly examine the rock before you. The most obvious slab hold is not always the best choice. Look for footholds to keep you in balance.

- Climb with control, confidence, and poise. Don't rush on slabs or you'll lose your balance. Be precise; sloppy footwork wears out your shoes.

VERTICAL CLIMBING

Climbing vertical cliffs requires balance, an erect body position, and attention to footholds

If you climb much, it's not going to be long before you're cranking vertical stone. A vertical face is simply a cliff tilted to 90 degrees or slightly under that. Most sport crags offer lots of vertical terrain. If you've been climbing slabs, you understand basic footwork. For vertical success, you need to translate that footwork to steeper cliffs.

As a rock face steepens, less of your body weight is supported by the feet and more by the arms and upper body. You need to use your feet, however, as much as possible to carry weight. Look for good footholds that allow you to keep your body erect, which forces gravity to transfer weight to your feet, giving you more shoe friction on footholds. Also

Vertical Faces

- Vertical faces are cliff sections angled at 90 degrees, although cliffs angled slightly less than 90 degrees are considered vertical by most climbers.

- You'll encounter vertical faces on most routes. Learn techniques to climb them or you're going to get

pumped and fall off.

- Keep your body weight centered over legs and feet and use your arms for pulling and balance.

- Practice vertical face climbing at your local indoor gym. Learn to use your feet before venturing to outside cliffs.

Body Position

- Keep an upright body position with your knees pointed to the side, not directly toward the wall.

- Use the X-body position. Find the center of balance in your torso and move arms and legs to stay in equilibrium. Strive for balance.

- Keep your body close to the wall so your weight remains on your feet. Turn a hip sideways toward the wall to pull your body inward.

- Coordinate pulling with your hands and pushing with your legs.

look for heel hooks and toe cams to relieve your arms.

Vertical face climbing is characterized by edging with your shoes rather than smearing. Edge holds on vertical faces hold you into the cliff and pull your body closer to the face. Look for holds for your toes and inside shoe edges. You'll also find holds that aren't either edges or smears but somewhere in between. Just roll your shoe onto the hold, a technique sometimes called smedging, and let friction do its work. Be aware which direction your knees point. Ideally they should point away from the face, which draws your hips into the wall and lets you reach higher holds.

Vertical climbing is about body positioning. Find a balance position in your torso and keep that in equilibrium as you climb. Move arms and legs in opposition to consistently maintain that centering balance. Strive to always have three stable points of contact with the rock—two arms and one leg or two legs and one arm. Move the fourth point to the next hold.

Using Hands and Feet

- Footwork is important for success on vertical faces. The angle is steep enough so that if you use just arm strength, you're going to fail.

- Keep weight over your feet. Look for good footholds. Use inside edging and smear holds. Stems also keep weight off your arms.

- Try to use sidepull handholds, which oppose your hands and feet. Grab the sidepull and twist your hips in to the wall to reach the next handhold.

Vertical Climbing Tips

- Constantly scan the rock for the best footholds. They're not always the biggest but the ones that keep you in balance. A small foothold below you is usually better than a big one to the side.

- Look for big rest holds for either hands or feet. Use them to recover and look ahead.

- Rest on straight arms rather than bent. Grab a good hold and lean back. Let bones hold you on the rock rather than muscles.

- Small steps use less energy and keep you balanced.

135

OVERHANGING CLIMBING

You need expert skills, strength, and perfect technique to swing up overhanging cliffs

Overhanging climbing requires both brute strength and impeccable technique. The essential fact of steep climbing is that your arms just aren't strong enough to support your weight for long. For success, learn how to position your body, use your arms and hands, and develop the foot and leg techniques required to keep your arms from getting pumped.

Body position is paramount on overhanging rock. Keep your arms straight whenever possible so the bones—not muscles—hold you. Bent arms pump out. Avoid locking off holds, which requires muscle, and push with your legs. Use counter-pressure between opposing arms and legs to climb upward. Look for crucial toe and heel hooks to take the

Overhanging Faces

- Overhanging faces are cliff walls angled beyond 90 degrees. The cliff-top overhangs the base.

- Overhangs require a lot of climbing skills. Footwork, strength, strategy, and technique are used in unison. Stay relaxed and climb efficiently.

- Practice overhangs in the gym to hone your technique. When hanging by your arms, climbing pace and speed are important.

- Roofs are horizontal overhangs that are strenuous and require heel hooks, toe hooks, foot cams, and knee bars.

Overhang Footwork

- The key to overhanging climbing is using the feet to keep as much weight off the arms as possible.

- The most common foot technique used on overhangs is the backstep, as it locks the hip in close to the wall. This places the maximum amount of weight on

the feet, as well as increases your reach.

- Overhangs require unique foot techniques to make the most of every foothold.

- Study advanced climbers to learn how to use your feet efficiently on overhangs.

weight off your arms, and knee bars, which allow quick rests. Dynamic moves are important, too, since it takes less energy to throw for a pocket than trying to move to it statically. Finding rests, like knee bars or straight-arm hangs, is crucial to send hard routes. If you can't rest on an endurance route, you'll never clip the anchors.

Climbing steep rock isn't easy to learn. It takes lots of work on both plastic and rock. Develop a relaxed mind, lower your expectations, and train like a fiend—only then will you get up hard routes.

ZOOM

To excel on overhanging climbing, train your abs and core muscles. Without a strong core, it's impossible to keep your feet on small footholds, let alone use them effectively. Do situps, crunches, and leg lifts.

Body Positioning

- Always hang with straight arms as much as possible to conserve strength. Bent arms sap muscle strength.

- Backstep as often as possible to keep your body weight on your feet. Also keep either of your hips close to the wall.

- When two footholds face each other, an over-exaggerated backstep, called a knee-drop can be used. Use this solid position to reach a higher handhold.

- Watch and mimic advanced climbers to learn the intricacies of overhanging body positioning.

Finding and Using Rests

- Climb hard by finding rests, which include jug holds, knee bars, stems, body jams, and scums. A scum is when you smear part of your body on a feature.

- To rest, hang straight-armed and dangle an arm toward the ground for ten seconds, then shake it above your

head for ten seconds. Alternate arms and repeat.

- No-hands rests are a blessing. Look for stems, knee bars, and large footholds.

- Identify rests pre-climb and pace around them. Climb fast between rests to save strength.

DYNAMIC MOVES

Dynamic moves are flying leaps between handholds on difficult routes

A "dyno," short for dynamic movement, is one of the most exciting climbing movements. Climbers, when confronted with a blank section of rock with handholds too far apart to reach, use dynos to leap vertically across the empty gap to the next hold. Doing a dyno on a route is both exhilarating and exacting. If you miss the top hold, you're going to fall.

Dynamic movements, first done by the great boulderer John Gill, not only allow you to bypass blank rock but also save energy. Doing a dyno or deadpoint, a modified dynamic move, is often easier than crimping across thin edges.

The wildest dynos are literal leaps. The climber grabs handholds and brings his feet high, setting them just below his

Dynamic Movement

- Lunge or throw yourself up to a high handhold using momentum and dynamic force. This movement lets you bypass short rock sections with no holds.

- A deadpoint is when a climber makes a dynamic move between handholds, but maintains four points of

contact with the rock.

- A dyno is an all-points-off leap to a faraway hold.

- Perfecting dynamic movement takes years of practice. Using dynamic moves saves energy and allows efficient climbing on hard routes.

Deadpoints

- A deadpoint involves firing a hand from one hold to another. Using your arms and legs, thrust your weight upward. Before gravity pulls you down, latch your hand on the hold.

- The "deadpoint" is the moment at the top of the thrust movement when you

hover for an instant before gravity pulls you down.

- Use a deadpoint when the holds are too small to hold and lock off statically with one hand.

- Before a deadpoint, set your body position as high as possible.

hands, and then rocks up and down building momentum. At the right moment he explodes, pushing his feet against the holds and jumping upward. At the last moment, he stretches his hands and grasps the target hold. It's usually easier to do two-handed dynos rather than one-handed ones, which can leave you twisting off the hold.

If you want to learn to dyno, watch the experts. Go to the zoo and observe the monkeys making spectacular dynamic moves with grace and balance. Then head to the gym to practice on big holds. Start with short dynos between good holds. As you improve, increase the gap between holds. Set your feet as high as possible and assume a frog position with feet splayed out and knees bent for maximum push. Keep your eyes on the target hold while jumping. When you explode up, push with your legs. Thrust your hips toward the rock rather than outward and extend your arms like a diver until you latch the hold. When you hit the handhold, hang on and don't let go.

Dynos

- A dyno is a full-blown dynamic leap or lunge to a hold otherwise out of reach.

- A dyno's momentum is always initiated and generated by your legs pushing up and your arms pulling down to escape gravity.

- Before dynoing, set your hands and feet solidly, usually close together. Focus on how you plan to grab the target hold, cock down, and lunge up.

- The dyno move is the only way to unlock sequences of moves on some hard routes, allowing you to pass blank rock sections.

Dynamic Tips

- Visualize your hand sticking on the target hold before launching. You'll stick it only if you believe you can. Confidence is critical for dynamic moves.

- Continue pulling down with your lower hand when making a dyno to avoid being tossed off.

- Set your feet as high as possible and push hard! It helps to push hard off your toe with your calf muscles to get an extra couple inches of oomph.

- Dynamic moves require good timing, accuracy, strength, and focus.

ADVANCED TECHNIQUES

Grow as a climber by learning new hand and foot techniques to climb more efficiently

To master climbing movement, learn advanced movement techniques including the rock-on move for shifting your weight onto a high foothold, using small intermediate holds between bigger holds, and refining your movement style.

A high-step move, where you lift a foot onto a waist-high edge, unbalances you and pushes your center of gravity away

from the wall. Although good flexibility helps you stay on the rock, learn how to rock onto the foothold to keep weight over your feet where it belongs. To rock on, use your foot to "grab" a high or faraway foothold. After placing your foot on the hold, shift your weight onto the hold and stand up. It takes leg strength but allows you to bypass intermediate

Rock-on Move

- "Rocking on" your foothold is when you high-step the inside edge on a foothold and essentially grab the hold with your foot, pulling your weight up and onto it.

- Next, "sit" your butt down on top of your upright heel and press your inside thigh against the wall, knee com-

  pletely bent. The other foot stands or dangles below for balance. Stand up.

- Turnout flexibility helps considerably to perform the "rock-on" move, as it allows the climber to suck her waist flat against the wall, placing the maximum weight on the foot.

Intermediate Holds

- Use intermediate hand-holds to aid in making long reaches.

- When cranking a long reach between poor holds, rather than making a long deadpoint or dyno, grab an intermediate hold to move the feet or to facilitate a shorter reach.

- When making high steps, it is often helpful to use an intermediate foot smear with the opposite foot. This moves your body into a higher position allowing you to bump your foot up more easily.

- Properly using intermediate holds is critical.

holds and provides resting opportunities for tired arms.

When you make dynamic movements, intermediate holds can mean the difference between success and failure. Small hand- and footholds often exist between large ones. These tiny holds allow you to move your feet and adjust your body position to make otherwise long reaches. When you make high steps or foot moves wide left or right, grab the small edges and shuffle your foot on a poor foothold to reach a better one.

Since most of us don't possess the strength to hang on a route for long, it's necessary to apply movement strategies so you climb efficiently. On steep routes, where your body weight remains on your arms for extended periods, climb fast and decisively. Grab and step mindfully. If your feet slip or if you constantly readjust them, focus on having precision footwork. Set your hand grip right the first time; readjusting on the hold burns power. The key to climbing hard routes lies in developing an efficient style and using the least amount of strength to surmount a climb.

Movement Strategy

- Climb efficiently. Move quickly and decisively; make as few moves as possible. Try to visualize the sequence of moves from the ground before climbing. Remember, wasted moves are wasted energy.

- Climb precisely. Indecision wastes energy.

- Pace your climbing around rests you find on the route. Take advantage of rests to recover. Climb swiftly between them.

- Don't forget to breathe. When facing the "pump clock," the more oxygen your muscles get, the longer your arms will last.

Movement Exercises

- Practice climbing slow and controlled. Place each foot and hand as precisely as possible, focusing on grabbing and stepping on each hold perfectly.

- Train your dynamic style—climb fast and fluid. Focus on climbing with momentum from each previous move, much like a monkey swinging branch to branch.

- Work on your footwork. Climb placing the maximum amount of weight on your feet. Grip as lightly as possible with your hands.

- Climb as many moves in as many areas as you can.

STRATEGY & GAME PLAN

A good mental attitude and positive thinking gets you up a lot of hard routes

To be a successful climber, learn the value of developing your own climbing strategy and always having a game plan when you go to the cliff. Climbing is a marriage of three important factors: strength, technique, and mind. Mental strength is the single most important factor for climbing success.

When you push yourself to the limits of your ability, fears and self-doubts can leave you grounded and unable to perform to your potential. Having fun, enjoying the process of climbing—including failure—and remaining positive and optimistic about success helps you climb many more difficult routes than burly muscles and long training sessions. If you think you're going to fail on a route, you will. Self-esteem and self-confidence are

The Mental Game

- Get in a rhythm. Steady breathing and a relaxed mind will give you the balance and control necessary to push your limits.

- Learn to control your emotions. Practice climbing in a meditative-like state of pure focus. Climb without fear or distraction.

- Develop your own pre-climb ritual, train on your focus, keep a clear mind, stay relaxed, and always visualize success.

- Always approach climbing with a positive attitude geared toward success—don't defeat yourself before you leave the ground.

The Power of Positive Thinking

- Unnecessary fears cripple your ability.

- Make it a habit to visualize success. When climbing moves at your limit, imagine yourself sticking the next hold from below.

- Let go of all your fears by dwelling on success and

self-confidence instead. The most important rule in climbing is to remember that you can do anything, if you believe in it enough.

- Lastly, make sure climbing is always fun. The minute it begins to feel like work, reevaluate your mental state and readjust your attitude.

critical for reaching vertical success. Furthermore, climbing requires equilibrium and continually readjusting your balance for every movement, requiring self-awareness.

Nature has created rock faces that have a limited number of features that can be used as hand- and footholds. As climbers, we must recognize how to use these particular features within the limitations of our bodies and minds effectively. Unlocking sequences of climbing moves, we create paths of upward momentum. Like solving a math problem, each climbing route requires completing a series of steps that lead to a solution.

········· GREEN ● LIGHT ··············

Focusing on the present is the most important mantra in climbing. Worrying about the past or future won't help you climb the route at hand. Practice using climbing as a meditation exercise. Get on the rock with a clear head, focusing all of your energy on each move you're engaged in performing.

Unlocking the Sequence

- Climbing is a puzzle. There are a limited number of holds, and it's your job to unlock the most efficient sequence.

- "Reading routes" is when the climber anticipates the moves ahead and plans accordingly. This invaluable skill saves strength.

- Learn to read sequences quickly by climbing as many routes in as many areas as possible.

- When working a difficult sequence, try as many different moves as you can, no matter how ridiculous they seem, to find the right moves that work for you.

Balance

- Balance gives you the control to hang in precarious positions and use small holds.

- Use flagging and backstepping to gain balance for sidepulling and laybacking movements.

- Practice climbing slabs one-handed and with no hands as a balance exercise. Since the hands should only be used for balance when possible, this trains you to keep weight on your feet.

- Anticipate when your weight needs to shift. Initiate the shift from your legs and core.

143

HANDHOLDS

Learn to grip various types of handholds to pull yourself up the rock

Every rock face provides the opportunity to use a variety of handholds or grips. Learn them in the gym and then use them outside. Practice every grip style to prevent tendon and joint injury and to gain the best hand techniques and strength. Once you've mastered the crimp and open hand grips, give yourself a hand—you're ready to climb!

There are two basic ways to grip a handhold—crimp and open hand. No rule applies as to which to use when you grab a hold—it's up to you. As you learn to climb, use both techniques and you'll find which you prefer. Most climbers use the open hand grip, which stresses the fingers less than crimps.

Crimps are small, narrow edge holds. Put the first pad of your fingers on the edge and hold on—that's a crimp. Curl your fingers over the edge for more power or press your thumb on the index finger. Crimping is hard on your fingers

Crimps

- Crimps are the most popular grip for small in-cut edges and flakes. Grab a small edge with the fingers bent at the middle knuckle and wrap the thumb over top of the index finger.

- In the half-crimp position, the fingers are clenched in crimp position but the thumb dangles to the side.

- The half-crimp is less secure than the full crimp. Experiment and see which crimp style works best for you.

- Overuse of crimps leads to injury. Use other grips whenever possible.

Open Hand Grips

- Grab a handhold with your fingers outstretched and the middle knuckle straight. This is the least stressful grip position since the joints are mostly straight.

- This grip is used for grabbing sloping holds or "slopers." Open hand gripping allows more of your finger's surface to contact a rock surface, increasing friction or "purchase."

- At first the open hand grip may feel like your weakest grip, but with training it becomes your strongest.

- The open hand grip should be your most used hand grip.

since it stresses the joints. Be careful or you'll pop a tendon.

Open hand grips are used on sloping holds as well as fat edges. It's not naturally a power hold like the crimp so train to increase strength. This grip relies on skin-to-rock friction so chalk up well.

ZOOM

Grip handholds lightly to increase endurance and limit muscle fatigue in the hands and forearms. Beginner and novice climbers often over-grip handholds, which quickly tire their arms. Grab lightly and climb quickly.

FACE CLIMBING

Friction Grip

- The friction grip, also called "palming," is similar to the open hand grip. Drape your palm over a hold and use skin friction to cling to it.

- Use this grip to climb arêtes and dihedrals. It's handy when other grips fail.

- Practice in the gym and on rock with your hand facing in both directions. Also practice inverting your palms on a sloping mantle hold.

- When climbing a chimney, press your palms and feet on the opposing wall to push up or hold in place.

Pinch Grip

- The pinch grip is a natural and widely used grip. To pinch grip, clasp a hold with a half crimp and use your thumb to pinch an opposing edge.

- Pinches are common on artificial walls. Beef up your pinch strength at the local gym.

- Outside pinches are also common on sport routes. They come in every form, from rock ribs to side-pulls with a "thumb catch" to brick-size pinches.

- Make training the pinch grip part of your gym regimen.

FOOTHOLDS

Learn to effectively use your feet and soon you'll be dancing up cliffs

Footwork is paramount to climbing success. Take time to learn, practice, and use every kind of foot placement. Determining the best foothold and foot position keeps you in balance, takes weight off your arms, and allows you to climb all day. Don't rely on your arms to muscle up a climb; give yourself a leg up with proper footwork.

When face climbing, you'll use your feet in two basic positions—edging and smearing. Edging is standing on either the inside or outside edge of your shoe on an in-cut hold. This is the most stable foot position. Stand on either the ball of your foot or the big-toe side of the shoe, depending on what feels best. Place your foot on the best part of the hold

Edging and Front-pointing

- Edging is stepping your foot on a flat or in-cut edge of a foothold with the front, inside, or outside edge of your shoe.

- Inside edging allows you to stand on micro holds.

- For outside edging, turn your foot and step on the shoe's outside edge to "backstep" for maximum reach.

- To front-point, place the shoe's toe on the hold. Front-point in pockets and on narrow edges. Front-pointing requires more leg strength than inside and outside edging.

Smearing

- Smearing is the foot position for standing on sloping, rounded holds via friction.

- Soft, flexible shoes are best for friction climbing or smearing. Slippers provide the maximum amount of contact with a foothold, letting you feel the rock for precise foot placement.

- Practice smearing by putting the maximum amount of weight over your foot on the friction hold.

- Learn to precisely place your shoe on a smear hold. If you throw your foot in a sloppy manner, chances are it will slip.

and you'll stick to it. Smearing is standing on a smooth, sloping hold where no edge exists. Stand on the front part of your shoe so you get the most rubber against the rock. The friction of rubber and rock keeps you from slipping. Keep your heels low to maximize weight on your toes.

After mastering edging and smearing, learn all the other advanced foot techniques like knee bars, heel hooks, high steps, and backsteps, and your climbing will dramatically improve.

FACE CLIMBING

Heel Hooks, Toe Hooks, and Knee Bars

- Use heel hooks on roofs, arêtes, overhanging faces, or anywhere else for balance. Set your heel carefully on an edge and then pull with the heel.

- Toe hooks are handy on overhanging walls and roofs.

- Try heel-toe combinations.

Sometimes a heel hook improves dramatically by camming your toe simultaneously against the rock.

- For knee bars, plant your foot and cam your knee against a flat or in-cut rock section. Use a Neoprene kneepad. Knee bars are great for resting on steep routes.

Rest and High Steps, Backstep

- High steps are just that—a high foot placement on an edge. Step up with your inside edge and "rock on" or shift weight onto the hold.

- Perform a rest step by stepping either the heel, arch, or ball of your foot on a foothold. Also stand on

top of your shoe with your other foot.

- To backstep, put the outside edge of your shoe on a foothold beneath your center of gravity. Weight your foot and lock your hip against the rock.

SIDEPULL HOLDS & UNDERCLINGS
Use a wide variety of different grips to utilize every handhold on a route

Handholds on cliff faces usually aren't horizontal edges like ladder rungs. Instead, the holds face every which way—vertically, upside down, and all other directions. To successfully climb face routes, you need to use these holds effectively. While climbing, you're constantly maintaining equilibrium by pulling in one direction while simultaneously pushing in the other, creating counterforce. This subtle balance between hands and feet working together allows you to use many features as holds.

Sidepulls are common hand grips. You reach out and grasp a vertical edge with palm in and thumb up, and pull it sideways toward your body. Lean away from the hold for maximum power. Laybacking is doing a long series of sidepulls, usually up a crack. Grab the crack edge with your hands, press your feet against the opposite wall, and lean back. Keep your feet high and your arms straight. Laybacking can be pumpy.

Side-pulls

- A sidepull involves grabbing the hold with your hand with your thumb facing up. Laybacking is when you pull the sidepull toward you. Place your foot in direct opposition to the direction of pull.

- Face holds are not the only sidepulls. You can use a crack for sidepull moves.

- Sidepulls allow you to make longer reaches than you can from horizontal holds.

- Dual sidepulls can be used together in an iron-cross position. The pulling opposition of your arms allows you to move your feet up.

Laybacking

- Laybacking is a continuous series of sidepull moves up a crack in a dihedral. Put both hands in the crack, lean back, and place your feet in opposition on the wall below your hands.

- Pull your hands toward you, gripping the crack, and press your feet on the wall.

- Keep your arms straight and make short moves up the crack. Alternate your hands or shuffle them up the crack.

- Keep your feet high, just below your hands. Look for footholds to make it less strenuous.

Gastons are the opposite of side-pulls. You crimp a vertical edge and pull outward: strenuous but effective.

An undercling is simply an upside-down hold, usually the down-pointing edge of a flake, which you grab with your palms facing up. Smear your feet on the face below, keeping them high for maximum opposition. Use straight arms to avoid the pump.

ZOOM

The gaston move is named for famed French climber Gaston Rébuffat, an alpinist and climber from the mid-twentieth century. To do a gaston, grab a vertical hold in front of your torso with your hand with the thumb down. Pull to the side like you're trying to open an elevator door.

FACE CLIMBING

Using a Gaston

- A gaston, pronounced *gas-tone,* is the opposite of a sidepull. Use a vertical hold. Grab it with your hand with your thumb facing down. Use your feet in opposition to hold the gaston.

- Pull a gaston with your right hand and push the left foot in opposition to keep in balance.

- Set your feet high before grabbing a gaston. It's difficult to move off the hold if your legs are extended.

- This advanced technique may feel uncomfortable. Use caution to avoid shoulder or back injury.

Underclings

- Underclings are upside-down holds, usually the edge of a crack, flake, or pocket. Grab the hold with your palm facing up.

- Keep the undercling between your waist and chest to feel stable. Place your feet high and lean back on your hands.

- For a high undercling, pinch the hold and work your feet high. Ease upward until the undercling is chest high and feels secure.

- Keep your arms as straight as possible, especially if your feet are smeared on the face. Move quickly to avoid getting pumped.

POCKETS
Stick your fingers in different-size pockets to climb limestone cliffs

Pocket pulling is a requirement for the modern climber. Most limestone sport climbing areas feature routes with a plethora of pockets from mono or one-finger pockets to huge jug pockets that both hands grab. These days a lot of climbers begin their careers outside on pocketed cliffs so it's important to know how to use them. Be aware that pocket climbing is rough on your fingers. It's easy to get injured hanging your weight from a couple fingers jammed in a pocket. Use caution, go slow, and don't overdo it. Finger strains are common injuries and take a long time to heal.

The ultimate climbing handhold is probably the one-finger or *mono-doight* pocket. You stick your middle finger, the strongest, into the hole and pray your tendon doesn't break. Two-finger pockets are more manageable. Slide your ring and middle fingers in or stack them one on top of the other. Bigger pockets that fit your whole hand are a blast to use.

Using Pockets

- Use an open hand grip or a half-crimp grip.

- Before using a pocket, inspect it and determine how to grab it. Slide your fingers in the pocket and feel around to discover the best grip, direction of pull, and finger combination.

- Many pockets have sharp edges or are a tight fit for your fingers. Don't stuff too many fingers in a pocket so they're stuck inside if you fall—you'll break them.

- Turn a pocket into a sidepull or undercling as you move up on it.

Mono Pockets

- Use caution while attempting to use these tiny one-finger pockets. Climbers pull tendons by pulling too hard and too fast on a mono. If you feel a pop—you're off to the emergency room.

- It takes time to build the needed finger strength required for hard moves off monos. Start by training with two- and three-finger pockets.

- Which finger should you use? Use the middle finger, the strongest, in an open hand or half-crimp grip, determined by each individual pocket.

150

Practice using pockets to find different ways to grip them. Think about turning a pocket into a sidepull or undercling. Before setting your fingers in a pocket, feel around. Make sure there are no sharp edges that cut. Think about your feet, too. Use a pointed shoe for cramming in pockets.

FACE CLIMBING

Finger Pockets

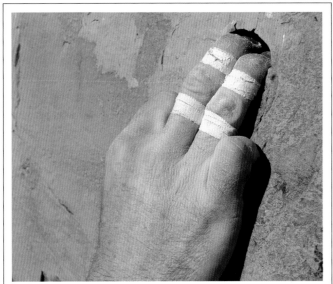

- Two- and three-finger pockets are commonly found in gyms and on limestone cliffs.

- Use combinations with your middle and ring fingers or index and middle fingers.

- For three-finger pockets, use the middle, ring, and pinky fingers or your three strongest fingers—index, middle, and ring. See which finger combinations are most comfortable.

- Train pocket strength religiously to prevent finger injuries. Try a variety of plastic pocket holds, which work great for bouldering strength training.

Split-finger Pockets

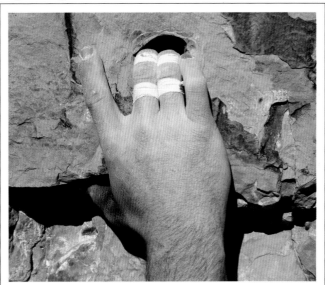

- A split-finger pocket is two small pockets right next to each other. They can be gripped with different fingers in different pockets simultaneously.

- Although not as common as two- and three-finger pockets, split-finger pockets are common.

- Pockets come in every combination! Don't get tunnel vision. Also keep a lookout for pocket and edge combination holds.

- Keep your attention focused on finding the best pocket grips. Try different finger combinations to find the best grip.

ADVANCED HAND TECHNIQUES

Hard routes require using your hands and fingers in strange and different ways

As you grow as a climber, you'll want to do harder climbs. The difference between moderate and hard routes is that on hard ones, the holds get smaller and the face gets steeper. The steeper the rock, the more important hand technique becomes. You just can't reach up and crimp and grab every hold because a lot of them aren't good. You need to learn and practice specialized hand work to be able to effectively use those holds. Before doing hard routes, you have to master mantling, palming, wrapping, and thumb use.

Mantling, an essential hand technique, is how you lift your body by pressing downward with your hands onto a narrow shelf or on top of a boulder. Imagine standing at a fireplace.

Mantling

- Imagine climbing out of a swimming pool. Set one or both hands palms down on the edge and push.

- Use mantles for climbing onto boulders, ledges, and shelves.

- Hanging from one arm, place a hand palm down,

high step the same-side foot, and press down until the other hand can flip to a mantle position. Ease your weight from your arms to your foot and stand up.

- Train by bouldering, doing dips, and weight-training the triceps, shoulders, and back.

Palming

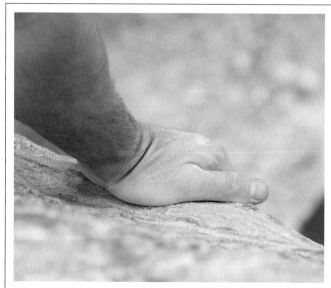

- Place the palm of a hand under or against a flat rock surface and press.

- Using your lower hand in a palm position with fingers pointing down lets you move your upper hand higher or your feet up. This is useful in squeeze chimneys.

- Palming is handy in dihedrals. Extend a palm and place it on the opposite wall, creating a counter-force hold.

- Like all sloping holds, the security of a palm hold is temperature dependent and improved by cooler conditions.

Put your hands on the mantel shelf and spring upward with your arms on the shelf. Now push down with your hands until your elbows lock, lift a foot onto the mantel, and stand up—that's mantling. It helps to kick a heel onto the shelf before cocking your arm—simple but strenuous.

Palming is a friction hand technique used for mantling on sloping holds or pressing against flat faces like the edge of an arête or the wall of a smooth dihedral. Palming is effective on slabby routes where you can place an inverted palm on a bump down by your waist, then press down on the palm and stand one foot up by your hand. When pressing, use the heel of your palm for the most friction.

Another technique is using your hands and fingers to wrap around holds rather than gripping them. Look for knobs and horns and simply wrap your wrist, hand, or fingers around the protrusion and hang on. Also remember to use your thumb whenever possible—it's your strongest digit.

Wraps

- For horns, points, and knobs, wrap your hand like you would grab a dowel on a peg board.

- On protruding knobs, wrap your hand around the hold with the pinky finger against the rock.

- Wrap your wrist around large knobs to save finger strength by transferring your weight onto the bones rather than muscle. Wrap the wrist, lock your arm, and relax your fingers.

- Also wrap your forearm around a horn, lock your arm, and relax your hand and fingers to rest.

Thumb Grip

- Use your thumbs for pinches, press downs, balancing, grabbing gastons and underclings, and hooking small edges or knobs.

- Use a thumb wrap to hold onto small knobs or crystals. Increase purchase by crimping one to three fingers on top of the thumb.

- For balance on gastons, grab the gaston with your thumb, hand open, and palm against the rock to step your feet up. Once you're in a higher and better position, flip the gaston to your fingers.

USING HANDS & FEET

Learn advanced techniques like matching hands, crossing feet, and stemming to climb rock features

Using your hands and feet is the primary way that you attach yourself to rock as you climb. Complex hand and foot movements include matching or crossing and using a variety of techniques to climb arêtes and dihedrals.

Matching or switching hands or feet on a hold is used on nearly every climb. Big handholds are easy to match your hands on; small ones are more difficult. It's best to weight your feet and then find a way to share the hold with both hands, even if it's only with a couple fingers from each hand.

The alternative to matching is crossing through, which saves energy by reducing the number of moves in a sequence. Often the key to crossing hands is to first place a

KNACK ROCK CLIMBING

Matching Hands

- Matching is replacing a hand or foot already on a hold with the other hand or foot.

- To match hands, grip with one hand then ease your other hand onto the hold one finger at a time. Slowly remove the first hand.

- To match feet, put your foot in a front-point position, then step your other foot on the open space. Remove original foot.

- For a dynamic match, place a free hand or foot above the hold and grab or step as soon as you let go or step off.

Crossing Hands and Feet

- Crossing a hand or foot over the other is a lateral climbing move. It's useful for traverses, when you can't match on holds, or during complex sequences.

- Use hand crosses on pockets, narrow holds, and sidepulls, either over or under a locked-off arm.

- Crosses save energy by climbing with the least amount of possible moves.

- Mastering cross moves takes practice. It's easy to twist your body out of balance. Learn to recognize when crossing through is effective and efficient.

foot ahead of you. Crossing your feet is also important, but it's often hard to match feet on tiny footholds. In that case, if your handholds are good, do a jump step to substitute one foot for the other.

Climb dihedrals and corners by stemming. Work on flexibility, palming techniques, and the use of counterforce opposition. You can climb even blank corners by stemming on smears. An arête is a feature shaped like a building corner. Use laybacking, toe and heel hooking, and pinch moves to surmount these precarious edges.

ZOOM

Practice your matching skills by doing a lateral traversing boulder problem. Match hands on each handhold and switch feet on each foothold. Try a similar crossing-through exercise. Do a low traverse, crossing your hands and feet on every move and never using the same hold twice.

Stemming

- Use your feet in opposition between two widely spaced footholds, usually on opposite walls of a dihedral or corner.

- Stemming takes weight off your arms, is great for resting, and allows upward progress in blank corners.

- In dihedrals, palm your hands on the opposing walls, which lets you move your feet up. Your back, hips, or shoulders are used in opposition against your stemmed feet for resting.

- Train flexibility. The wider you can stem, the more footholds you can stand on.

Arêtes

- An arête is the sharp edge on the outside of a corner. Climbing arêtes requires balance, sidepulls, and finesse.

- Arêtes are usually climbed by laybacking the edge and heel or toe hooking around the arête.

- Use the frog technique to climb an arête straight on and to move from side to side. Keep a leg on each side of the arête; squeeze them together at tenuous sections.

- Grab the arête using a pinch grip for extra security. Combat the barn door effect by using sidepulls.

THE ART OF JAMMING

Get jamming on natural cracks and fissures to enjoy climbing cracks of all sizes

Traditionally, most climbs ascended crack systems up cliff faces since these features offered natural weaknesses, allowing climbers to easily place protection and anchors. Crack climbing or jamming is the process and techniques developed by climbers to ascend various-size cracks. Cracks, naturally occurring lines that split rock walls, are usually described by the appendage used to climb them, such as finger cracks, hand cracks, or fist cracks. Wider cracks are called off-width cracks, while those that accommodate your entire body are known as chimneys.

Jamming, the technique used to climb cracks, is a learned technique that at first seems unnatural. Jamming is simply

What Is Jamming?

- Crack climbing involves ascending cracks by wedging or jamming your body or parts of it into vertical cracks.

- Jamming is hard to learn because it is counterintuitive. It's not like face climbing where you use hand- and footholds to push and cling upward.

- To jam a crack, wedge your hands in it and expand them, exerting opposing pressure on the crack's sidewalls to hold you in place.

- Jamming can be painful since you're placing skin against rock, but it's also rewarding since it gets you to wild places.

All About Cracks

- Cracks are natural weaknesses in rock. Routes follow cracks because they're easier to protect with gear than blank faces.

- How you climb a crack depends on what size it is—finger, hand, fist, off-width, squeeze chimney, or chimney.

- A crack's difficulty depends on hand and finger size. A man's hand crack is a woman's off-width crack.

- Don't be discouraged by crack difficulty ratings. Hand and fist cracks are easiest. Off-widths, even easy ones, are hard. Finger cracks are hardest.

wedging fingers, hands, fists, arms, feet, and legs into a crack, depending on its width or what climbers call its size. Crack climbing is not intuitive like face climbing. You can't just step up to a crack and start jamming it. You have to learn specific ways to place your hands and feet. It can also be painful since cracks are often rough inside and crystals may cut your skin.

With skill and practice, however, you can become proficient at jamming and even love it. Crack climbing is not a natural or easy skill to learn, but with practice at your local cliff, jamming cracks will be a lot of fun.

GREEN ● LIGHT

To improve your crack skills, get lots of jamming practice. Go to your local cliff and set up top-ropes on different-size cracks. Do lots of laps on them. Figure out the jams, see what works best, and experiment with foot placements. Downclimbing also helps to improve your crack technique.

Basic Crack Technique

- Several variables determine how you climb a crack. What is the width? Which direction does it angle? How steep is it? Is it parallel-sided?

- The easiest way to jam is to wedge your appendage above a constriction in the crack. Pull or push against the constriction, using it as a handhold.

- If the crack is parallel-sided and without constrictions, you have to torque or twist your appendage in it and use the opposing pressure to move up.

Crack Climbing Tips

- It takes practice and time to master jamming the different crack sizes.

- Learn from an experienced crack master and you'll improve faster than by trial and error.

- Athletic tape protects your hands and fingers from abrasions and scrapes.

- If you can't jam it, layback it. Laybacking can be easier but less secure.

- Stemming feet away from a crack takes weight off hand and finger jams.

- Look for face holds as you climb for both hands and feet.

CRACK CLIMBING

157

HAND CRACKS
Start with the hand jam and build your crack climbing technique from there

Hand jams are a basic crack technique. Start crack climbing by learning how to hand jam and you'll have a sound basis to climb other crack sizes. Hand jams are simply that—your hands wedged into cracks that just fit them. Hand jams often use little strength because you're hanging on your arm bones, not your muscles.

Jamming a hand crack is like climbing a ladder without rungs. Your hands, jammed in the crack, keep you balanced. Stand on a foot stuffed in the crack, then step the other up to calf level and slot it in. Keep moving up. Shuffle your hands. Keep your feet stepping one above the other. Find a rhythm and economy of movement. After you've learned to jam a

The Sweetest Crack

- Hand cracks are the right width to accept both hands and feet, making any jam a jam bomber.

- Hand cracks range from thin hands to regular hands to wide hands. Thin hands are hardest. Wide hands can be strenuous.

- When jamming, feel for the best jam. Do most hand jams with your thumbs up. Also shuffle your hands and feet up, keeping one above the other.

- Hand cracks can be abrasive. Tape your hands if the rock is rough or come home bloody.

Classic Hand Jams

- The secure hand jam is simply your hand crammed inside a 2- to 3-inch-wide crack.

- Bring your thumb diagonally across the palm. Cup your hand and insert into a crack like you're shaking hands. Wedge the hand and create pressure with fingers

- and the back of the hand.

- For loose jams, put the hand in thumb down. This twist increases torque.

- Jam with your thumbs facing each other. Keep the thumb-down jam at the top and the thumb-up jam below. Shuffle up the crack.

158

hand crack, take those basic techniques and begin climbing other crack sizes. It's best to learn finger cracks next, since you'll encounter them more than off-widths.

For aspiring crack climbers, the hardest part is learning to create holds in a crack from nothing. Jamming a hand in a crack is not like grabbing an edge on a face climb. Instead you need to practice and find the best jams. Focus on body position, repetitive movement, and shifting your balance from each hand and foot as you jam.

ZOOM

The key to hand jamming is good footwork. Look for great foot jams and find edges outside the crack to keep your feet solid. Remember to always move from your feet, and that even an insecure hand jam will keep you on the rock.

Thin and Wide Hands

- Thin hand cracks are strenuous since you can't get the meaty part of your palm inside.

- For thin cracks, keep your thumb on top of the hand. This lets you insert the hand farther into the crack. Use your fingers to press against the sidewall.

- To jam wide hand cracks, cup your hand with the thumb in the palm. Stuff it in the crack and torque with the back of the hand and fingers against the sidewalls.

- The more you cup, the more insecure the jam.

Foot Jams

- To make a foot jam, twist your foot sideways so the big toe faces skyward. Slide it into the crack. Release the tension and let the shoe's rand and sole cam against rock.

- Take small steps. Shuffle your feet with one always above the other or alternate jams, walking your feet above each other. Do what feels best, but keep your heels below your toes.

- Use your legs to push you up the crack. Look for face holds outside the crack for your feet.

CRACK CLIMBING

FINGER CRACKS
Finger jams give you leverage on the thinnest cracks to test your jamming skills

Finger cracks range in size from narrow slits that fit fingertips to ones that require stacking two fingers. The best finger cracks swallow your fingers to the third knuckle and offer constrictions where you slot your fingers like a nut. These jams, called fingerlocks, are your best friends in a finger crack. For a fingerlock, insert your fingers and slide them down the

crack until they lock in the constriction. The sequence and placement of each hand is critical on finger cracks. Strategize before starting to find fingerlocks when you need them.

You can insert your hand in two ways—thumbs up or thumbs down. You'll use both as you jam a finger crack. Thumbs up allows you to reach farther between jams, your

About Finger Cracks

- Finger cracks are narrow cracks from ½- to 1½-inches wide. Thin finger cracks are extremely difficult, while wide finger cracks, called off-fingers, are the most insecure.

- The easiest finger cracks accept your fingers to your knuckles and are a bit wider

than your fattest finger.

- Look for constrictions in the crack where you can find secure fingerlocks above. Feel around for the best finger fit.

- If the crack's a bit too wide, then layback for a few moves.

Jam a Finger Crack

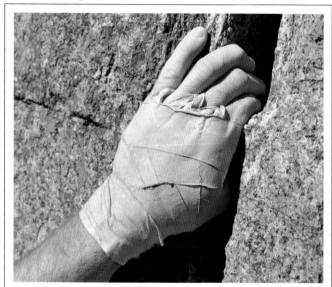

- Slot your fingers in the crack as far as they'll go. Wedge the middle joints by twisting your hand.

- For best results, look for constrictions in the crack. Slide your fingers in the wider part above the constriction, placing your fingers like you are placing a nut.

- Move your fingers around, up and down, until you find the best fit. Turn your elbow down, keeping your forearm parallel to the crack to keep your fingers from levering out.

fingers don't twist to lock, and it's less strenuous. Thumbs down lets you torque your fingers, creating pressure and locking you in. It's secure but can be painful.

Good footwork is essential on finger cracks. The cracks are too thin to accept more than the toe of your shoe. It's important to find good foot placements to take weight off your fingers, otherwise you'll get pumped out. Look for face holds on either side of the crack, stemming holds, and flares where you can jam shoe rubber.

ZOOM

Look for rests when you're jamming steep finger cracks so you recover arm strength. The best rests are usually pods where you find a good hand jam or a face hold where you stand on one foot.

Thumbs Up or Down

- Your thumbs can point either up or down, depending on the torque you apply and which way you face the rock.

- For thin cracks, jam thumbs down for maximum torque. Place your thumb under the first joint of your index finger and twist.

- Thumb up is great if your fingerlocks are perfect, but you don't always get enough torque to stay in the crack as you move up on the jam.

- Try thumb up or thumb down to find the best jam.

Footwork

- Footwork is key to jamming finger cracks. Finger cracks will only accept the smallest part of your shoe's toe.

- Use thin-toe shoes like slippers for jamming the toe or smearing on the outside edge of the crack.

- In wide or flared finger cracks, twist your foot sideways, keeping the big toe up, and slot the shoe's toe in the crack.

- Look for smears and edges on the face away from the crack. If there aren't any footholds or decent toe jams, then paste your feet on smears.

CRACK CLIMBING

FIST & OFF-WIDTH CRACKS
Fist jams offer a secure hold, while off-widths require true mastery of jamming technique

Fist cracks are wide fissures that accommodate your clenched fists. They're usually not difficult to climb since they're wide enough to slot your feet inside and carry your weight. Look for constrictions in the crack where you can securely wedge a fist above. Jam the fist with palms up for the most security.

Off-width cracks are problematic. Most are strenuous and technical since your appendages don't easily fit in the crack. These are the cracks you need to practice. Anyone can jam a hand crack, but only a true crack master can float an off-width crack. It's good to become proficient at climbing wide cracks since most long routes have mandatory climbing up off-width and chimney sections.

Fist Jams

- Fist cracks are just that—cracks big enough to jam a fist inside.

- To make a fist jam, ball your hand into a fist and stuff it in the crack with knuckles either up or down. Tense your hand muscles like you're squeezing a lime and you're wedged.

- Thumb placement varies depending on crack width. For narrow cracks, put the thumb inside the fist. Try your thumb over or under the fingers for other widths.

- Torque half your foot or make a heel-toe wedge between the crack sides for secure foot jams.

Off-width Cracks

- Off-width cracks are strenuous, awkward, painful, and hard to master. Jamming off-widths is a slow-moving game of inches.

- Like all cracks, jamming an off-width is about creating opposing pressures on the crack's sidewalls to hold you in place.

- Off-width cracks range from 4 to 12 inches wide. Climb with either your left or right side in the crack, depending on features.

- Specialized techniques beyond the scope of this book are required to climb many off-widths. Learn the basics first.

Off-width cracks are the awkward size between fist cracks and squeeze chimneys. They're often strenuous and difficult with upward movement measured in inches. Footwork is crucial for success since off-width cracks wear you out fast and require lots of muscle tension. First decide if you're climbing it right-side-in or left-side. Then jam your leg, knee, and thigh into the crack and torque it against the sidewalls. Use your outside foot with a heel-toe or a foothold to propel upward. To move your torso up the crack, traditional off-width climbing uses arm bars and chickenwings.

Off-width Technique

- Learn these techniques and you'll get up lots of wide cracks.

- For an arm bar, put your arm in the crack and lever by pushing against one side with your hand and your elbow on the other. Press your other hand on the outside edge of the crack.

- Chickenwings or arm locks are secure. Bend your arm and stick your elbow in the crack. Press triceps against one wall and palm on the other. Press the outside arm on the crack edge.

Off-width Footwork

- Good footwork propels you to off-width success. Be warned, however; using your feet is strenuous and awkward. Climb with high-top shoes and kneepads.

- One foot is outside the crack, the other is inside. The inside foot does a heel-toe jam. Torque your foot with the toes on one wall and the heel on the other.

- The other foot does a heel-toe jam on the outside of the crack, with the toe and heel smeared against the edges.

- Look for footholds outside the crack to make it easier to move upward.

CHIMNEYS

Climbing chimneys challenges all your jamming skills and adds some new ones, too

Chimneys are fissures wide enough for your body to fit inside. These range in width from squeeze chimneys, which you squeeze inside, to gaping chimneys, which you climb by bridging arms and legs on opposite walls. Climbing chimneys is straightforward, but it takes practice to develop skills. Learn to climb chimneys because, as with off-width cracks, most multi-pitch routes have mandatory chimney sections.

Climb chimneys by using opposing pressures with hands, back, knees, and feet on the sidewalls. Advance by pushing and pulling, moving in short spurts rather than big moves. Press the front wall with your feet or in tight chimneys with your knees, pushing your back against the back wall to hold

Climbing Chimneys

- Chimneys, cracks that are wide enough to fit inside, are the easiest cracks to climb.

- You'll find two basic chimneys—squeeze chimneys and full-body chimneys, which range from 2 to 6 or more feet wide.

- Use both sides of the chimney to climb, making progress by pushing and pulling against opposing walls.

- Chimneys are difficult to protect unless you find cracks inside. The lack of protection is not a big deal because it can be hard to fall out of chimneys.

- Practice chimney climbing at small cliffs. On every long route you'll encounter a chimney. Know how to climb it and you'll have more fun.

Squeeze Chimney

- Your body fits inside a squeeze chimney. Some are tight and progress is made by inches. Wider ones allow you to slither.

- Basic technique is the secure heel-toe used in off-widths. Use pressure and sticky rubber to move upward. Stiff shoes work best.

- In wider squeezes, use T-stacks. Heel-toe with one foot by putting the heel in the instep of the other shoe, which presses against the wall lengthwise.

- Use chickenwings with one arm and press the outside edge of the chimney with the other hand.

your body in place. In tight chimneys, cock one arm in a chickenwing as in off-widths and use the other on the outside of the crack, or push down with your palms.

Squeeze chimneys, the tightest of the big cracks, are secure and relatively simple to climb. Make small moves in squeeze chimneys to conserve energy. In very tight chimneys, inhale to hold in place with your chest and exhale to move upward.

The back-and-foot chimney, usually 3 feet wide, is the easiest to climb. Use arms and legs in an alternating scissor position, which keeps your back pressed against the wall. After planting your legs opposite, push against the back wall with your palms and scoot your back up. It's a game of inches. Don't make big moves unless your feet are on good holds. For wider chimneys, keep your feet in front or bridge the gap with an arm and leg on each wall.

Most chimneys are difficult to protect. Look for cracks for gear; otherwise you'll be climbing scared. Like other cracks, practice chimney technique at your local crag and you'll gain competence.

Back-and-foot Chimney

- A back-and-foot chimney is climbed by pushing your back against one wall and pressing your feet against the other.

- Ascend by putting one foot below your butt and leaving the other on the opposite wall. Press against the wall and straighten your leg, pushing your body up.

- Use your hands to push, too. After moving up, trade leg positions. Look for face holds to put a foot on or grab with a hand.

- On wider chimneys keep your feet on the opposite wall and hands behind.

Full-body Chimney

- Wide full-body chimneys can be easy or hard depending on the width and what holds are inside.

- Stem up the chimney with one arm and leg on one wall and the other arm and leg on the other. Advance by pressing against the walls and scooting a foot then a hand and repeat.

- For wide chimneys, do a full-body stem with hands on one wall and feet on the other—scary, strenuous, and fortunately, rare.

- Most wide chimneys are unprotected. Look inside for cracks for protection.

USING YOUR FEET

There's nothing fancy about proper footwork; learn the skills and give your arms a break

How you use your feet is the most important aspect of crack climbing. You can learn all the hand and finger jams but if you don't know how to effectively use your feet, then you're going to struggle. Every time you jam a crack, think feet first. Let your feet support your body weight as much as possible rather than jams, which pump you out. Let your feet propel

you up the rock. Hand and fist cracks are the best size for learning basic crack footwork since they're both the same width as your foot. For hand cracks, slide your foot in the crack to the ball of your foot and stand on it. Imagine a crack as a ladder with invisible rungs; let each foot jam become a rung. If the crack is narrower than your foot, drop your knee

Tips on Footwork

- Good footwork is key to successful crack climbing. Your feet support you and take weight off your arms.

- Keep your legs straight. If you bring your feet high, it forces your butt out and puts weight on your arms.

- Keep your heels low to keep the toe and rand rubber smeared on rock for friction.

- Jamming cracks hurts your feet, especially on long routes. Get well-fitting crack shoes. High-tops are best for wide cracks, but are hard to find.

- Do lots of cracks at your local cliff. Find what works and feels secure. Sticking your feet in cracks initially feels awkward, but with practice you'll get the hang of it.

Thin Crack Footwork

- Footwork is important for finger cracks since they're too small to get more than your toe tips into. Thin cracks without footholds are usually strenuous.

- Find good jams that support your body. Use your feet and legs to push up the crack.

- Look for flared sections of crack for your toe box to jam. Twist your foot, cram the toe in, and keep your heel low.

- Look for sections you can jam with your fingers and stem with your legs. Stemming takes weight off your arms.

sideways and wedge the foot inside, straighten your leg, and feel the torque. Foot jams in hand cracks can be painful, especially if you're jamming long vertical stretches. Wear socks and a comfortable stiff shoe, preferably a bit larger than your normal shoe, and scan for rest holds outside the crack to relieve the ache.

Finger cracks are tough on the feet. If you're not careful with your feet, you're going to get pumped and fall. Sometimes all you'll get is the toe of your shoe in the crack, forcing you to look for footholds outside the crack. Keep one foot smeared in the crack and the other on edges. Use jams as laybacks to bring each foot up. If there are no outside edges, stick the toe tip in vertically and weight it.

Off-width cracks and tight chimneys require the heel-toe technique, which is surprisingly secure. Also use knee jams and counter-pressure to push your body upward.

Hand Crack Footwork

- Hand cracks offer the best foot jams since they're the same width as your feet. A good foot jam easily supports your weight.

- Twist your foot, slot it in the crack to the ball of your foot, and weight it.

- Don't jam your foot in so deep that it gets stuck.

- For thin hand cracks that are too narrow for your foot, twist your foot and insert with the pinkie toe pointing down. Turn your leg upright with the knee above the foot. The camming action holds you in place.

Wide Crack Footwork

- If the crack is too wide, twist your foot to get toe rubber on one wall and your heel on the other.

- For off-width cracks and squeeze chimneys, use the heel-toe technique. Insert your foot in the crack and twist your ankle, pushing toes on one wall and the heel on the other. Use opposing pressure and friction to move.

- If the crack's wide, push your whole leg inside. Press the knee against one wall or jam your thigh. Heel-toe with your other foot on the outside.

167

TOP-ROPING

When top-roping, the rope always protects the climber from above

Top-rope climbing is fun as well as safe. It's the perfect way to get climbing outside when you're starting out. Top-roping offers all the rewards of climbing without the extreme risks. Top-roping is, of course, dangerous like any rock climbing activity, but you do everything possible to minimize and control those risks so you'll come home safe.

Top-rope climbing is simply ascending a cliff with the rope always anchored above you. That way you're protected by the rope from above. If you fall, and you will fall, you usually drop only a few feet before the rope catches you. It's hard to get injured top-roping if you do everything right, like building sturdy anchors, following proper belaying and lowering techniques, wearing good equipment and a helmet, and not goofing off.

Top-roping is the first introduction to climbing for most folks, whether it's in the local rock gym or at a small cliff. It's

Top-rope Skills

- Anchors. You need to know how to create a safe and equalized anchor at the top of a route or cliff-top for the climber.

- Belaying and lowering. You need to be able to safely belay and lower a climber.

- Rope management. You need to know how to tie into the rope and then handle the rope for climbing and belaying.

- Safety. You need to be able to create a safe climbing environment by assessing the site and then managing it to minimize danger.

Basic Top-rope System

- The slingshot belay is the best and most common climbing setup at top-rope cliffs.

- In a slingshot belay, the rope runs up the cliff from the belayer, through the anchor master point at the cliff edge, and then back down the cliff to the climber.

- The climber is always protected by the rope above, which the belayer on the ground pulls through the anchor and her belay device.

- If a climber falls on a top-rope, it is always a short distance since the rope is tight.

KNACK ROCK CLIMBING

168

a great way to learn the basics of climbing movement, how to rig anchors, how to belay, and to just have fun climbing. Top-roping is ideal for beginners because they don't have to worry about falling but can concentrate on learning to move over stone.

·········· GREEN ● LIGHT ··········

If you've never climbed outside before, hire a guide from a climbing school. She'll supply the gear and take you top-roping at a nearby crag. Ask questions and learn everything you can about climbing techniques and safety. It's cash well spent.

Top-roping from Above

- Sometimes you can't do a slingshot belay and belay on the ground, but instead have to belay on the cliff-top.

- Build the anchor back from the edge and equalize it. The belayer clips into the master point and stands near the edge to see the climber below.

- Run the rope through a carabiner on the anchors for a redirected belay rather than belaying him from your harness. It's easier, safer, and his weight comes on the anchor, not on you.

- The climber should either rappel or be lowered to the cliff-base.

Top-rope Chain of Safety

- The three parts of the top-rope safety chain are as simple as ABC—anchor, belayer, and climber.

- Anchor. You need a great anchor to be safe. Any top-rope climb is only as safe as its anchor. If the anchor fails, the climber hits the ground.

- Belayer. You need to be a great belayer to hold a fall and manage the rope. Learn to belay in a gym before trying it outside. If you can't hold a fall, your buddy's going to crater.

- Climber. Have at least one experienced climber with you. He can check knots, check anchors, and make sure you're belaying right.

169

TOP-ROPE EQUIPMENT

Top-roping doesn't require lots of gear—personal equipment, a rope, and carabiners

Top-roping is the best and easiest way to get outside climbing on real rock. It's not only safe, but it also doesn't require a lot of gear beyond basic personal equipment. You also don't have to make a huge investment in expensive climbing gear to start out. There is so much good climbing gear available now that you can easily find great deals on versatile equipment that will keep you safe and happy.

You're going to need personal equipment. While you can wear sneakers for your first time on the rocks, nothing will make you love climbing more than wearing a pair of snug rock shoes with sticky rubber soles. If you're starting out, buy a pair of inexpensive, all-around shoes. When the soles wear

Personal Gear

- You'll climb best in a pair of rock shoes, although if you're just starting out, a snug pair of sneakers will work.

- Each climber should have a harness. You can get by with just two—one for the climber and one for the belayer.

- You need a belay device with a locking carabiner to attach to your harness belay loop.

- A helmet is essential safety equipment for climbing, belaying, and standing at the cliff-base.

Rope

- Use a dynamic rope.

- Don't use a thin rope. They wear out faster. Lots of top-rope climbers use a beefy static rope because they wear better—just don't use it for lead climbing.

- Carry your rope in a rope bag. Spread its tarp out

below the cliff and stack your rope on it to keep it out of the dirt.

- Look after your rope—it's your lifeline. Store it in a dry, cool place. Keep it away from chemicals and auto supplies.

out you can get them resoled. You'll also need a comfortable climbing harness, a belay device with a locking carabiner, and a helmet. Get in the habit of always wearing a helmet when you're top-roping. Bits of rock are regularly knocked off top-rope cliffs, and your head will hurt if one finds you.

Get a good climbing rope. Start out with a 165-foot (50-meter) cord rather than a longer one. Most top-rope routes are less than 85 feet long and the shorter rope is easier to manage. Thick ropes with a diameter between 10mm and 11mm are best. They wear better and last longer.

You'll also need a handful of locking carabiners to clip into the anchors and to run the rope through. Steel carabiners, while heavy, are super strong and won't wear out. If you use aluminum carabiners, rope grooves quickly form from repeated top-roping. You'll also need slings and long loops of webbing for equalizing anchors. Leave anchor building with gear for expert climbers. Take an anchors class from a certified guide if you want to learn.

Locking Carabiners

- Make it a habit to only use locking carabiners on your top-rope anchor.

- Use two locking carabiners at the master point on your anchor so the rope can never come unclipped. Steel carabiners are best because they're strong and long-lasting.

- Rope grooves quickly form in aluminum carabiners, significantly weakening them. If your biners are grooved, it's best to retire them from service.

- It doesn't matter if you use screw gates or auto-locking carabiners, but screw gates can come undone.

Anchor Gear

- If your top-rope route has bolt anchors, all you need is some locking carabiners and slings to rig it.

- Advanced climbers can use nuts and cams to build a gear anchor.

- Bring a selection of 2-foot slings as well as a length of

rope or webbing tied into a 20-foot-long loop for tying off trees and equalizing your anchor.

- Take an anchors class from a certified guide before attempting to build your own top-rope anchors. If you don't have the skills, it's a recipe for disaster.

171

TOP-ROPE ANCHORS
A safe top-rope route requires secure anchors; learn to build one before climbing

Learning to rig a safe top-rope anchor is an essential skill to climb on your own outside. Your top-rope anchors are the most important part of your safety system. If the anchors fail, then the climber relying on them to hold a fall will be killed or injured.

Always remember that creating top-rope anchors is serious business, and if you don't know what you're doing then you have no business making them. Don't fool yourself into thinking you know how to make safe anchors by reading a book about climbing. Take an anchors class from an instructor or serve as an apprentice to an experienced climber so you learn how to rig safe anchors.

Select Anchor Site

- The first step to build a top-rope anchor is to select the best site for it.

- Evaluate the cliff-top. Are there bolt anchors at the top? Can you tie off trees and place gear? What routes do you want to climb? Can you safely extend the rope over the edge?

- Reach the cliff-top anchor site by leading a route or scrambling around the side of the cliff.

- When you're on top, clip yourself into a rope so you don't fall off while rigging your anchor.

Rig Anchors

- Next, build a safe, equalized anchor using bolts, gear, trees, and boulders. Use two or three primary anchor points.

- If there is a two-bolt anchor, clip in two slings, make a magic-X, and clip into it with locking carabiners for an equalized top-rope anchor.

- Use gear for primary anchors and natural anchors for secondary ones.

- Now equalize the anchor points with slings, webbing, or rope to a master point, which extends over the cliff edge. Thread the rope through two locking carabiners in the master point.

Top-rope anchors are the points, including bolts, cams, nuts, trees, and boulders, on a cliff-top or partway up a cliff that you use for securing your rope. The rope is clipped to anchors with locking carabiners at its midpoint, and each end drops to the ground. A climber ties in one end and the belayer to the other. If the anchor fails, the rope and climber will fall to the ground. Make a fail-safe, bombproof anchor with redundancy. Use two bolts or at least three other anchors for safety.

········· RED ● LIGHT ·············

Be careful on the cliff-top when you're rigging a top-rope anchor. Don't scramble around unroped. It's easy to trip, lose your footing, and fall off. Instead tie your rope to a tree and clip yourself to it before setting your anchor at the cliff edge.

S.E.C.U.R.E.

- Evaluate your anchor using SECURE and make safety corrections.
- Is the anchor Strong enough?
- Is the anchor Extended over cliff edge?
- Is the anchor Centered over your proposed route?
- Is the master point an Unbroken ring of metal (carabiners)?
- Does the rope Run easily through the carabiners?
- Is the rope below the cliff Edge so it doesn't get cut?
- If all answers are "Yes," climb on.

Top-roping Anchor Tips

- Don't scramble around on the cliff-top without being tied into a rope.
- Don't trust any fixed gear, but always use your own gear to build an anchor.
- Don't trust natural anchors—trees can break and boulders can move.
- Don't trust your life or your partner's life to a single anchor. Always use three anchor points for redundancy.
- Don't run your rope through anchors, including bolts or carabiners. Equalize the anchor with slings and use locking carabiners.
- Equalize your anchors to a master point and hang the rope from carabiners clipped to it.

TOP-ROPE BELAYING

Top-roping is only safe if you have sound belaying skills and can lower your partner from the top

Belaying is an essential skill that you need to know to go top-rope climbing. You have to be an attentive belayer to look after your climbing partners, to hold falls, to lower them, and to manage the rope. If you're a bad belayer, you're going to drop your buddy to the ground. Learn to safely belay and lower a climber, preferably in a gym, before heading out to a top-rope cliff. Usually you'll use a slingshot belay setup with the rope going up the cliff from you to an anchor and then down to the climber. Anchor to a tree at the cliff-base to ensure that you're not dragged across the ground if a climber falls, especially if he weighs more than you. When you belay, never let go with your brake hand. Always keep it ready to

Belay Anchor

- You need to be anchored when top-rope belaying, especially if the climber weighs more than you do.

- If you're not anchored, you risk being pulled off your feet and dragged into the cliff by a falling or lowering climber.

- A single anchor like a tied-off tree or a good cam is usually fine for a ground belay anchor.

- Stand near the cliff-base if you're not anchored down.

Slingshot Belay

- The slingshot belay is the best and safest belay for top-roping from the ground.

- The middle of the rope is anchored at the cliff-top. The two ends hang down with one for the climber and one for the belayer.

- As you belay the climber, never let go of the rope with your brake hand.

- Practice top-rope belaying in the gym. If you're inexperienced, use a backup belay with another climber to be safe outside.

174

hold a possible fall. Keep the rope snug on the climber so you feel him climbing.

Besides doing a ground belay, learn to belay from the cliff-top since you can't always belay at the base. Keep yourself tied into the anchors and run the rope through a carabiner on the anchor rather than letting it go directly down to the climber from your harness. This keeps his weight on the anchor, not on you.

Lowering the Climber

- Lowering is one of the most serious jobs the top-rope belayer does.

- Make sure you're anchored to a tree or piece of gear when lowering, especially if the climber weighs more than you.

- Keep both hands on the rope below the belay device. Two-handed lowering offers redundancy and less chance that the rope will get away from you.

- Lower slow and steady, not fast and jerky. Let the rope run gently through your palms.

Belaying from Above

- Sometimes you have to belay on the cliff-top because you can't easily access the bottom.

- Cliff-top belays are tricky. Make sure you have a bombproof anchor.

- Belay the rope through a carabiner attached to the anchor rather than directly off your harness. If you have to hold a fall or lower a climber, her weight comes on the anchor.

- Instead of lowering a climber from the cliff-top, have them rappel down. It saves wear and tear on your rope.

TOP-ROPE CLIMBING

LOWERING

Every belayer and climber needs to know how to lower back down the cliff

Lowering is another important top-rope skill to learn in the gym before you head to the cliffs. After you've belayed a climber up a cliff to the anchors, the easiest way for her to return to the ground is for you to lower her with the rope. Lowering, like other climbing skills, is very dangerous if done improperly. If you start climbing in a gym, you'll get lots of

practice lowering your partner off the walls and learn how to control her descent.

If you're the climber, lowering is all about trusting your belayer, the rope, the anchors, your tie-in knot, and the top-rope safety system. You trust that your belayer is safe, knows what he's doing, and that he's going to lower you slowly. If

How to Lower Down

- The best way to get back to the cliff-base after top-roping is to have the belayer lower you down.

- Lowering is one of the hardest parts of climbing for beginners. It's also a leading cause of accidents.

- You must trust your belayer, the knot, the rope, the anchors, and the climbing safety system.

- To lower, simply sit back in your harness seat and let the rope and gravity take you down. Ask your belayer to lower you slowly and smoothly.

Body Position

- If you use the wrong position, you'll flounder and flop on the way down. In the gym you'll quickly learn how to lower and the right body position to use.

- Sit down in your harness and let the rope tighten on you.

- Keep your legs shoulder-width apart and place your feet on footholds as you lower or paste them on the face.

- Don't grip the rope above you. It introduces slack into the system and makes you feel unsafe. Instead grab your tie-in knot.

you don't, then evaluate your safety system and belayer and make necessary changes.

The proper technique to lower is to sit down in your harness, put your legs shoulder-width apart on the cliff, and let gravity and your belayer lower you down. Keep your legs straight and don't pull on the rope above you. It's an unnatural feeling but after a few times you'll get the hang of it. Like other rock skills, practice lowering in the gym so when you get outside you already know how to lower.

Lowering Tips

- Before leaning back to lower, warn your belayer. Say, "Ready to lower. You got me?" Don't assume the belayer is ready for you.

- Ask your belayer to tighten the rope so you can feel tension. Only then should you unclip from the master anchor point.

- Before lowering, double-check everything. Is your knot right? Is the rope through both anchors?

- Ask the belayer not to lower you fast. Speed can cause the belayer to lose control. Make sure the rope isn't running over sharp edges. If so, flip it to a safer spot.

Clean Fixed Anchor

- If you're last up, clean the anchor so you can retrieve your gear and rope. Descend by rappelling or lowering.

- Cleaning the anchor is dangerous. Pay attention to what you're doing and double-check everything.

- To clean the anchor, clip into the anchors with a daisy chain, quickdraws, or knot. Any of these work fine, but they must be girth-hitched directly to your harness, not a gear loop. Tie a knot and clip the rope to your harness so you don't drop it.

- Thread the rope through the anchor, retie, and double-check your setup. Now unclip the rope from your harness.

- Ask the belayer to "Take" you tight. Unclip yourself from the anchors and lower away.

177

TOP-ROPE SAFETY

Keep your top-rope partner and yourself safe with mandatory buddy checks and attentiveness

Top-roping, like all climbing activities, is potentially dangerous. You need to be vigilant and do everything possible to create a safe climbing environment. Before you think about setting anchors and climbing, look at the top-rope site and evaluate it for safety.

Consider the site by asking questions. What kind of climbing

are you doing—vertical, overhanging, or slab? Does the area offer routes for beginning climbers or are they difficult? How do you get to the cliff-top to rig anchors? What kind of anchors can you use? Are there bolt anchors or do you have to rig a multi-directional gear anchor? Can you easily lower from the top? Is the cliff-base safe and is there an anchor for

Do a Buddy Check

- Use the buddy system to make sure each of you is safe before climbing. Don't get annoyed. Mistakes happen. Check each other out.

- Check your harness. Is the buckle doubled back? Are the leg loops not twisted?

- Check your tie-in knot. Is it properly tied and does it have a backup knot? Is the tail at least 6 inches long?

- Check the belay setup. Is the rope properly rigged in the belay device? Is it clipped to the harness belay loop? Is the locking carabiner locked?

Take Precautions

- Because top-roping is easy to do, it's easy to be careless. Take precautions for a safe climb.

- Don't climb beyond your ability and experience or use skills that you're unfamiliar with, such as creating a gear anchor. Have an experienced climber check

everything before committing to your safety system.

- Let beginners practice belaying so they understand the mechanics before attempting a real belay.

- Use bolt anchors whenever possible when you're learning. They're easiest to rig.

the belayer? Do you have to worry about loose rocks falling off? Do you have the technical skills to safely rig an anchor and manage the site for others? Answer these questions and you can begin to manage top-rope danger and minimize risky situations.

When you start climbing, use the buddy system to take care of your climbing partners. Make sure harnesses are doubled back, that the rope is properly tied into the harness, and that the belayer is anchored and has rigged her belay device.

Top-roping seems benign and safe. You're sitting at the cliff-base and enjoying the company of your pals as you take turns climbing. But don't let your guard down; accidents happen in an instant. Be attentive when belaying and lowering. Make sure no one sits below the climber or against the cliff—falling rock kills. Don't be distracted by conversation; you might forget to double back your harness belt, put on a helmet, or finish tying your knot. Minimize danger by following basic safety precautions and staying alert.

Cliff-base Management

- Before top-roping, especially with a group, assess the area and potential dangers.

- Identify and avoid hazards, including loose rock, sharp edges, and limited anchor placements.

- Make sure other climbers don't sit at the cliff-base but are at least 10 feet away. Loose rock can fall and kill.

- Check the access to the cliff-top, exposure to sun and weather, difficulty of routes, and danger from other climbers.

Top-roping Is Dangerous

- Double-check all knots, including at the anchor and on the climber.

- Make sure both ropes run side by side and are never crossed.

- Watch for rocks knocked off the cliff-top. Wear a helmet at the base.

- Pay attention to the climber when belaying. Anchor yourself to a nearby tree or other stationary object.

- Make sure the rope runs through at least two locking carabiners at the anchor master point.

- Never use a single anchor. Two is good. Three is best.

- Pad sharp edges at the cliff edge so the rope doesn't abrade or cut.

ALL ABOUT SPORT CLIMBING

Make sport climbing part of your routine and improve your rock skills by leaps and bounds

Sport climbing focuses on movement and the pursuit of difficulty. It's about the commitment to climb your best, to get stronger, and to push through barriers to become a better climber.

Sport climbing limits the dangers of getting injured by using preplaced, permanent bolts hammered into drilled holes in cliffs for protection. The lead climber doesn't place protection, but rather carries quickdraws to clip his rope into each bolt as he climbs. Since sport climbers aren't limited by crack systems or by placing their own gear, the difficulty of the climbs they can do is greater. When you sport climb you concentrate on movement, on figuring out how to climb

What Is Sport Climbing?

- Sport climbing is ascending rock faces with your hands and feet and using bolts for protection. The climber follows a predetermined route, clipping the preplaced bolts, and ends at a fixed bolt anchor.

- Sport climbing is about pushing your limits and cranking hard routes with gymnastic moves and minimal risk.

- Most sport climbers are willing to take falls to work out difficult moves. The satisfaction is in climbing the route without falling rather than reaching a summit.

Sport Climbing Protection

- A bolt hanger, a metal angle with a hole for clipping a carabiner, is permanently attached to each bolt.

- The climber clips the top carabiner of a quickdraw into the bolt hanger. The rope is clipped into the quickdraw's bottom carabiner.

- Bolts, usually used in construction, come in different sizes and types, including wedge bolts and sleeve bolts. Most are either ⅜-inch or ½-inch in diameter and 3 to 4 inches long. Stainless steel bolts are the strongest.

hard sections, and succeeding on difficult routes.

Sport climbing also requires less of a time commitment than traditional climbing since most sport routes are less than half a rope-length long. A climber ascends to anchors near the cliff-top, clipping bolts for protection, and then lowers back to the ground so his buddy can try it.

Sport climbing is also practical for the urban climber since many bolted crags are near cities and easily accessed. Hiking approaches are usually short and quick, and with preplaced bolts you don't have to own and carry a lot of equipment.

If you've already learned to climb and belay in the gym and then gone outdoors and top-roped lots of routes, then you might be ready to go sport climbing. On bolted cliffs you learn about lead climbing and hone safety skills. It's best to go with an experienced climber who already knows about clipping bolts, cleaning anchors, lowering, and leading. You'll learn a lot more and come home safe.

The sport game also has rules. The main rule is that you climb from bottom to anchors without falling, hanging on the rope, or grabbing quickdraws.

Skills to Sport Climb

- If you learned to climb in a gym, you've already learned the basic skills for sport climbing—belaying, lowering, and movement.

- But gym climbing doesn't give you judgment, safety sense, and environmental awareness. That comes from outside experience.

- On bolted cliffs, you take your climbing to a higher level by practicing new techniques, climbing harder routes, and graduating to lead climbing.

- Sport climbing doesn't require placing gear, making it safer than trad climbing.

Sport Climbing Safety

- Climbing is dangerous. A fall can be fatal. Check and double-check all your systems to make sure you're safe before leaving the ground.

- Don't rely on what you've learned from any instructional book. Learn skills to lead, follow, and belay sport climbs at a gym or from a guide.

- Accidents happen at the anchors. Double-check your tie-in knot to make sure it's right and check to make sure the rope threads through both anchors. Don't make assumptions.

- Don't let the belayer take you off belay when you thread the anchors.

- Ask your belayer to pay attention when you lead and lower. Accidents happen because of a lack of communication.

SPORT CLIMBING EQUIPMENT
Your personal gear and basic climbing equipment gets you outside on fun sport routes

Sport climbing requires minimal equipment to get vertical. All you need is personal gear—rock shoes, harness, helmet, chalk bag, and belay device—and basic climbing equipment.

Any pair of rock shoes is good when starting out. Whatever shoe you use in the gym works fine on most sport cliffs. Hardcore sport climbers, however, wear tight shoes to feel the rock better. Slippers are great for many areas. If the cliff offers steep, technical routes, a pair of snug lace-up shoes for edging is ideal.

Sport harnesses are light and streamlined. Wide cushioned leg loops and waist belts aren't necessary since you won't be hanging in your harness all day. Make sure it has four gear

Personal Gear

- Start with all-around rock shoes. Later, as you improve, use slippers on steep rock.

- Lightweight harnesses are great because you're not hanging for long periods. Make sure it has a belay loop and four gear loops for racking quickdraws.

- Start with a belay tube or plate. Make sure you can feed and take rope easily. Get an auto-locking carabiner to clip the belay device to your harness.

- Use a medium-size chalk bag that you can dip your whole hand inside. Hang it around your waist on a belt.

Rope

- Buy the best rope you can afford.

- Buy a 200-foot (60-meter) rope rather than a 165-foot (50-meter) one. Many sport routes are 100 feet from base to anchors, so the longer rope will allow you to safely lower.

- Use a 10.5mm or 11mm diameter rope rather than a thinner, lighter rope, which wears out faster. You won't notice the weight difference.

- You don't need a dry rope. They're used for mountaineering and ice climbing where it's important for the rope to stay dry.

loops for toting quickdraws. Also get a belay device and locking carabiner as well as a medium-size chalk bag and belt. Bring extra chalk in a plastic bottle to replenish your bag. Some climbers use belay gloves to keep their hands clean and a toothbrush for scrubbing chalk off critical handholds.

Sport climbing is hard on ropes. They get lots of action—leading, falling, and top-roping takes a toll on your rope. Buy a quality UIAA-approved single rope, preferably 10.5 mm or 11mm in diameter and 200 feet (60 meters) long. Thicker ropes hold up better. Get a rope bag, too. It protects your

rope from sun, sand, and grit and ensures that it has a long and happy life.

Quickdraws are another sport climbing necessity. Invest in twelve to twenty quickdraws, depending on where you regularly climb. Make sure each has a straight-gate carabiner on one end for clipping bolt hangers and the other has either bent-gate or wire-gate biners for clipping the rope. Buy mostly short draws but a few long ones as well as a couple 2-foot slings with carabiners.

Quickdraws

- A quickdraw, which is a piece of sewn webbing with a carabiner at each end, is essential sport climbing gear.

- Have a straight-gate carabiner at one end for clipping into a bolt hanger. On the other end use a bent-gate

or wire-gate carabiner, which is easier to clip the rope into while leading.

- Put locking carabiners on the rope end of a couple quickdraws to use in spots where you don't want the rope coming unclipped.

Other Gear

- A rope bag that unfolds into a tarp is essential at most sport crags. It keeps your rope out of the dust and grime.

- A daisy chain, while not essential, is ideal for quick-clipping a bolt or anchors to rest or safely clean and thread the anchor.

- Some climbers carry a stout toothbrush or denture brush to whisk chalk and dirt off key handholds before their ascent.

- Ropes get dirty and your hands get black. Bring a pair of leather gloves for belay duty.

CLIPPING TECHNIQUES

Learn the right way to clip quickdraws to bolts and the rope to carabiners

Sport routes are protected by bolts, metal shafts hammered into drilled holes by the first ascent party and outfitted with a bolt hanger, which provides an attachment point for a carabiner. The technique of attaching quickdraws to a hanger, usually called a bolt, and to your rope is called clipping.

When you lead a sport route, count the number of bolts, add two for the anchor, and rack that many quickdraws on your harness. As you lead, simply clip a quickdraw and your rope to each bolt as you climb. Use straight-gate carabiners on the quickdraw tops for clipping bolts and bent-gate carabiners at the bottom for clipping your rope.

It's an art to clip bolts safely and correctly. There are two

Clipping Bolts

- Attach a quickdraw to each bolt and clip your rope into its bottom carabiner for protection.

- Carry quickdraws on your harness, half on each side. Clip straight-gate biners to the harness. Carry two quickdraws with locking carabiners to clip bolts

- where you don't want the rope to come unclipped.

- Don't backclip! Backclipping is when the rope passes through the carabiner toward the rock. The rope must be against rock, passing out of the carabiner. The rope can unclip if it's backclipped.

How to Clip

- For the thumb clip, grab the carabiner with your thumb on its spine and your middle finger just below the gate. Push the rope through the gate with your index finger.

- For finger clips, put your middle finger in the bottom curve below the gate. Lift

- the rope between your thumb and index finger and push the rope through the gate with the thumb.

- Practice clipping at the gym to get the technique down. You don't want to be sketching a clip on a steep climb and blow it.

ways to clip your rope to draws hanging on bolts—finger clip and thumb clip. Know both so it's a quick action to pull rope and clip. Look for clipping holds as you climb. The bigger the hold the better since you'll be hanging from one hand while you clip with the other. Make sure the biner gate faces away from the direction you're climbing so you don't risk the rope popping out. Also avoid backclipping. A correctly clipped rope runs out through a carabiner to the leader.

RED ● LIGHT

Place the quickdraw so the gate on the bottom carabiner faces away from the direction of travel. If you're climbing up right, the gate should face left. This keeps the rope from accidently unclipping itself if it runs across the gate.

Clipping First Bolts

- Clipping the first bolt is the most dangerous. If you fall, you hit the ground. Have your belayer use his arms to keep you upright if you fall.

- If the first moves are hard or the first bolt is high, consider using a clip-stick to affix a draw with the rope in it.

- A clip-stick is an extending pole with an attachment on the end to hold a carabiner with its gate open. A stick-clip can save a broken ankle.

Clipping Tips

- Make sure the gate on the bottom carabiner doesn't push against rock edges. It can open and the rope can pop out. Use a longer sling.

- Look for the best hold to grab for clipping. You'll hold on with one hand while you pull the rope up with the other and clip it into the draw. Try to find the biggest hold possible.

- Don't try to clip bolts that are too high. If you can't make the clip and fall with slack, you'll injure yourself.

185

BELAY SPORT CLIMBING

Know and practice the principles of safe belaying; your partner will appreciate it

Belaying is the most important sport climbing job that you do. The more you climb, the more you'll belay since you swap climbs with your partner. Never feel that you're so experienced that you can belay on autopilot. To be a great belayer, you need to always be attentive, alert, and ready for any situation. Be prepared to catch a fall at any time.

If you learned to belay in a climbing gym, then you already know the belay basics for leading, lowering, and top-roping. All those skills are the same when you're sport climbing. The big difference is that situations happen outside that you won't encounter in a gym setting. For example, your belay stance might be rocky or loose rocks can peel off above and hit you.

Anchor Yourself

- If the leader weighs much more than you, always anchor yourself.

- Also anchor yourself if you might get pulled off a ledge or boulder at the base, if you have to belay away from the base, or if you could be jerked headfirst into an overhang.

- Belayer mobility can be good. You can step forward to give slack or step backward to tighten the rope.

- Never sport belay sitting down. Stand up. Lounging might be comfortable but it's hard to control the rope.

Pay Attention

- Watch the climber. Don't chatter at the base or answer your phone.

- Anticipate when the climber will need slack for clipping or if you need to pull excess rope in.

- If the rope pulls against your belay device or you feel the climber move through the rope, then you're keeping it too tight. Loosen up!

- Most leaders need about 4 feet of slack rope to clip a bolt. This is usually done in two pulls. Be ready to feed rope, now.

Anchor yourself if you can, especially if the leader weighs more than you. Find a tree to tie off or stick a cam in a crack and clip into it. Try to belay directly below the leader to avoid being jerked off your feet and doing a face-plant on the cliff if he falls. Being anchored limits your mobility but keeps the leader from hitting the ground.

Belayers drop leaders to the ground by not paying attention, running out of rope, and not tying a stopper knot in the loose end. Take belaying seriously; don't chatter with your buddies on the ground or dig in your pack for a water bottle.

Give the leader your full attention—he deserves it. Watch the rope when lowering to make sure you don't run out. Tie a knot in the end to keep the tail from slipping through your belay device—a common cause of sport climbing accidents. Lastly, communicate with the leader. If you see something unsafe, tell her. Belayers look after the leaders. Communication between climber and belayer is essential.

Sport Belaying Tips

- Spot the climber until he clips the first bolt so if he falls he's not going to break a leg.

- Always tie a stopper knot or tie into the loose end. Never assume your rope is long enough to climb and lower.

- Always face the leader and be prepared to dodge rockfall if a handhold breaks.

- Your belay position is important. It's best to stand below the first bolt. Don't stand to the side or face away. If the climber falls, you could drop him to the deck.

Communication

- "Slack" means give the climber extra rope, usually for clipping a bolt.

- "Take" means "Hold me tight with the rope."

- "Up rope" means to reel the rope in and take slack out of the system.

- "Watch me!" means to pay attention and be prepared for a possible fall.

- "Falling" means that you better lock down the rope in your belay device and prepare for a catch.

- When you reach the anchors, never say "Off belay!" if you intend to lower. If you say this, the belayer thinks you want to be taken off belay.

- "Ready to lower" means just that—"I'm ready to lower now. Dirt me!"

THREAD THE ANCHOR
Learn the system for threading the rope through anchors so you can safely lower down

When you reach the anchors after climbing, you need to thread the rope through the bolts so you can lower down without leaving gear. Most sport climbing accidents happen after climbing when you're threading the anchor and lowering. Pay attention to these important tasks to avoid problems. The accidents are usually from not tying back into the

rope properly, unclipping from the anchor and leaning back without warning the belayer, or the belayer losing control while lowering.

To clean the anchors, clip yourself securely into them. Tie the rope to your harness so you don't drop it, untie your knot, thread the anchors with the loose end, and retie your

Cleaning the Anchors

- When you reach the anchor, you have to thread the bolt anchor and lower back down.

- Threading an anchor and lowering are when most sport climbing accidents occur. Use extreme caution and double-check everything.

- Accidents happen by not properly tying in with the rope. If your knot is wrong because of inattention or distraction, then it can untie and you'll fall to the ground.

- Practice the process on the ground. Then use the same system every time you clean an anchor.

How to Thread

- Clip your belay loop into both anchors with quick-draws, keeping the gates opposed or using at least one locking biner.

- Pull up 6 feet of slack, tie a backup loop knot, and clip it to your harness so you don't accidently drop the rope.

- Untie your lead knot, thread the rope through both anchors, and retie the knot on your harness.

- Untie the backup loop and drop the rope. Ask the belayer if you're still on belay. Double-check your knot. Unclip the draws from the anchor and lower away.

climbing knot. Double-check your knot and setup, then, before lowering, confirm with your belayer that you're still on belay and that you're ready to lower. Never assume that the belayer is ready for you. Get verbal confirmation.

As you lower, clean the quickdraws off the route. Take each one off the bolt and rope and clip it to a harness gear loop. Make sure your rope is long enough to climb and lower off the route. Accidents happen with short ropes when the rope slips through the belay device, dropping the climber to the ground. Tie a stopper knot in the end to prevent ground falls.

Sometimes you might rappel the route rather than lower because the anchors might be worn or the rope runs over a sharp edge. In this case, clip into the anchor and have your partner take you off belay. Untie, thread the anchor with the rope, and rig your rappel device. Again, double-check everything before committing to the rappel.

If you're planning on top-roping the route after leading it, don't thread the anchor. Never top-rope on bolts, it quickly wears out the anchors. Instead use quickdraws or slings equalized with the sliding X.

Sport Anchor Tips

- As you're lowering, remove quickdraws from the route. If it overhangs, clip the rope with a draw on your harness and pull yourself in as you're being lowered to clean gear.

- Don't thread the anchor if you're top-roping. Instead put the rope through quick-draws to avoid anchor wear.

- Instead of securing yourself with quickdraws at the anchor, use a daisy chain or girth-hitch a sling to your harness and clip in with a locking carabiner.

- Never unclip from the anchor without verbal confirmation that you are on belay.

Rappel the Route

- Rappel from sport anchors if the anchor is worn, your belayer is inexperienced, or edges could damage the rope.

- Clip into the anchor. Tie a loop knot in the rope and clip it to your harness so you don't drop it. Untie your knot.

- Thread the loose end through both anchors. Tie a stopper knot in the end, then untie the loop knot and feed the rope through the anchors until each end touches the ground.

- Rig both ropes in your rappel device, clip to your belay loop, and rappel.

SPORT CLIMBING TIPS
Climb hard, climb safe, and push your limits to the max by sport climbing

When you sport climb, you're going to feel safe, especially with beefy bolt protection and short fall potential. That doesn't mean, however, that you're safe. Sport climbing, like all climbing, is dangerous. Never forget that. Every time you go climbing, no matter how much fun you're having, you run the risk of being in an accident. Your safety is your responsibility. Learn the skills, knowledge, and judgment to safely sport climb.

Taking falls is part of sport climbing. When you climb harder routes, you're going to log air time because you'll never do them first try. Sport climbing falls are always on good bolts, minimizing the risk of injury. As you work up the grades and

Falling

- You've got to learn to fall before you learn to fly. Falling is a fact of sport climbing. Push your limits and you're going to fall.

- When you fall, warn your belayer. Yell "Falling!" Push away from the rock. Try to impact with hands and feet.

- Stay upright. Don't grab the rope.

- Injuries happen when you hit ledges or the rope tangles around your leg, flipping you upside down.

- Practice short falls off a steep section of cliff to become more comfortable falling.

Working a Route

- Your goal is to climb a hard sport route from base to anchors without falling. If you clip bolts, it's called a red-point ascent. If draws are already hanging, it's a pink-point ascent.

- Hard climbs are a commitment. You have to work at them.

- Practice the route over and over on top-rope and lead. Work on tough moves. Learn to link tricky sequences. Find rests. Take falls. Get stronger.

- Then try the route. If you fall, rest thirty minutes and try again.

do harder routes, learn how to fall. Take practice falls to learn the right way. Most injuries happen because you get tangled in the rope or flip upside down. If you're going to fall, pick a landing zone, stay erect, and keep calm.

Before sport climbing outside, learn the necessary climbing and rope-handling skills to be safe at the gym and by top-roping. Don't rely on information in books or videos; instead learn by doing. Your safety depends on sound judgment. Think through the consequences of your actions at the cliff and always err on the side of caution.

Sport Climbing Safety

- Learn climbing skills in your gym before heading outside. Safety depends on judgment and experience. Hire a guide. Take a class.

- Avoid letting the rope run between or behind your legs as you climb above a bolt. If you fall, you'll flip upside down. It's a good way to fracture your skull—wear a helmet.

- Bolts are safe, but they can break. Never trust your life to a single bolt.

- Always tie a stopper knot in the belayer's end of the rope to prevent accidents.

YELLOW ●LIGHT

To keep from flipping upside down and sustaining a head injury, keep the rope over your thigh when leading. The rope between or behind your legs can tangle in a fall and invert you. Step around the rope rather than straddle it. If you're belaying, warn the leader. Wear a helmet.

Sport Climbing Glossary

- On-sight ascent is climbing a route with no info. Walk up and crank it first try. Way to go!

- Flashing is climbing a route for the first time but with information from someone else or after watching someone climb it.

- Red-point ascent is climbing a route from base to anchors without falling and clipping the bolts as you climb.

- Pink-point ascent is climbing a route with the draws already hanging on it. Less strenuous than red-point.

- Bolt is a metal shaft hammered into a hole drilled in rock. A bolt hanger is attached for clipping a quickdraw.

- Backclip is when the rope runs backwards through a carabiner, increasing the chance of the rope coming out.

ABOUT TRADITIONAL CLIMBING

Trad climbing is an expression of freedom and a chance to blaze a new route

Traditional, or trad, climbing is simply that—the traditional way of climbing before the proliferation of bolts on routes in the 1980s. Before then, all rock climbing was trad climbing. Climbers started from the base of a cliff and climbed to the top. To do this, they developed and refined fundamental climbing skills—placing removable gear for protection and anchors, jamming cracks, routefinding, and rope management—that are still used in climbing.

Trad climbing is all about vertical adventure. You need competent trad skills to get to wild places like desert towers or big walls. If you're a sport climber accustomed to following bolts, you'll never experience those routes. Traditional

What Is Trad Climbing?

- Trad climbing is adventure. It's heading up the rock and figuring out where to go to reach the top.

- Trad skills include placing removable gear for protection and belay anchors, routefinding, and rope management.

- Traditional routes usually follow crack systems that accept gear for protection.

- Most trad routes require more climbing skills than sport climbs since the climber places gear, finds the route up the cliff, creates equalized anchors, and makes lots of decisions.

High Adventure

- Traditional climbing makes you a better climber because you learn lots of skills and techniques; it also takes you to wild places.

- Trad routes range from single-pitch crack routes to thirty-pitch climbs up big walls like El Capitan in Yosemite Valley.

- To be a trad climber, you need to know anchor systems, how to evaluate anchor sites, and how to build multi-directional belay anchors.

- Trad climbing requires routefinding skills to figure out how to ascend a cliff since there are no bolts to follow.

boltless routes are everywhere. Some of the best American areas are Yosemite Valley, Joshua Tree, the Utah canyon country, Eldorado Canyon, and the Shawangunks.

To climb at these places, you need to be well-versed in basic climbing skills. Learn how to place protection while hanging from one arm, build complex anchors on small ledges, find your way up cliffs, and make sound judgments. Traditional climbing is less about you and more about following nature's rules and having a conversation with the rock.

Trad climbing requires gear. Slowly build your rack as you grow as a climber. Start with sets of passive gear like tapers and Hexes. Later buy more expensive cams as you need them.

You need to learn how to properly place gear for anchors. Be an apprentice to an experienced trad climber. Follow her up lots of pitches. Ask questions about protection and anchor systems. Or take classes from a certified guide to learn the ropes. This measured approach pays dividends later when you lead trad routes on your own. Remember that trad climbing is dangerous. You're relying on your own expertise for your personal safety. Don't blow it.

Traditional Gear

- Trad climbing requires placing gear for protection. This is active protection with moving parts like cams, and passive protection that doesn't have moving parts.

- It's a big investment to transition from sport climbing to trad climbing. You need to invest in a basic rack, which costs at least $500.

- Learn from a guide, then practice placing gear at the base of a cliff.

- Climb easy routes where you can place gear in cracks. Learn about good placements and how to remove gear.

Your Trad Rack

- Size up your route and figure out what you need, or ask someone who's climbed it for suggestions.

- Most routes don't require specialized gear like micronuts or wide crack cams.

- Organize gear on a shoulder sling and harness gear loops.

- On the sling, rack big cams at the back and small cams on the front. Clip wired nuts, quickdraws, and slings with carabiners to gear loops.

- Use a 200-foot (60-meter) 10.5 mm rope. Fat ones wear better than thin ones and are less likely to cut on edges.

ESSENTIAL TRAD SKILLS
Put all your climbing skills to the test and learn new ones, too

Climbing a trad route is not like climbing a sport route where you just follow a line of bolts up a cliff to preplaced anchors. Nope, part of the trad challenge is finding your way upward. Sometimes the route is obvious since it follows a crack system. On long routes it's more difficult. The route often changes crack systems, edging across crackless sections to another crack. The belay stances aren't easily found either.

If it's a well-traveled route, look for signs of previous climbers —maybe a dusting of chalk or a shoe scuff mark on a hold. Eyeball the route from the ground before climbing. Try to figure out exactly where the route goes and where you'll find each belay ledge. Get out your trusty guidebook and see how it describes the route. If you do get off route, look around. You may have to reverse moves to get back on route.

Long trad routes have loose rock, especially on low-angle sections. Be extremely careful on loose rock. Test holds; pull

Routefinding

- Trad routes wander up crack systems and are not always apparent. Scope from the ground with binoculars.

- Use a guidebook and compare rock features to the route topo.

- Trad climbers look for protection placements, not

holds. Follow the line of least resistance and look for fixed protection. Don't get suckered off route by dead-end features or off-route chalk marks from lost climbers.

- If you feel off route because the climbing's hard or there's no pro, downclimb to find the route.

Loose Rock

- If you climb long trad routes, you're going to find loose rock. The routes aren't precleaned like sport climbs.

- Look for loose holds, hollow flakes, perched blocks, and crumbling cliff sections. Test your holds. Tap on flakes. Use caution.

- Try to climb around loose sections instead of through them. Warn your belayer to be alert before weighting a suspect block or hold. Set up belays out of the line of fire.

- Wear a helmet. Climbing helmets are made to withstand top impacts from falling rocks.

down not out; warn your belayer if something might break off. Wear a helmet. It's a valuable skill to know how to downclimb rock. Practice at small cliffs. Also, make aid moves to get past tricky sections. It's fast and efficient.

············· RED ● LIGHT ·············

Expect long runouts—unprotected sections—on trad routes. Look at the rock before climbing. Figure where to place your next pro. Assess the danger level. If you fall, will you get hurt? It might be wise to back off to avoid injury. It's easier than rescue. When climbing runout rock, keep a cool head and know how to reverse the moves.

Runouts and Downclimbing

- Sometimes you run out of gear placements but you have to keep climbing.

- Learn how to keep a steady hand and cool head to climb above protection. Before starting up a runout section, look above to see where you can find the next gear placement.

- Learn to downclimb. It'll save you time after time. It's useful if you get off route, you get scared, or you need to rest. Downclimbing is about survival.

- Practice downclimbing top-rope routes to improve your skills.

Other Skills

- On long climbs, haul a pack rather than carry it. Use a thin rope to pull it up behind you.

- Learn to make aid moves. Don't be afraid to grab gear to pass a hard section.

- To lower off a pitch, leave at least two good nuts or cams. If the cliff is small, rappel down to clean gear.

- If you need to rappel, use good anchors. Don't be a cheapskate and not leave gear. It's your life we're talking about!

PLACING PROTECTION

Protection forms a chain of safety from belayer to climber; every link counts

Placing gear for protection is the single most important skill you need for safe traditional climbing. If you don't know how to place and evaluate gear, then you're an accident waiting to happen. Think of trad climbing as rock engineering. As you climb you install a system of anchor points with gear to protect yourself in case of a fall. This forms a closed safety system that links the leader to the belayer with the rope.

As a leader it's your responsibility to place sufficient gear to keep the route safe. If you're a novice, put in lots of pro. Every time you can slot a good nut or cam, take advantage and place it. When you gain experience, you'll take a more tempered approach. Placing gear uses energy and costs time.

Learn to Place Pro

- Placing gear is the most important skill to safely trad climb. Without dependable protection, you will die if you fall.

- To climb a trad pitch, you create a system of protection points, which are linked to you with rope and carabiners.

- Place lots of gear, especially if the climbing is hard. Never pass good gear placements.

- Place gear when needed. Get pro at the start of a pitch. Slot a nut before a hard move. Place gear to keep you off ledges if you fall.

Using Nuts

- Look for narrow slots and constrictions to fit nuts.

- Insert the nut, make sure it won't pull out, and jerk down to seat it. Clip a quickdraw to keep it from tugging up and out. Get maximum contact between nut face and rock.

- A large nut is usually more secure than a small one. For Hexentrics, look for bottlenecks and cracks that pinch down. Practice placing before using them.

- Tri-Cams are useful in holes and pockets. Wedge one in, put the fulcrum point inside the pocket, and pull to seat.

Sometimes it's advantageous to use fewer but better pieces of gear, but that's a judgment call. Be aware of the hazards of leading above your gear and remember that the protection system is only as good as the last piece you placed.

To decide if you should place protection, ask two questions: "Is there the possibility that I could fall?" and "What will happen if I fall?" If the climbing is hard and you could fall, place the best gear you can find. If you fall and could be injured, again, place gear.

Also consider protecting the second climber on traverses; not using all the gear so you have stuff for the belay; and planning ahead so you have gear left for above. At hard sections, place gear before starting the crux so you don't waste energy while your forearms flame out. If you have to place pro at the crux, look ahead for the best handhold and what piece you need before moving up.

Placing Cams

- Spring-loaded camming devices (SLCDs) or cams are the workhorses of your rack. Cams, despite being expensive, are versatile, safe, and easy to use.

- Look for parallel-sided cracks. Pick the largest cam that will fit. Don't over-cam; leave it about 50 percent expanded. The stem should point in the direction of loading, usually down. Large cams are stronger than small ones.

- Cams can swivel and walk in the crack when the rope pulls upward. Use a sling or quickdraw to reduce rope drag.

Protection Tips

- Never rely on a single piece of gear. Back it up. Redundancy is safety.

- Don't trust fixed pitons or old bolts. Both can fail.

- If you take a lead fall, you fall on gear you placed below. Know what you're doing so the gear does its job.

- Look for natural pro. Tie off trees, chickenheads, and chockstones. Loop slings over spikes and flakes. Find holes for threads.

- Don't place gear behind loose flakes or in fractured rock.

- Make sure your rope runs straight and avoid rope drag by using lots of slings.

- Save gear to build a belay anchor at the end of the pitch.

197

LEARNING TO LEAD
Leading is dangerous but rewarding if you're a cool and competent climber

Leading a trad climb is dangerous business. The leader is the climber who assumes the risks of climbing by hauling the rope up the cliff, placing protection, and setting up belay stations. The leader makes routefinding and safety decisions. The leader puts his neck on the line because he could fall and be injured.

Becoming a trad leader is your ultimate test as a climber since it requires knowledge of climbing skills, experience, good judgment, and a cool head under pressure. When you take what climbers call the "sharp end" of the rope, you're ready to accept both the challenges and fears of climbing.

The best way to learn is to lead sport climbs. They're usually

Follow the Leader

- Part of the climbing game is risk, and nothing you do is more risky than lead climbing. Lead climbing is about taking charge of your climbing.

- The leader is the first person up the cliff, the one who drags the rope up, places protection, risks falling and getting injured, finds the way up, and sets belay anchors.

- Lead climbing is the final step in becoming a climber. It's risky. Your decisions have consequences, sometimes disastrous. It requires mental commitment and lots of climbing skills.

Lead Sport Climbs

- Sport climbing is the best way to learn to lead. The only gear you need are quickdraws.

- Pick easy routes with lots of bolts or routes you already know. Take your time. Pay attention that you clip into the bolts and rope correctly.

- Rack your draws evenly on both sides so they're quickly available. Climb with the rope over your leg so you don't flip if you fall.

- After leading a lot of sport routes, you'll be ready to make the jump to leading trad climbs and placing gear.

well protected with preplaced bolts so you don't have to worry about climbing and placing gear at the same time. Plus you're out there on the sharp end, pushing your limits, and learning how to fall. Start with easy routes, ones you've already climbed, so you feel safer above the bolts. Later, after leading sport routes and following an experienced climber up trad routes, you'll be ready to take off the training wheels and lead a trad route.

Follow this lead strategy: Pick routes within your technical ability—go down in difficulty. Most climbers lead harder sport routes than trad ones. Study the guidebook and route ahead of time so you know where to go. Bring enough gear to protect it. Plan ahead as you climb so you know when to place gear for cruxes or to protect the second climber. Climb quickly and efficiently. Don't waste time on easy moves because you're scared, just do them. Downclimb if you're pumped or off route. Don't overplace gear; it's hard to remove. Keep the rope free of tangles. Manage your fear and have fun.

Trad Lead Basics

- Don't try trad leading until you're competent. Know basic safety skills, develop good judgment, be comfortable with movement, learn to place gear, and do lots of top-roping.

- The best way to learn is to follow experienced climbers up lots of routes.

- Practice leading on top-rope. Pick a crack climb and pretend to lead it while being belayed from above. Have an experienced climber critique your gear placements.

- Lower your expectations and climb easy routes. Concentrate on understanding the systems and skills.

How to Lead Trad

- The leader climbs, trailing the rope up a cliff. A belayer below protects the leader from a long fall.

- The leader places gear in cracks every 10 feet and clips the rope into a carabiner attached to the gear. If the leader falls, the belayer holds the rope and the leader falls twice the distance she is above the last gear.

- When the leader reaches a ledge, she creates an anchor system, clips in, and shouts "Belay off!" She pulls up slack rope and puts the second on belay. The second follows the pitch, cleaning gear.

199

MULTI-PITCH CLIMBING

Multi-pitch routes offer a world of new adventures to expert climbers

The best part of trad climbing is learning the skills to climb multi-pitch routes. When you start out, it's fun to do single-pitch sport climbs. Those seem pretty high. But once you start doing longer routes, you climb to high and wild places. You ascend with only air beneath your feet, feeling a rush of exposure as you climb higher. After the climb, you bask on a hard-earned summit, the world spread below your eagle aerie.

Multi-pitch climbing is more complex than doing a two-pitch trad climb. There are lots of challenges and work involved. You need to be competent at not just climbing but also rigging anchors, placing gear, routefinding, and belaying. You put all the skills you learned on short cliffs to the test.

Climbing Long Routes

- Multi-pitch routes are what trad climbing is about. You get high and climb terrain that goes somewhere—often to a summit.

- To climb multi-pitch routes, you have to be fast, efficient, and safe at placing gear, rigging anchor systems, routefinding,

belaying, and leading. Learn on short routes and you'll have more fun.

- To climb a big route, you need to be in good physical condition. Go running or hiking and build fitness. Climb sport routes so you're stronger, and can execute hard moves easier.

Before Climbing

- Step back from the cliff and eyeball your route. Look at the cracks it follows and where belay ledges are. Compare the guidebook description to the route.

- Stash your packs. Rack gear on a shoulder sling and gear loops. Fill a day pack with shoes and water.

Flake out the rope.

- Get communication signals clear with your belayer, especially if it's noisy. You need a system of rope tugs if you can't hear each other.

- Study the first pitch. Look for obvious gear placements, key holds, and rest stances.

Swinging leads, when a pair of climbers alternate leading pitches, is the usual method to climb long routes. One climber leads a pitch or rope-length until he reaches a ledge with good anchors to clip into. He makes a belay and brings the second climber up, who cleans gear along the way. At the ledge, they reorganize the rack and the second climber continues by leading the next pitch. The climbers alternate leading and following successive pitches to the cliff-top, never untying from the rope.

When swinging leads, climbers are usually of similar ability.

Often an experienced climber leads the hard pitches or all the pitches. Swinging leads is efficient because the second climber doesn't have to tie into the anchor but simply picks up the rack and starts climbing.

As you lead, think about the second climber below. Don't knock off rocks. Warn him if you're climbing a loose section or doing hard moves and might fall. Protect the second, especially on traverses—put in lots of gear so he doesn't pendulum.

The Second Climber

- Give the leader a solid belay. Pay attention if she's out of sight. Feel movement through the rope.

- Let the leader know when half the rope is out and again when 50 feet is left.

- Don't take the leader off belay until you're sure she's anchored. Don't unclip yourself from the anchor until the rope is tight and you know you're on belay.

- Alert the leader to dangers you see. Make sure she puts in gear on traverses so you don't take a sideways fall.

Cleaning a Pitch

- Use a nut tool on stuck gear. Use the tool's hook to retract cam triggers or loosen cams.

- After cleaning gear at cruxes, leave it on the rope until you get to a stance. Then rack it on your harness.

- Be careful not to drop gear—you might need that piece up higher. Clip it to yourself before unclipping it from the rope.

- Don't climb above gear before removing it. Figure out how it was placed for easier removal.

TRAD CLIMBING STRATEGIES
How you climb a route is more important than getting to the top

Traditional climbing has its own strict ethics. How you do a climb is more important than just getting up the rock. That style affects other climbers. Your main ethical concern should be to climb a wall without changing the natural environment, leaving it as unchanged as possible for the next party. Other considerations are the placement and addition of bolts to routes and creating handholds.

It's best to climb the route in the same manner as the first ascent climbers and not bring it down to your level. As the great climber Royal Robbins wrote, "Better to raise our skill than lower the climb."

The mental aspect of climbing is as important as movement techniques and safety skills. The mental game is an important part of trad climbing. You can be strong and possess the experience to climb any big wall but sometimes you're afraid of heights and falling. To be a successful leader

Traditional Ethics

- Trad climbing ethics place success and trust in your skills and confidence rather than in equipment and tactics. You go for it, finding natural weaknesses in the rock. You don't force your way by drilling bolts.

- Leave a route as unchanged as possible so the next

climber enjoys the same quality ascent as you.

- Bolts permanently alter the rock. Some view bolts as cheating.

- The purest ethic is climbing a route from bottom to top, placing and then removing all your gear.

The Mental Game

- Leading is not just about skills and techniques, it's about the other half of climbing—the mental game. Leading is about conquering your fear of heights and fear of falling.

- Leading is scary. You're going to be afraid of falling. Think calm, cool, and col-

lected and be safe.

- Don't let fear rule you. Relax, the belay is good. Look around, you can get gear up there. Slow down and ground yourself in the moment.

- Concentrate on climbing. Be in control and breathe.

you have to deal with fear.

Develop mental strategies to combat fear. Remember that everyone gets scared climbing. Focus on what you're doing, not on outcomes. Concentrate on the movements, then move. Climb ledge to ledge, one step at a time. Break the climb into manageable segments and before you know it, you're cruising for the summit.

Rope Management

- Efficient rope management is vital.

- Avoid rope drag by extending gear with slings and quickdraws. Strive to keep the rope running straight, not zigzag.

- Keep the rope free of tangles and kinks when you belay. Carefully stack it on a ledge or do a lap coil as you belay your second up.

- Don't let the rope hang down from the belay. It can snag on flakes or blow around a corner. You don't want to have to rappel down to free it.

Trad Climbing Tips

- Look at the route before climbing it.

- Compare the route to a guidebook description.

- Use binoculars to familiarize yourself with its features.

- Carry the right gear to protect the route.

- Plan where to place gear and belay.

- Look for rest stances to catch your breath and relax.

- Keep on route by following clues like chalk marks and fixed gear.

- Place protection that's easy to set and remove.

- Stack the rope when belaying. Don't let it hang down.

LET'S GO BOULDERING

Bouldering celebrates the joy of moving over stone without a rope and with little risk

Bouldering, the art of climbing without a rope on boulders and small cliffs, is about moving across stone. It's a simple and pure climbing discipline, just yourself and the rock. Nothing gets in the way of climbing—no ropes, gear, or partner. Bouldering is about challenging yourself to climb harder routes than you do on cliffs, improving your technique, and getting

stronger. Bouldering is convenient, too. You can do an hour session at the gym or on local rocks during the lunch hour. It requires a limited time commitment, little risk, and lots of benefits.

When bouldering you climb boulder problems or short routes that are usually difficult and challenging. You seldom

What Is Bouldering?

- Bouldering is the essence of climbing. It's just you and the rock. No ropes. No gear.

- Bouldering is all about doing hard moves and pushing your limits. Bouldering makes you a stronger and better climber.

- Bouldering is convenient. It's easy to go bouldering for an hour after work.

- Bouldering is good for beginners since they can practice climbing moves close to the ground and learn the basics of climbing movement.

Bouldering Equipment

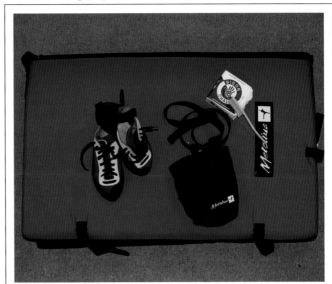

- You don't need much gear to have fun bouldering—just rock shoes. Any shoe will do. High-tops give ankle support. Use slippers for steep problems.

- Chalk and a chalk bag are essential. Don't overchalk and leave ugly white stains.

- Crash pads are thick mats put under boulder problems to cushion your landing if you fall.

- Bring a toothbrush for cleaning holds and a carpet patch for wiping your shoes clean.

do a worthy problem on your first try. Instead you work on it, figuring out the moves, and teaching your body and mind to work together until you solve the problem. Bouldering makes you a better climber; you learn about sequences of moves and how to link them together. Later, when climbing a roped route, you can bring those technical skills and strength to the vertical world.

Most boulder problems or short bouldering routes ascend blocks of rock and cliffs that are less than 15 feet high. Because you're climbing close to the ground, bouldering is usually safe. It's easy to manage the risks of bouldering by using a spotter to direct your fall, crash pads, and a safe top-rope on high problems.

You need less gear for bouldering than other types of climbing. All you really need are rock shoes, chalk bag, and chalk. Other gear includes crash pads, which are thick pads that you put on the ground to cushion falls, a toothbrush for cleaning holds, and a short rope for top-roping. With a minimalist approach, you don't have to spend much money to go bouldering.

Great Training

- Bouldering offers a way to train your muscles as well as practice hard moves. You'll learn techniques for hard climbs and to get stronger.

- Bouldering helps build confidence. If you can bust a hard move 5 feet off the ground, you can do it 500 feet up.

- Bouldering makes you stronger and more flexible. Do traverses to learn how to use your feet better.

- You can get injured bouldering. Sprained ankles are common. Use a crash pad and a spotter for safety.

Where to Boulder

- You can go bouldering anywhere you find rock, from highway road cuts to New York City's Central Park.

- Popular American bouldering areas are Hueco Tanks, Texas; The Buttermilks, California; Horsetooth Reservoir, Colorado; Pawtuckaway State Park, New Hampshire; and Horse Pens, Alabama.

- Most indoor climbing gyms have bouldering walls and caves where you can practice your technique.

- If you don't have a nearby gym, you can build a small bouldering wall in your garage.

INDOOR BOULDERING

Go bouldering at your local gym and quickly improve your technique and strength

Gym bouldering is the quickest way to improve your climbing strength and technical skills. You can push your limits, develop strong fingers, and learn foot placement. Every serious climber uses bouldering to improve. In the gym, you practice many sequences by doing lots of problems so when you climb on a rope, you'll rarely encounter new situations.

Plus the weather's always great inside, you can boulder alone, or you can meet pals after work for a bouldering session.

Most gyms have special bouldering areas with steep walls and lots of holds. Sometimes specific problems are mapped with colored tags, but you can also make your own. Create your own gym problems to work on your weaknesses.

Push Your Limits

- Indoor bouldering offers a safe haven to push your limits.

- Try a difficult boulder problem over and over until you achieve success.

- Once you "wire" a boulder problem, do laps on it to practice climbing the moves as efficiently as possible. Try the same moves differently to practice and perfect your rock technique and style.

- Bouldering allows you to practice unlocking tricky sequences of moves, master dynamic moves, refine your technique, and do climbing-specific strength training.

Make Up Problems

- Rather than trying one problem at your limit fifty times, train by cranking many different problems in a session. This works more muscles and gives more technical practice.

- Use as many body positions, types of holds, and different movements as possible.

- Make problems harder by "tracking" your feet. This means that, rather than using all the footholds on the wall, you use only the same holds that you do for your hands.

- Boulder with experienced climbers to learn how to make up good problems.

Look for ways to practice footwork, heel hooks, straight-arm hangs, gastons, laybacks, and other technical moves. Also work on body positioning and balance.

Since problems are close to the floor, it's easy to jump off and try again. To start, pick problems you can do first and climb them until your muscles warm up. Also work on a couple hard problems every session until you can finally climb them. In addition to doing power moves, improve climbing endurance by traversing the base of the walls until you can't hold on anymore.

Training for Success

- Bouldering on artificial walls is the most effective training you can do to improve, and you can train no matter how bad the weather is outside.

- Indoor bouldering is safe. You can boulder alone or with a group of bouldering buddies.

- Since indoor bouldering allows the execution of the hardest possible moves, a good workout is achieved faster and more thoroughly than climbing routes.

- Gym bouldering allows you to train specific weaknesses systematically and quickly become a stronger climber.

More Training Tips

- A partner provides a safety spot and inspires friendly competition to enhance the intensity of a training session.

- Variety is key. Mix it up by traversing, doing lots of moderate problems and problems at your limit, and playing bouldering games.

- Difficult bouldering is extremely hard on the joints, ligaments, tendons, and muscles. Warm up, stretch, and warm down thoroughly during every session.

- If you are training to climb a particular boulder problem outside, set up indoor problems with similar moves.

BOULDERING

SPOTTING

Learn how to spot and save your bouldering buddy from breaking his leg

Ground falls are a regular part of bouldering. If you boulder, you're going to fall. Even though most boulder problems are short, you can still get injured by a fall. Boulderers do as much as possible to mitigate sprained ankles or broken legs by using a top-rope, crash pads, and a spotter. Spotting, a safety technique, is when a climber on the ground helps break the

boulderer's fall and steers him to a safe landing zone.

An experienced spotter and crash pad are the two most important things to bring bouldering. When you boulder, do it in pairs so one of you can climb and the other spot. Your goal as a spotter is to soften the fall, helping the climber protect his head and back from injury. Before spotting, note any

Protect the Climber

- The hips usually indicate the direction of a fall. Catch the climber from his center of gravity just above the hips.

- Always make sure that a climber's head and back are protected from hitting rocks or anything else.

- Your partner's life is in your hands. As a spotter, be attentive and make sure he lives to climb another day.

- Only volunteer to give a spot if you're confident you can catch your partner. Practice spotting on easy problems before giving a spot on high ones.

Watch the Landing

- Spotters must inspect the landing and identify any possible hazards.

- Move sticks, logs, and boulders out of the potential fall zone to improve the safety of the landing area.

- If the ground slopes away or boulders litter the landing,

be prepared to shove the climber away from hazards. Once pushed to a clear area, the climber is responsible for his own landing.

- Protect the climber and yourself. A spotter is often hurt worse than the climber if he doesn't size up the landing zone properly.

ground problems like branches, roots, or rocks. Place a pad beneath the anticipated fall area so the climber has a safe landing.

As the climber moves up, stretch out your arms toward his hips or torso. Focus on the hips; if he falls this is where you will control him. Don't worry about arms and legs; they'll only distract you. If the climber falls feet first, steer him toward the landing zone, usually a crash pad, and let his legs take the shock. If he falls from an overhang, grab toward his armpits and above his center of gravity to rotate his feet down. Watch

his head and back so they don't hit anything. Cup your hands when spotting. Don't stick your thumbs out because they're easy to sprain.

Spotting is a serious duty. When your buddy is 10 feet up and starts to sketch out, pay attention. Be ready for a fall. If you're bouldering, make sure your spotter is ready before climbing. Ask, "You got me?" Then send your problem.

Don't Touch

- While it's crucial to keep your hands close to the climber, don't touch or support him.

- The purpose of a spot is to catch the climber if he falls, not to assist his ascent in any way.

- On spots close to the ground, keep your hands 6 inches to a foot away from the climber's center of gravity, usually his waist or chest.

- To a serious boulderer, even the slightest touch from a spotter degrades the integrity of the ascent, especially if it's a hard problem.

Break the Fall

- The spotter's job is to break a fall and absorb as much impact as possible before the climber hits the ground.

- During a fall, the spotter steers the falling climber to a crash pad. Don't make it worse by pulling him on top of you.

- Once you break the fall, grab the climber around the torso or armpits to keep him upright.

- By grabbing the falling climber, you can steer him away from hazards and to a safe zone.

BOULDERING TECHNIQUES

Bouldering improves your technical skills, making you a better rock climber

Bouldering is all about technique. Sure you can power up steep problems, but when you get on the real toughies, it's technical skills that get you up. No technique is more important than precise footwork. If you know how to use your feet and find the right holds, you'll take weight off your arms. Try to get as much weight on your feet as possible and they'll

stick better. Also remember to keep an eye on your toe until it's firmly placed on the hold. If you look away, you risk falling. Make decisive foot movements and minimize the number of times you move and place your feet; each foot position uses strength.

Bouldering makes you a better climber because you

KNACK ROCK CLIMBING

Footwork

- As with all types of climbing, footwork in bouldering is paramount.

- Since every bouldering fall is a ground fall, try to maintain an upright "X" body position to prevent landing on your side, back, or head. Consider the fall trajectories in the event a foot does pop off.

- Always place each foot with extreme precision. Surprise foot slips in bouldering lead to bad falls.

- Be creative with your footwork and don't get tunnel vision. Carefully examine the rock for small footholds.

The Mental Game

- Always approach a boulder problem with an open mind. Often sequences that work for other people may not work for you. Be creative and find the holds and sequences that work best for you.

- Develop a pre-climb ritual to get focused and set your

- mind at ease.

- From the ground, visualize all the moves on the boulder problem. Knowing exactly which hand- and footholds you will use saves strength and increases confidence.

- Constantly try different sequences.

become a student of movement by paying attention to body, foot, and hand positioning. Do lots of easy problems to build body awareness. Every time you boulder, work at becoming a better technical climber. Work toward using the least energy possible to do a problem or sequence and learn how to position your body in the most efficient ways to succeed. Women need to figure out their own method for doing problems. Men are bigger and built differently, so their sequences often don't work for women boulderers.

Always warm up before bouldering because you'll be cranking extreme moves and have big injury potential, especially to your fingers, hands, elbows, and shoulders. Go for a short run or use the hike to the boulders to get blood flowing. Do calisthenics and stretching. If you feel any abnormal twinge in your joints, quit for the day.

Build bouldering success by strategizing every bouldering session. Do lots of problems to work technique and strength. Pick harder projects to work on every session. Use friendly competition with your climbing mate to push yourself to climb higher and have more fun.

Warming Up

- Always warm up thoroughly to prevent injury.

- Start out by hiking, jogging in place, or doing jumping jacks or similar aerobic exercise.

- Next, stretch out completely to make sure your muscles are loose and ready.

- Climb a handful of easy problems, continuing to stretch between ascents, to make sure your muscles and fingers are ready to climb.

- If it's cold outside, warming up before bouldering can be difficult. Warm up at home on a fingerboard or in the climbing gym.

Bouldering Strategy

- Prevent disaster by checking the top-out of tall problems from above. Look for hidden hand- and footholds that may help to avoid a nasty fall.

- Rest between attempts. Bouldering hard moves tires your muscles fast, and recovery is crucial.

- Always assess the landing and possible fall trajectories with your spotter. Be prepared for the worst case scenario.

- Make sure your climbing shoes are clean, and that critical holds are dry, brushed, and grime-free.

BOULDERING OUTSIDE
Use crash pads to cushion bad falls and a top-rope for protecting high-ball problems

Crash pads, which came into bouldering in the early 1990s, revolutionized bouldering safety. Before pads, every fall was potentially serious since the ground is unforgiving. But with a pad below, landings became soft and cushioned and ankle damage was minimized. Pads, however, only work if they're placed thoughtfully. Look at the landing before climbing and

place the pad in your fall zone where it reduces the risk of injury. Be careful placing it over large rocks or branches. If you fall and hit one of those, you could still break a leg. Also let the spotter reposition the pad as you climb higher.

Cheater stones are simply rocks placed on the ground below a boulder problem, allowing a climber to stand high

Using Pads

- If a pad slips out from the climber, it can make a fall worse.

- Ask advanced climbers for tips on pad use. Decide where the fall trajectory is and set your pads accordingly—protect against the worst-case scenario.

- Use pads to cover boulders, fill holes between boulders, and to block trees. Don't land in gaps between pads or on the seam of folding pads, as this can cause injury.

- The spotter can reposition the pads as the climber ascends—especially helpful on traversing problems.

Don't Cheat

- Cheater blocks are rocks stacked on top of each other under a boulder problem to assist in reaching a high first handhold.

- If you fall on a cheater block, you can injure your legs, ankles, arms, ribs, or even your head.

- Cheater blocks are dangerous. When bouldering, you want a clear landing without any hazards.

- Instead of cheater stones, stack a few pads on top of each other and have your spotter pull them out as soon as you leave the ground.

enough to grab good holds and avoid a hard start. There's no rule against them, but serious boulderers view them as cheating. While their use is discouraged, if you insist on using one, place it close to the wall so you won't break an ankle if you crash land on it.

One of the joys of bouldering is doing first ascents. If you find an unclimbed boulder, be environmentally conscious. Don't destroy vegetation or damage the ecosystem. Do scope the problem and get to work climbing it.

BOULDERING

First Ascents

- Always clear objective hazards, including rocks, boulders, sticks, and logs, away from the base of the boulder problem. Be environmentally sensitive and don't overdo the cleaning.

- Carry a brush for cleaning dirty, dusty, mossy, or lichen-covered holds.

A brush mounted on an extension pole aids in cleaning holds out of reach from the ground.

- Always fully scope out the descent before climbing. You don't want to get stuck on top with no way down except jumping.

Bad Landings

- Many boulder problems have bad landings with big rocks, tree trunks, and holes between rocks. Climb these problems using extreme caution, or don't climb them at all.

- Use as many spotters and crash pads as necessary to stay safe. Climb focused and aware of the dangers lurking beneath your feet.

- Boulder at your own risk. Be aware of the consequences of falling and proceed with caution.

- Always have a good spotter and pads; decide if it makes sense to use a top-rope.

ADVANCED BOULDERING
Use dynamic monkey moves on hard boulder problems to save strength and have fun

When you go bouldering, come with a strategy and you'll get up more problems. Adopt the French approach to bouldering and put together circuits of problems of similar grades, then link them together. You'll get a killer workout and have fun, too.

Never be afraid to put a top-rope on a high problem. Long falls not only hurt, but they bust legs and heads. Using a top-rope on risky problems keeps you safe, especially if the landing has rocks, roots, and sloping ground. It's easy to rig most boulders with a short rope, slings, and carabiners. Also use a top-rope to practice all the moves before trying a problem ropeless.

Use a Top-rope

- Use a top-rope when the problem is too tall to safely fall from, if the landing has boulders and gaps, if the landing slopes away, or if there's loose rock.

- It's not worth getting hurt over your ego. On serious problems use a top-rope.

- Although tall boulders may have a preplaced bolt on top, look for natural anchors utilizing cracks, trees, and boulder tie-offs, so you can brace yourself back from the edge and belay sitting down.

Highballs and Sit-Starts

- A highball boulder problem is one that's high and scary, with a potentially bad landing. Use a top-rope to avoid serious injury.

- Highballs are risky business. If you climb without a rope, be prepared for serious consequences. Have health insurance!

- Many climbers start a problem from a sitting-down position on the ground to add a few extra moves.

- If you've mastered all the problems on your local boulders and done the sit-starts, make problems more difficult by eliminating holds and "contriving" the problem.

Climbing a highball problem without a rope is dangerous. Some are as long as sport routes, minus the bolts. If you fall, the consequences are serious and life-changing. Don't let peer pressure push you to do something you'll regret. Leave highballs for expert climbers who understand the consequences. If you do one, use lots of pads and spotters. You'll reach the point, however, where they can't do anything and you're on your own.

Before climbing a boulder, find the descent route, which can be tricky. Usually you'll downclimb the backside or a tree next to the boulder, or as a last resort, jump.

Retreating

- Retreat from a high problem consists of three scenarios—jumping off on purpose, falling off, or downclimbing.

- If you fall, always stay as upright as possible. Try to land on your feet first. Know your landing and be prepared to push off obstacles if necessary.

- If you're facing a bad fall and you're too high to jump, downclimb a few moves until you can safely dismount.

- If you jump, run or roll once you hit the ground to reduce impact on your legs.

Dynamic Moves

- Dynamic gymnastic-style climbing is an important part of bouldering.

- A swing start is a dynamic leap from the ground to the first holds. While standing, grip a hold with one hand, then jump from the ground and latch the next with your free hand.

- Use a pad and spotter for dynos and deadpoints. Unpredictable falls happen during dynamic moves.

- Climb focused and confident. Trust your spotter and don't hold back. Remember, if you're thinking about falling, you're not thinking about the move at hand.

CLIMBING SAFELY

Staying safe is your responsibility; take it seriously and enjoy a lifetime of climbing

Climbing is dangerous, so you need to do everything possible to lessen the dire effects of gravity and falling. Learn all the basic climbing techniques and safety skills to keep yourself and your climbing buddies safe. Pay attention to what you're doing. Remember that no matter how much fun you're having, everything can change in an instant. Your world can

fall apart. Always be attentive, aware of your surroundings, and responsible for yourself, and use gear properly. Do those things and you'll have more fun and climb more safely.

Beginning and novice climbers are vulnerable to accidents because they simply don't know better. In this case, ignorance is not bliss. Ignorance kills. Learn about climbing from

Stay Alive

- Falls can be fatal. Check and double-check your systems before leaving the ground.

- Don't rely on books. Learn the skills to lead, follow, and belay at a gym or from a certified guide.

- Accidents happen at anchors. Double-check

your tie-in knot and check to make sure the rope is threaded through both anchors. Don't make assumptions.

- Ask your belayer to pay attention when you're leading and lowering. Accidents happen because of a lack of communication.

Use S.T.O.P.

- Follow the letters STOP to stay safe climbing.

- Stop what you're doing if you see something unsafe like an improperly tied knot or a bad anchor.

- Think what the problem is and how it can be corrected. Use your head to find a calm solution and don't get too excited.

- Observe the big picture before doing anything. Consider if your solution will make the problem better or worse.

- Proceed with your course of action to correct the situation.

216

experts and certified guides. Their job is to teach you to be safe on the rocks.

When you climb, always use sound judgment; respect the dangers of climbing; don't climb beyond your ability and skills; ask for advice and help from more knowledgeable climbers; be self-reliant and cautious; and find an experienced mentor or take climbing lessons to learn all the ways to climb safe. Remember that most climbing accidents happen because of climber error, rather than objective dangers beyond your control.

Evaluating Fixed Gear

- Never trust fixed gear without inspecting it thoroughly. If it's funky, don't rely on it for your safety.

- Always back up fixed gear with a nut or cam. Use a sling to equalize the new and old gear.

- Check old bolts carefully for rust and corrosion on the bolt shaft and signs of wear on the hanger. Don't trust ¼-inch bolts or homemade hangers.

- Inspect old pitons for rust and a bent or cracked eye. Check the placement. Most work loose over time and can be pulled out.

······· • GREEN ● LIGHT • ·······

Make a ritual of double-checking your personal safety system before climbing. The top three on your checklist are: buckle doubled back on your harness; proper knot completely tied to your harness; rope threaded through belay device and clipped to your partner with a locking carabiner. Check your partner, too. Come home alive.

Ten Safety Tips

- Always check harness buckles.

- Always check your knots.

- Always wear a helmet.

- Always check to make sure your rope is through the belay or rappel device and a locking carabiner.

- Make sure your rope is long enough for your route.

- Always pay attention when belaying.

- Bring enough gear for your climb.

- Climb with the rope over your leg.

- Properly clip the rope through carabiners.

- Use safe anchors.

CLIMBING SAFETY

217

BEING PREPARED

Take these precautions *before* you get into trouble and you'll come home safe and sound

When you rock climb, you're out in a world that can change from a sunny day to a rainy deluge, changing a fun outing to a survival story. Be prepared for unexpected events. Your climbing partner can slip and break a leg, get struck by lightning, get benighted on a cliff-top, get soaked by rain, or get lost. Every climbing trip has the potential for dangerous situations.

Be prepared for emergencies and rely on yourself for rescue. Carry the "Ten Essentials," ten special items that have a place in every climber's pack, especially if you're heading into the backcountry. When you're out there, you need to take care of yourself and your partners if things go wrong. You can't rely on a cell phone to call a rescue service to extricate you from

The Ten Essentials

- Be prepared for emergency climbing situations by bringing the Ten Essentials:

- Navigation

- Sun Protection

- Insulation

- Illumination

- First-Aid Supplies

- Fire

- Repair Kit and Tools

- Nutrition

- Hydration

- Emergency Shelter

Know Your Location

- When you're out climbing, you need to know where you are so in an emergency you can tell rescue personnel how to find you.

- Remember where you parked your car and what trail you followed to the cliff.

- Bring a cell phone to call for help. You just might get service, saving precious search and rescue time.

- Tell your climbing partners where your car keys are located. Also tell someone at home where you'll be climbing and when to expect you back.

a bad situation. Carry the Ten Essentials and you can survive and respond to emergencies.

What you carry is not as important as knowing how to use what you have. There's no sense carrying the Ten Essentials if you don't have a clue about using half the stuff. Knowledge, emergency preparedness, first-aid skills, and a cool head are the most important things you can carry. The number one item on your essentials list is your brain. Use your head to survive an emergency.

Know what you're doing with the "Three Knows:" your location, your limits, and your route. Know your location so if someone is injured you know where to direct emergency personnel. Tell someone where you're going and when you'll return. Know your limits. Don't climb beyond your ability or attempt routes that you're not ready for. You're responsible for yourself when you go climbing. Use good judgment to be safe. Know your route. Bring a guidebook and read it. Figure out where your proposed route goes and the descent route.

Know Your Limits

- Climbing is about accountability for your actions, self-reliance in difficult situations, and responsibility for your decisions.

- Know your limits. Know what you can and cannot safely do.

- Use your best judgment.

Evaluate what you're doing and ask if it's safe. Don't let ignorance, distraction, or pressure lull you into peril.

- Climbing is dangerous. Every time you climb, you could die. Don't assume anything. Take climbing seriously so you can play another day.

Know Your Route

- Know a cliff and its routes when you're learning to climb. If you're an advanced climber, you can venture onto unknown routes. As a novice, stick with what other people climb.

- Before climbing, look at a route from the ground. Figure out where the belay ledges are and if there are fixed anchors for rappelling.

- If you get off route or start up the wrong route because of ignorance, you may have an epic fall and put yourself at risk unnecessarily. Use a FalconGuides book or reliable Internet information.

COMMON CLIMBING MISTAKES

From novice to expert climbers, avoid these climbing pitfalls by using common sense

Climbing is an intensive skill-based activity. It requires lots of techniques, knowledge, and experience to be safe. Climbers not only need to be proficient with the sport's tools and skills, but also need to develop the subtle art of calculating risk and making decisions based on their calculations. It's called climbing judgment.

Many times novice climbers are safer than experienced climbers because they're new to the sport and unsure about their judgment so they err on the side of caution. That's a good thing. As you climb and improve your skills and gain experience, it's easy to become nonchalant about climbing, develop bad habits, and use shortcuts that might speed up

Over Your Head

- Don't lead climbs that are beyond your ability and experience.

- If you have premonitions of disaster, pay attention to them. Is your partner experienced and trustworthy? Are the conditions good for climbing? Can you place good gear and retreat easily?

- Never feel bad about retreating from a route that you're not up to doing or you have a bad feeling about. Intuition may save your skin.

- Climb for your own reasons, not for someone else's reasons. Don't let peer pressure put you in a dangerous situation.

About Retreating

- Sometimes retreating from a route is the prudent thing to do. The cliff will still be here tomorrow, but you may not be.

- Retreat is advisable if a thunderstorm approaches or loose rock endangers your belayer.

- Retreat is easy if there are good anchors or a bolt on your route. Clip a carabiner on the bolt and lower or rappel.

- Never retreat from a single anchor. Your life is worth more than all your gear. Build a good anchor that gets you down safely.

your climbing but lessen your safety. Don't do that. Don't think that you can take more chances because you're good, because those mistakes can easily catch up with you.

You can make many mistakes when you climb. Some are no big deal, but others can be fatal. To live long and prosper, avoid making these critical mistakes: don't climb over your head, don't be afraid to retreat off a route, don't let miscommunication ruin your day, and don't leave essential gear on the ground.

Communication Problems

- Use formal voice commands to communicate with your partner and avoid misunderstandings.

- Bad communication makes for dangerous situations. Never take your partner off belay unless you're sure he just yelled, "Off belay."

- If the cliff is crowded, use your partner's name as part of the command.

- Work out a system of non-verbal commands in advance if it's windy or you're climbing above a noisy river. Usually a series of tugs is enough to understand each other.

Not Enough Gear

- The sin is never in taking too much gear, but in not taking enough.

- Before climbing a route, eyeball it and see what you might need. Don't implicitly trust a guidebook description about necessary gear. Decide for yourself.

- Climbing a route without enough gear is dangerous. Otherwise be prepared for runouts, rope drag, bad cam and nut placements, and insufficient gear for a good anchor.

- On sport routes, count the number of bolts yourself. Bring two extra quickdraws.

FIRST AID FOR CLIMBERS

With first-aid gear and knowledge, you'll be a valued member of your climbing team

Every time you climb, there's the possibility that someone could be injured, sometimes severely. Be prepared for climbing injuries by carrying a first-aid kit in your pack every time you climb, and know the first-aid skills to use the kit and save a life.

If you've done a first-aid course in the past, you already have

the basic skill set to assess and treat injuries. The knowledge, however, drains away if you don't use it and you don't take refresher courses. The American Red Cross regularly offers first aid and cardio-pulmonary resuscitation (CPR) courses. You can even take one online. Just do it. You'll be thankful later. After that you can take a Wilderness First Responder

First-Aid Kit

- Keep a first-aid kit in your climbing pack.

- Your brain is the most valuable part of your first-aid kit—use it.

- Let fellow climbers know where the first-aid kit is and what's in it. Keep your kit up to date. If you use sup-

plies, replenish them before going out again.

- It's difficult to treat severe and traumatic injuries with a basic first-aid kit. Consider bringing a larger kit if you have a big party or will be climbing at a remote location.

Climbing Injuries

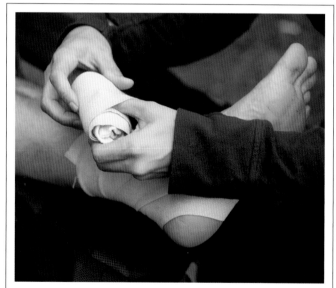

- Most climbing injuries are either minor or catastrophic.

- Minor injuries include cuts, scrapes, blisters, pain, headaches, and sprains.

- Major injuries are tendon and ligament injuries, broken bones, head injuries,

severe bleeding, and traumatic internal injuries.

- Treat traumatic injuries as best you can but get help immediately so the victim can be evacuated to a hospital. Bring a cell phone in case you get service.

(WFR) course and learn essential first aid for every backcountry and climbing accident.

There are three types of climbing casualties. At either end are those who will live no matter what you do and those who will die not matter what you do. It's the middle group that demands your attention; maybe your buddy who lives because you stopped severe bleeding or opened his airway. What then are the first-aid basics every climber should know? Remember ABC—airway/assess, breathing, circulation. Check for those first.

GREEN ● LIGHT

Learn self-rescue techniques to deal with climbing accidents. Rescues aren't always available, but you are. Learn to use climbing skills and gear to build and use a self-rescue system. Buy and study *Self-Rescue*, a FalconGuides book, for all the techniques for safety and self-reliance on the rocks.

First-Aid Classes

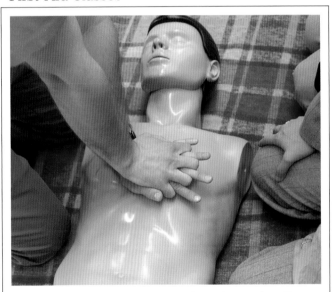

- A first-aid kit is only useful if you know how to use it.

- Take an American Red Cross first-aid and CPR course and learn how to deal with life-threatening emergencies. Follow up with a refresher course every year to keep your first-aid skills up to date.

- The Red Cross also offers online courses so you can work at your own pace.

- If you're going to be a competent climber, then you need to know first aid.

Injury Prevention

- Climbing, especially in gyms or on sport routes, stresses muscles. Always warm up thoroughly before climbing to avoid injury.

- Climbing moves shouldn't hurt. If you feel pain in your hands or a twinge in your elbows, let go and lower down before doing damage.

- It's easy to overdo it. If you're tired, quit while you're ahead. Tired muscles make for sloppy technique and bad habits.

- Don't climb every day. Take rest days to allow your muscles and joints to recover. Do cross-training to be a complete athlete.

LIGHTNING SAFETY

Lightning doesn't care if you're having a good time; it can strike you anyway

Lightning is one of the biggest outdoor hazards encountered by climbers in the United States. Lightning kills over one hundred people a year, and another 300 survive a strike. Victims are usually those who spend a lot of time outside, including climbers. Lightning generates huge amounts of electricity, millions of volts, that dissipates almost instantly in heat and

light. It's enough electricity to kill you instantly.

Lightning is an electrical charge generated by water molecules bumping together in clouds. The bumping causes electricity to build, which eventually discharges between the clouds and ground or between clouds. Since air is a poor conductor of electricity, it's discharged through better

Lightning Likes High Places

- Lightning is one of the biggest climbing hazards in the United States.

- Lightning seeks the path of least resistance and the shortest distance from cloud to ground, usually striking high points.

- Most lightning strikes hit mountains and high ridges, the same places that climbers like.

- Over one hundred people are killed by lightning each year. Your chances of being struck by lightning are 1 in 600,000.

Avoid Lightning

- Check the weather forecast before going climbing.

- Climb in the morning before afternoon storms build up.

- Change or abandon your climbing plans if you see or

hear lightning. Get off high places before a thunderstorm arrives.

- Follow the 30-30 Rule: If you hear thunder within thirty seconds of seeing lightning, avoid climbing for thirty minutes.

conductors like rocks, trees, and humans. Lightning seeks the path of least resistance and follows the shortest distance from cloud to ground, usually hitting high points.

Climbers also like high points. That's why it's important to get off ridges, summits, and cliff-tops before lightning storms. Be proactive before a thunderstorm arrives. Get off the rock quickly to avoid being caught by lightning. Climb in the morning before storms build up and be ready to change your plans. If you hear thunder and see lightning, watch out! You're in danger. Remember—there are no safe places in a lightning storm.

Lightning First Aid

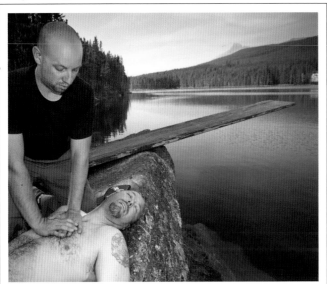

- Go or call for medical help immediately if a member of your party is hit by lightning.

- Assess the situation. Move the person to a safe place. Don't expose yourself to possible strikes.

- Check for breathing and heartbeat. Check for pulse at the carotid artery in the neck. Lightning causes cardiac arrest.

- Administer CPR if the victim isn't breathing—two rescue breaths followed by thirty chest compressions in thirty seconds. Get CPR certified.

Lightning Safety Tips

- Quickly descend to a lower elevation.

- Don't be the tallest object around.

- Keep away from metal objects that conduct electricity. Abandon metal gear and electronics until the storm passes.

- Wet ropes carry current.

- Squat or kneel down on the ground on top of your pack to insulate yourself from a ground strike.

- Spread your group out. Don't hide under overhangs on cliffs and boulders.

- Avoid rappelling in lightning storms.

LOOSE ROCK

Falling rocks gain momentum quickly; avoid dangerous situations and protect yourself from rockfall

It's a geological fact that cliffs fall apart and rock crumbles to dust. Time coupled with ceaseless erosion ravages even the mightiest rock walls. As a climber, you deal with loose rock all the time. In the Utah canyon country, you'll find loose blocks and wedged boulders on sandstone cliffs. On big walls at the Black Canyon and Yosemite Valley you'll find loose rock. You'll even find loose rock on your local crag.

Loose rock is one of the greatest dangers you face as a climber. Accidents happen because of loose rock and rockfall. Most of these occur when a climber above dislodges a rock that impacts a climber below. Be careful while climbing that you don't pull off loose rock that could injure your belayer or

Wear a Helmet

- Rock is hard and your head is soft. If you want to protect your head and life, always wear a helmet.

- Get in the habit of wearing a helmet from your first day of climbing.

- Wear a helmet when you're belaying at the base of a cliff or if you're climbing below another party. Many climbing fatalities occur from rockfall.

- Always wear a UIAA-approved climbing helmet with maximum protection on the crown, where you're most likely to be hit by falling rocks.

Don't Climb Below Others

- Avoid climbing below other parties, especially on cliffs with loose rock. Rocks get knocked off by careless climbers.

- Rockfall from others is not part of the game. Change your plans and pick another route to climb.

- Most long routes and big walls have loose rock sections on them. Even a helmet might not save you if a dislodged rock hits you.

- Remember, a small stone or piece of gear that falls 500 feet will kill you.

yourself. If you do accidently dislodge a rock, yell "Rock!" to warn climbers below. At many cliffs, you get lulled into a false sense of security, while danger lurks everywhere. The rock we play on is unforgiving. It doesn't yield. It doesn't care if it hurts us.

Protect yourself from rockfall by always wearing a UIAA-approved climbing helmet. A helmet protects your head from falling missiles, rock projectiles, and dropped gear. The consequences of not wearing a helmet and sustaining a head injury are severe and life-changing. One small stone that falls 500 feet can kill you.

Avoid climbing on cliffs with loose rock to avoid rockfall. It's that easy. If you don't climb on rotten rock, then you don't have to deal with loose flakes and stacked blocks. Look for popular routes that get traffic so loose rock cleans off. Avoid climbing below other parties. Instead, change your plans and do a different climb. Most multi-pitch routes have loose sections—you're asking for trouble to climb below others. Also don't sit at the base of sport cliffs. Get out of the line of fire and be safe.

Climb Cautiously

- Evaluate rock quality as you climb so you don't yank off loose blocks.

- Test suspect handholds before using them. Be suspicious of anything that looks loose. Inspect holds visually and ask: Is it solid? Are there fractures? Can I avoid it?

- Tap a block or flake with your knuckles. If it sounds hollow, it could break. If there is movement or vibration, avoid it.

- If you can climb around loose rock, then do it. Easier low-angle sections of cliff are usually looser than steeper sections.

Loose Rock Tips

- Always wear a helmet.
- Avoid climbing below other parties.
- Don't sit or stand at the base of cliffs.
- Evaluate rock quality as you climb.
- Test suspect holds before using them.
- Don't place protection behind flakes or blocks.
- Don't belay directly below the leader.
- Watch for loose rock when pulling a rappel rope.
- Yell "Rock!" if you knock anything off.
- Keep your rope away from loose rock.

RESOURCES
What's next?

Rock climbing is a complex and varied world. After reading and using this book to learn all about climbing and to develop a lot of the skills and techniques required to become a safe and competent climber, you need to continue to grow as a climber. The following list of recommended resources, including books, organizations, magazines, Web sites, and manufacturers, will provide you with a good start to find more information about rock climbing.

While lots of information about climbing is available online, much of it is worthless, dangerous, or poorly written. Use the three recommended Web sites included below. Two of the Web sites, Mountain-Project and SuperTopo, offer lots of worthwhile information about climbing areas and routes, while the third at About.com gives plenty of excellent information about climbing skills, knots, techniques, and a blog about timely climbing events.

The long list of recommended books below, most published by Globe Pequot Press as part of their excellent How to Climb series,

have lots of specific and detailed information about rock climbin[g] you want to grow and progress as a climber, consider buying s[ome] of these books to add to your climbing library. The books on climb[ing] anchors, training, advanced techniques, and the generalized gu[ide] books to some of the great climbing areas around the United St[ates] are all valuable resources.

Climbing, while fun, is also dangerous. Never forget that. [Take] classes or hire an experienced guide to improve your skills and l[earn] from an expert. Hands-on training is preferable to strictly book le[arn]ing—learn by doing. Also join your local climbing gym to beco[me] part of a network of climbers and to make new friends to have cli[mb]ing adventures with outside. You can also join an online forum to [dis]cuss your new passion with other climbers around the world. All [that] said, let's go climbing! Have fun and be safe.

Books About Climbing

Florine, Hans and Wright, Bill. *Speed Climbing!* (2nd Edition), Globe Pequot Press, 2004.

Gnade, Lisa and Petro, Steve. *Crack Climbing!*, Globe Pequot Press, 2008.

Green, Stewart M. *Rock Climbing Arizona*, Globe Pequot Press, 1999.

Green, Stewart M. *Rock Climbing Colorado* (2nd Edition), Globe Pequot Press, 2010.

Green, Stewart M. *Rock Climbing Europe*, Globe Pequot Press, 2006.

Green, Stewart M. *Rock Climbing New England*, Globe Pequot Press, 2001.

Green, Stewart M. *Rock Climbing Utah,* Globe Pequot Press, 1998.

Hörst, Eric J. *How to Climb 5.12* (2nd Edition), Globe Pequot Press, 2003.

Hörst, Eric J. *Learning to Climb Indoors,* Globe Pequot Press, 2006.

Hörst, Eric J. *Training for Climbing* (2nd Edition), Globe Pequot Press, 2008.

Hurni, Michelle. *Coaching Climbing,* Globe Pequot Press, 2002.

Lewis, S. Peter. *Toproping,* Globe Pequot Press, 1998.

Long, John. *Gym Climb,* Globe Pequot Press, 1994.

Long, John. *How to Rock Climb!* (5th Edition), Globe Pequot Press, 2010.

Long, John. *Sport Climbing* (3rd Edition), Globe Pequot Press, 1997.

Long, John and Gaines, Bob. *Climbing Anchors* (2nd Edition), Globe Pequot Press, 2006.

Long, John and Gaines, Bob. *Climbing Anchors Field Guide,* Globe Pequot Press, 2007

Long, John and Luebben, Craig. *Advanced Rock Climbing,* Globe Pequot Press, 1997.

Long, John and Middendorf, John. *Big Walls,* Globe Pequot Press, 1994.

Luebben, Craig. *How to Rappel,* Globe Pequot Press, 2000.

Luebben, Craig. *Knots for Climbers* (2nd Edition), Globe Pequot Press, 2003.

Luebben, Craig. *Rock Climbing: Mastering Basic Skills,* The Mountaineers Books, 2004.

Mountaineering: The Freedom of the Hills (7th Edition), The Mountaineers Books, 2003.

Presson, Shelley. *Climbing: A Woman's Guide,* Ragged Mountain Press, 2000.

Sherman, John. *Better Bouldering,* Globe Pequot Press, 1997.

Periodicals

Alpinist
P.O. Box 190
Jeffersonville, VT 05464
(888) 424-5857
www.alpinist.com

Climbing Magazine
2291 Arapahoe Avenue
Boulder, CO 80302
(303) 225-4628
www.climbing.com

Gripped
344 Bloor Street West, Unit 510
Toronto, ON Canada M5S 3A7
http://gripped.com

Rock and Ice Magazine
417 Main Street, Unit "N"
Carbondale, CO 81623
(970) 704-1442
www.rockandice.com

Climbing Web Sites

About.com Climbing
http://climbing.about.com

Mountain Project
www.mountainproject.com

SuperTopo
www.supertopo.com

Climbing Organizations

The Access Fund
P.O. Box 17010
Boulder, CO 80308
(303) 545-6772
www.accessfund.org

American Mountain Club
710 10th Street, Suite 100
Golden, CO 80401
(303) 384-0110
www.americanalpineclub.org

American Mountain Guides Association
P.O. Box 1739
Boulder, CO 80302
(303) 271-0984
www.amga.com

Appalachian Mountain Club
5 Joy Street
Boston, MA 02108
(617) 523-0655
www.outdoors.org

Colorado Mountain Club
710 10th Street, #200
Golden, CO 80401
(303) 279-3080
www.cmc.org

Leave No Trace
P.O. Box 997
Boulder, CO 80306
(800) 332-4100 or (303) 442-8222

www.lnt.org

The Mountaineers Club
300 Third Avenue West
Seattle, WA 98119
(206) 284-6310
www.mountaineers.org

Education

National Outdoor Leadership School (NOLS)
284 Lincoln Street
Lander, WY 82520
(800) 710-6657 or (307) 332-5300
www.nols.edu

Outward Bound
910 Jackson Street
Golden, CO 80401
(866) 467-7651 or (720) 497-2340
www.outwardbound.org

Climbing Guides, Schools, and Gyms

You can find climbing guides and schools at most major climbing areas as well as indoor rock gyms in the United States. For a nearby gym, check your local telephone listings or do an Internet search. For a climbing guide or school, do an Internet search for the climbing area you want to visit. Reputable guide services are found at any national park with climbing as well as in major cities near climbing areas. Call and ask about the guide services. Check for certifications. Make sure they have insurance and permits for the areas they guide at. Ask for references and check them out.

Gear Manufacturers

Acopa Shoes (Rock shoes)
www.acopausa.com

Arc'teryx (Harnesses and soft goods)
www.arcteryx.com

Black Diamond (All gear)
www.blackdiamondequipment.com

Bluewater Ropes (Ropes)
www.bluewaterropes.com

EntrePrises (Climbing holds and walls)
www.epusa.com

FiveTen Shoes (Rock shoes)
www.fiveten.com

La Sportiva Shoes (Rock shoes)
www.sportiva.com

Mammut (All gear)
www.mammut.ch

Marmot (Soft goods)
http://marmot.com

Metolius Climbing (All gear)
www.metoliusclimbing.com

Misty Mountain (Harnesses)
www.mistymountain.com

Mountain Hardware (Soft goods)
www.mountainhardwear.com

Nicros (Climbing holds and walls)
www.nicros.com

Omega Pacific (Climbing gear)
www.omegapac.com

Patagonia Clothing (Clothes)
www.patagonia.com

Petzl (All gear)
www.petzl.com/us/home

PMI Ropes (Ropes)
www.pmirope.com

prAna (Clothes)
www.prana.com

Sterling Ropes (Ropes)
www.sterlingrope.com

Trango (All gear)
www.trango.com

GLOSSARY

Aid Climbing: Climbing rock faces by using gear, rather than hands and feet, to progress upward. Used to climb blank walls that do not have features to free climb.

AMGA: American Mountain Guides Association. An organization that sets and certifies standards of quality for guiding businesses and individuals.

Anchor: Any permanent or removable piece of gear used to attach a climber to a cliff, cliff base, or climbing wall, either directly or by clipping a rope to the anchor and climber.

Autoblock Knot: A rappel safety knot that connects a climber's harness to rappel ropes. The knot cinches on the rope if the climber lets go while rappelling.

Backclip: Clipping the rope the wrong way in a carabiner, with the rope running from the front through the carabiner toward the rock. Dangerous because the rope can unclip.

Backstep: Stepping on the outside edge of a climbing shoe with the hip against the rock.

Belay: The action of holding and managing a climbing rope that a climber is tied onto.

Belay Device: A metal device, attached to a harness, that is used to hold a climber's fall. The rope runs through the device, using friction to hold the climber.

Belay Loop: A loop of sewn webbing attached to the waist and leg loops of a harness; used as the attachment point for belay and rappel devices.

Beta: Helpful information about the moves, protection, or approach to a climb.

Bight: A loop of rope used for tying knots.

Bolt: A permanent metal anchor hammered into a drilled hol[e] rock.

Bomber: Refers to a solid and secure anchor or piece of gear th[at] so strong it could withstand a bomb blast. Also called "bombpro[of]"

Bouldering: The discipline of climbing boulders or short cliffs; u[su]ally done without a rope.

Brake Hand: A belayer's bottom hand, which holds the rope be[low] a belay device and stops a fall.

Bucket: A large handhold that is grasped like the edge of a buc[ket]. Also called a jug or "Thank God" hold.

Cam: A mechanism, called a spring-loaded camming device (SLCD), with retractable cams that is wedged or cammed in cracks for climbing protection. It's also a verb, referring to the act of using a downward force as an opposing outward force in a climbing move like a jam.

Carabiners: Various D-shaped, oval, and pear-shaped snap links, made from high-strength lightweight aluminum or steel, used to connect climbers to the rope safety system.

Chalk: Magnesium carbonate is powdered chalk used to absorb moisture and sweat. Chalk keeps a climber's hands from sweating and slipping on rock.

Chickenhead: A large knob that protrudes from a rock wall. It makes a big handhold or it can be wrapped with a sling and used for protection.

Chickenwing: Technique for climbing off-width cracks. The climber inserts his elbow into the crack with his arm bent and cams the palm of the hand against the rock.

Chockstone: A chunk of rock wedged inside a crack that can be tied off with a sling as a piece of protection.

Contact Strength: A climber's raw strength for hanging onto small handholds with his fingers.

Cordelette: A 20-foot section of small-diameter cord, wrapped up in a small coil, used for self-rescue and equalizing anchors.

Core: The braided center and strongest part of a climbing rope.

Crimp: A crimp is a small edge hold that is grabbed with the fingers bent at the middle joint.

Crux: The hardest move or set of moves on a route or a pitch.

Daisy Chain: A length of sling with small sewn loops that is used to attach a climber's harness to an anchor with a carabiner.

Deadpoint: The highest point of a dynamic thrust or dyno before gravity pulls down; the point when the climber feels weightless before grabbing a handhold.

Dihedral: A cliff feature that looks like a book that is standing open. A small dihedral is called a corner.

Dyno: An upward thrust move where the climber generates dynamic momentum from the hands and feet and "jumps" to an out-of-reach hold.

Edging: A foot position used to stand on small holds with the inside or outside edge of a climbing shoe.

Endurance: The power and stamina to endure prolonged hard climbing for an extended period of time.

Equalize: Linking two or more anchor points together with slings or rope so that they share equal amounts of weight.

ERNEST: An easy to memorize set of guidelines for building belay anchors: Equalized, Redundant, No Extension, Strong, and Timely.

Etrier: Ladder steps made from webbing that are used for aid climbing. Also called "aiders" and "stirrups."

Fixed Protection: Any gear that is left permanently in the rock, including pitons, bolts, and stuck nuts.

Flash: Successfully climbing a route with no falls on your first try, using prior knowledge or beta to assist the ascent.

Footwork: How you use your feet on different types of footholds. Good footwork is the key to good climbing.

Free Climbing: Using only your hands and feet to climb a rock face and using gear only for safety in the event of a fall.

Frog Position: When the climber assumes a stance with both feet close together, at knee-height or above, and the knees/hips bent open to each side.

Gaston: A backwards sidepull. Grab a vertical edge with your thumb facing down and pull out from your body to hold yourself in place.

Gobies: Cuts, scrapes, or abrasions on your hands.

Guide Hand: The top hand that guides the rope through the b[e] device while belaying or rappelling.

Hangdog: Climbing a route that is above your ability level by ha[ng]ing on the rope to rest, allowing you to master the sequence[ ]moves.

Highball: A high, scary boulder problem with a potentially dang[er]ous fall.

Hitch: A knot that ties the rope around another object and can[ ]untied easily.

Horn: A spiked projection of rock that can be tied off as an anc[hor] or used as a hold.

Jam: The art of wedging your fingers, hands, fists, arms, feet, or other body parts into a crack, crevice, hole, fissure, or chimney, allowing you to move upward.

Jug: A huge positive handhold, like a jug handle, that you can wrap your hand over.

Layback: A technique for climbing a crack in a dihedral. Grab a vertically-oriented edge or crack and pull with the hands while pressing the feet in opposition. Also called "lieback."

Leader: The first climber of a team of two or more to ascend a route. The leader assumes most of the risks of climbing.

Lock-Off: Holding your body's weight on one arm, as the other arm and hand reaches statically up to the next handhold.

Mantle: Imagine climbing onto a mantleshelf above a fireplace. You press your weight onto your hands while lifting a foot up, allowing you to stand up. Also spelled "mantel."

Master Point: The primary point of attachment for the climbing rope and carabiners in an anchor system.

Mono-Doight: A small pocket usually found on limestone cliffs that fits only one finger.

Munter Hitch: An emergency safety knot used for rappelling and belaying. It's ideal to use if you lose or drop your belay device.

Natural Protection: An anchor constructed from a natural feature, including cracks, boulders, horns, chockstones, trees, and roots, that the rope can be attached to with slings and carabiners.

Nut: A metal wedge-shaped anchor that is fitted into constrictions in cracks as a type of passive protection.

Nut Tool: A thin metal blade that is carried to help remove stuck nuts and cams from cracks.

On-Sight: Climbing a route with no falls on your first try, without any prior route information. This is the best style to climb any route.

Opposition: Using opposing forces to counterbalance each other, creating a solid hold. Also used in anchor systems when pieces of gear are placed opposing each other to furnish a more solid placement.

Pink-Point: The act of successfully leading a route with the quickdraws preplaced on bolts and no falls.

Pitch: A length of climbing between belay stations on a route. Pitch lengths are determined by the length of the rope as well as by the location of ledges used for belays.

Piton: A pointed metal spike of various shapes that is hammered into cracks for protection. Types of pitons are knifeblades, angles, and Lost Arrows.

Protection: Gear placed as anchor points on a pitch that the leader clips into with carabiners and rope to protect himself from the effects of a fall. Shortened to "pro."

Prusik Knot: A friction hitch that is used for self-rescue and as a safety backup knot when rappelling. The act of using two Prusik knots to ascend a rope is called "Prusiking."

Quickdraw: Two carabiners attached by a short sewn length of webbing; used to clip the rope into bolts or gear, minimizing rope drag and letting the rope run easily.

Rack: An assortment of slings, quickdraws, and passive and active protection, including cams and nuts, that is carried up a route so that both protection and anchor safety systems can be created.

Rand: The portion of rubber that wraps around a climbing s above the sole and underneath the leather upper.

Red-Point: The act of successfully leading a route, placing the qu draws while leading, with no falls.

Rope Drag: The friction of the rope running over rock feature protection pieces.

Runout: A long distance between bolts or other protection route. Runouts are usually dangerous.

Second: The climber that follows the lead climber on a top-rop rope from above, removing protection as he climbs. The act of cli ing second is called "seconding."

Sidepull: A vertically-oriented handhold that is grabbed with a hand, which pulls the hold toward your body. That sideways force holds you in place.

Smear: A smooth foothold that the entire front of a rock shoe's sole is pressed against. The friction of the rubber and your body weight allows you to stand. The technique is called "smearing" or "friction climbing."

Spotting: A bouldering technique that protects a climber during a ground fall. The spotter, standing on the ground, steers the falling climber to a safe landing zone.

Stance: A small secure ledge or position that is used for resting or to belay.

Stemming: A climbing technique for dihedrals. The hands and feet are bridged in opposition across the inside of the dihedral, taking weight off the arms.

Tail: The section of rope left over after tying a knot.

Toe-In: Also called front-pointing. Stepping straight onto a small pocket or narrow edge with the toe of the rock shoe.

Top-Roping: The act of climbing with the rope protecting the climber from above. Top-roping is the safest form of climbing since falls are short.

Topo: A map of a route that provides information with symbols for cracks, overhangs, ledges, fixed protection, and ratings.

Traverse: Climbing sideways, across a rock face and parallel to the ground.

Undercling: An upside-down handhold, usually a crack, that is grasped with the palm facing up.

UIAA: Union Internationale des Associations d'Alpinisme. An international organization that establishes safety standards for climbing gear. Never use climbing gear that is not UIAA approved.

Webbing: Flat, extremely strong lengths of nylon that are used for slings and other climbing applications.

INDEX

PROTECTING CLIMBING **ACCESS** SINCE 1991

| JOIN US |
WWW.ACCESSFUND.ORG

Jonathan Siegrist climbs the Third Millenium (14a) at the Monastery, Colorado. Photo by: Keith Ladzinski